RELIGION
& Popular Culture

RELIGION

& Popular Culture

A CULTURAL STUDIES APPROACH

CHRIS KLASSEN

OXFORD
UNIVERSITY PRESS

OXFORD
UNIVERSITY PRESS

Oxford University Press is a department of the University of Oxford.
It furthers the University's objective of excellence in research, scholarship,
and education by publishing worldwide. Oxford is a registered trade mark of
Oxford University Press in the UK and in certain other countries.

Published in Canada by
Oxford University Press
8 Sampson Mews, Suite 204,
Don Mills, Ontario M3C 0H5 Canada

www.oupcanada.com

Copyright © Oxford University Press Canada 2014

The moral rights of the author have been asserted

Database right Oxford University Press (maker)

Library and Archives Canada Cataloguing in Publication

Klassen, Chris, 1972–
Religion and popular culture : a cultural studies approach / Chris Klassen.

Includes bibliographical references and index.
ISBN 978-0-19-544918-1

1. Religion and culture—Textbooks.   2. Popular culture—Religious aspects—Textbooks.   I. Title.

BL65.C8K53 2013   201'.7   C2013-901311-3

Cover image: © Wong Yu Liang, Malaysia

Oxford University Press is committed to our environment.
This book is printed on Forest Stewardship Council® certified paper
and comes from responsible sources.

Printed and bound in Canada

7 8 9 — 20 19 18

MIX
Paper from
responsible sources
FSC® C004071

Contents

Preface

I must admit that I first got interested in the study of religion and popular culture by accident. I was asked to teach the Religion and Popular Culture course in my department at the last minute after someone else backed out. Since I was studying a group of popular alternative religious people—contemporary Pagans—it was thought that I would make a good substitute. I certainly did have an interest in the popular representations of witchcraft and the occult that had surfaced in recent Western popular culture, but that was the extent of my knowledge at the time.

That was over 10 years ago, and since then I have taught Religion and Popular Culture to thousands of students and expanded my own knowledge and interest in the area. I have published essays on TV shows and movies with religious themes. I have become co-editor of the *Journal of Religion and Popular Culture*. And I have become increasingly frustrated with the lack of a good theory-based text to introduce students to this fascinating study. Don't get me wrong—there are lots of excellent studies of religion and popular culture out there. Most of them, though, are collections of essays that look at a specific example using various theories without fully explaining how the theory has come about. These are useful resources and I would hope that some of them would be used in conjunction with this book to expand the breadth of the case studies students can address.

There are also some very good texts that outline cultural studies theories. I have relied heavily on cultural studies as it is the theoretical area I find most useful for studying popular culture in my teaching and research; however, none of these texts address religious issues or analyses. After teaching many years trying to have students read a cultural studies primer alongside a religious studies primer with some added case studies, I decided it was time to write a textbook that put these together. I hope that this text will give enough depth of the theories with some brief case studies that specifically address religion and popular culture together. I also hope that because this text is not monstrously large, professors will be able to add their own favourite topics and case studies alongside this text. That is my intention.

I would like to thank some very important people who helped me immensely through this project. First I would like to thank the very helpful and encouraging editors at Oxford University Press: Stephen Kotowych, Meg Patterson, Leah-Ann Lymer, and Karri Yano. Without their help this book would still be an idea in my head pounding to come out. I would also like to thank all of the students who ever took Religion and Popular Culture with me, and yes, there are literally over a thousand of you. You taught me what worked and what did not work, and introduced me to many specifics of the popular culture of your generation (such as emo and metrosexuality). I would like to thank the following colleagues for their participation in many conversations about this book and religion and popular culture in general: Brent Hagerman, Carol Duncan, Scott Daniel Dunbar, Mary Ann Beavis, Ryan Weston, Scott Kline, and Carmen Celestini.

I also want to thank the reviewers of the manuscript who were so positive and provided feedback that made this into a much better book:

Leona Anderson, University of Regina
Catherine Caufield, University of Alberta
Siobhan Chandler, University of Waterloo
Carlos Colorado, University of Winnipeg
Ellen Goldberg, Queen's University
Wynne Jordan, Saint Mary's University
Jennifer Porter, Memorial University of Newfoundland
Anne White, University of Calgary

Finally, I want to thank my extremely supportive partner, Akio Saito, and my kids, Maxwell and Simon, for their patience as I worked, complained, anguished, and finally completed this project.

Chris Klassen
June 2013

Introduction

Images, Icons, and Identities

James Cameron's blockbuster film *Avatar* (2009) has it all: adventure, high tech graphics, romance, religion, politics, and violence, and provides amazing special effects with its new 3D technology. Integrated into this film is a story about colonization and an indigenous population's fight for freedom. The indigenous people represent a holistic spiritual worldview that seems to have resonated with many viewers.

Why might it be significant for religious studies scholars to take a Hollywood film like *Avatar* seriously? Popular culture is a body of cultural productions (films, music, books, TV) which are consumed and recognizable by a significantly large proportion of, in this particular case, the North American population regardless of class, race, gender, sexuality, etc. This is not to say that everyone consumes these cultural productions in the same way. But box offices, best seller lists, and music charts show us that popular culture is just that—popular. Though everyone reads (engages with) popular culture in differing ways depending on race, class, gender, politics, religion, sexuality (and the list goes on), it still has a power of representation which cannot be ignored. When popular culture takes on the themes of religion and spirituality, religious studies scholars cannot afford to cast it aside as simply entertainment. These products, and the way people interpret them, say much about the religious aura and attitudes of our societies.

The above example is one way of thinking about the relationship between religion and popular culture. Another example comes in the work of John Walliss (2012) who has studied the implications of playing role-playing games (RPGs) such as *Dungeons and Dragons* for evangelical Christians. There has been a strong critique of RPGs by evangelical Christian groups who see the magical worldviews and inclusion of monsters and occult practices as a sign that these games are Satanic. However, there are also some evangelical Christians who are very interested in playing these games, though they face considerable criticism by their Christian peers. Walliss shows that evangelical Christian gamers have developed three strategies for playing RPGs that allow them to remain true to their Christianity while enjoying their hobby. First, some Christians simply remove the elements of the game they find questionable. For example, one participant in Walliss' study plays *Dungeons and Dragons*, but cuts out the demons, insisting that one does not need them to be able to play the game. A second strategy is to Christianize the game. One example of this is to model a druidic character on Celtic Christianity rather than on traditional

Druidry. The third strategy is to create and play specifically Christian RPGs such as *Holy Lands*. Interestingly, Wallis found that the majority of evangelical Christians chose the first two strategies rather than the last.

Why should scholars care how evangelical Christians play their games? Is this really a serious study? A study like Walliss' shows both the opposition to some popular culture by religious groups as well as the use, and at times the adaptation, of popular culture by religious people. Again, this study shows how people interact with their world through, and sometimes in spite of, their religious belief systems.

In his book *For God, Country, and Coca-Cola* (1993), Mark Pendergrast suggests that Coca-Cola is a religious icon because it provides a symbol of the American dream and elicits religious responses, not only from consumers' devotion, but from company executives, such as Harrison Jones in the 1920s, who referred to the drink as "holy water" (Pendergrast 1993, 146). Coca-Cola has become a global image that many consume "religiously," and far more frequently than, say, the Catholic mass. Key to this global image, according to Jeffrey Scholes is the branding of Coca-Cola, that is, it is less the taste of the drink than "the *meaning* of the brand, which encourages consumers to think of the relationship between themselves and the product in a deeper way" (2012, 139). The advertising for Coca-Cola indicates its almost magical qualities not only to quench thirst but to bring peace and harmony to the world. The missionizing of the product has resulted in a global presence.

Why should a religious studies scholar care about what is essentially a completely secular, non-nutritious, beverage? James Twitchell suggests that "Brand stories act like religion not just by holding people together but also by holding individual experiences together [. . .]. We cluster around them as we used to cluster around sacred relics" (2004, 24). Though Coca-Cola is not actually a religious icon, it functions as such, pointing to consumer identities of happiness, satisfaction, and group identity.

Religious studies scholars who study these interesting parallels learn something not only about the object/subject of study (Coca-Cola), but how popular culture can be understood and function in similar ways to religion, in any given society.

Intersections and Integration

What do you think about when you think of religion and popular culture? Some people have a hard time putting these two arenas together. They think religion is serious, sacred, and otherworldly while popular culture is frivolous, profane, and part of the everyday. Increasingly though, religious studies scholars are seeing the intersection and even integration of these two arenas as we begin to take more seriously the religious practices of people outside of the institutions. Even in institutional religion, we are seeing an increased engagement with, not just resistance to, popular culture. There are many texts out there that will give you examples of studies exploring these engagements. What this text provides, to complement these many case studies, is an introduction to some of the theories that scholars have used to think about the relationships between religion and popular culture. I have focused on a cultural studies framework as it seems the most useful for a religious studies approach that explores multiple kinds of popular cultural productions and processes. Cultural studies, as we will see, allows for a variety of interpretations, exploring both producer and consumer understandings of popular culture. Cultural studies scholars also take very seriously questions about race, gender, sexuality, class, age, etc.

Chapter Summaries

In Chapter 1 we look more closely at the main themes of our study: religion and popular culture. There are multiple ways scholars have approached religion and popular culture as disciplines. First, we will look at the history of the academic study of religion, leading to the recent trend to move away from formal definitions of religion to the "lived religion" in the lives of individuals in a community. Second, since we are focusing on a cultural studies approach, we will look at the development of cultural studies and examine its significance for a study of religion. We conclude Chapter 1 with a discussion of the relationships between religion and popular culture to give a preliminary sense of the kinds of discussions we will have in the larger text.

Chapter 2 jumps into the first real cultural studies approach to popular culture: one that draws on Marxist theory. Marxist thought focuses on historical materialism and the relationships between modes of production and the superstructures designed to support those modes of production. Drawing on Marxist theory, later theorists have moved out of the specifically economic realm to use Marxism to examine the production of culture. These neo-Marxists base their theories on the concept of hegemony, which is explored more fully in this chapter. We also focus on the work done by a group of neo-Marxist scholars known as the Frankfurt School and a critique of this approach. To demonstrate how scholars have applied these neo-Marxist theories—such as the Frankfurt School's culture industry thesis—to religion and popular culture, we will explore some analyses of self-help spirituality, such as *The Secret* by Rhonda Byrne, as well as the commodification of religion in Hollywood films.

Chapter 3 takes us into a prominent response to the Frankfurt School: culturalism. Culturalism suggests that there is more to popular culture than what the producers intend. Rather scholars must also look to consumer use and the overall "structures of feeling" of any given culture. Stuart Hall's theorizing about the encoding and decoding of meaning in documentary cultures has been significant for all cultural studies following after. To explore these theories more closely, we look at what Christopher Partridge calls the growing occulture within Western culture. Specifically, we address how one might determine and analyze the structures of feeling tied to differing representations of zombies. Zombies, as characters from within Haitian vodou and Hollywood horror films, defy singular definition. They are both religious and popular cultural figures; they can represent both the importance of community and the importance of individuality. In an attempt to make the application of culturalism clearer, we also explore multiple meanings given to vampires, another popular occultural figure within film and literature. Finally, we address some evangelical Christian responses to the occult.

Chapter 4 takes us into the theories of performativity. This includes both ritual studies and the postmodern theories of Judith Butler. Ritual, whether specifically religious or not, is often seen by ritual studies theorists as performative utterance. For both ritual studies theorists and Judith Butler, whose work on performativity focuses on gender and sexuality, performance *does* something that is more interesting than intended or interpreted meanings. These theories can be complex and confusing, so we will make them clearer by analyzing performances of religion and gender by Madonna and Lady Gaga, as pop icons, and the performance and fandom in sport, particularly hockey. Performativity asks us to think about what ritual, performance, and utterance does and how effective they may be.

Chapter 5 continues our discussion of gender and religion by looking specifically at feminist theories and their uses in the study of popular culture. Feminism begins early in eighteenth and nineteenths centuries largely with the fight to get women the vote. In the 1960s we get a second wave of feminism that begins to explore multiple ways of understanding women's equality or liberation. This chapter explores a number of different feminisms and demonstrates how they can be used to understand representations of the feminine divine, particularly in the famous Dan Brown book and film, *The Da Vinci Code*, as well as representations of girl power in comics, television, books, and film.

Chapter 6 explores the anti-racism theories of Paul Gilroy and bell hooks and shows how race is a significant analytical framework to view popular culture. We will see how racism and anti-racism are structured in larger society and how these structures affect religious depictions and engagements in popular culture, particularly in rap music, demonstrating that an understanding of race and racism is integral to understanding contemporary Western popular culture. An important piece of this understanding comes from recognizing the continuing importance of the trans-Atlantic slave trade and the resistance to that slavery. It is through that oppression and migration that West African religio-musical styles and content entered Western popular culture blending with European, Indigenous, and other religions and musical styles to create very unique and influential genres: blues, jazz, rap, and hip hop. This chapter explores the religious history of rap music, the continuing dialogue between music and religion within rap music, and the legacy of slavery and racism.

For Chapter 7 we take the discussion of oppressions into the relationship between Westerners and Easterners. In Edward Said's articulation of Orientalism, we use a theoretical apparatus to see how figures and cultures from the Middle East, Far East, and even Indigenous Americans have been constructed in very narrow and limiting ways. Orientalism has a long history in European contact with the East. In some contexts it has morphed into a more specifically antagonistic Islamophobia. Our explorations in this chapter will look at the constructions of the Arab/Muslim terrorist in Hollywood as an Orientalist and Islamophobic phenomenon. However, not all Orientalist imagery is overtly negative: some is more positive, but equally restricting. Thus, we also explore the Western romanticization of the Oriental Monk and Eastern spirituality. In addition, we look at how both the negative and positive stereotypes from Orientalism have been also used in Hollywood to characterize a narrow and limited figure of the American Indian. This Orientalist lens has not been left unchallenged, however, and we look at a couple of examples of reframing identity in popular culture in direct response and resistance to Orientalism.

Chapter 8 explores the worlds of subcultures and post-subcultures. Subcultural studies scholars tend to approach subcultures as resistance to dominant mainstream culture, often based on class or race categories. Post-subcultural studies scholars tend to dispute the existence of one dominant mainstream culture and the distinct boundaries between various subcultures. We will look at the differences between these two approaches and apply them to two examples: Goth and the Burning Man festival. Both of these examples include religious, or parareligious, elements.

Our final chapter takes us into the virtual world with a discussion of digital media and hyper-real religion. We first look at the shifting media environments from print to electronic to digital and then think through the implications of these kinds of media for the practices of religion, particularly online. In exploring what Jean Baudrillard calls the hyper-real, we see how the growth of digital media is tied to the development of hyper-religions. Then we apply these theories to two main environments: *Second Life* and *World of Warcraft*, and explore the implications of practising evangelical Christianity in *Second Life* and the digitizing of prayer. We then look at the practice of religious ritual in the role-playing game world and what, if any, significance it may have for real-life religious or spiritual identity.

Throughout this text we focus on theoretical approaches. When we look at specific examples of the relationship between religion and popular culture, it is through cases that we flesh out the use of the theoretical approach. The examples demonstrate how to use the theory; but they are not the sole examples available for these theories. I encourage you to think about other cases in which these theories may be useful.

Useful Resources

Print

Pendergrast, Mark. 1993. *For God, Country, and Coca-Cola: The Unauthorized History of the Great American Soft Drink and the Company that Makes It*. New York: Charles Scribner's Sons.

Scholes, Jeffrey, 2012. "The Coca-Cola Brand and Religion." In *Understanding Religion and Popular Culture*. Eds., Terry Ray Clark and Dan W. Clanton, Jr. London: Routledge. 139–56.

Walliss, John. 2012. "The Road to Hell is Paved with D20s: Evangelical Christianity and Role-Playing Gaming." In *Handbook of Hyper-real Religions*. Ed., Adam Possamai. Leiden: Brill. 207–23.

Video

Cameron, James. 2009. *Avatar*. 20th Century Fox.

1

Religion and Popular Culture

OBJECTIVES

This chapter will help you develop an understanding of

- the variety of ways scholars approach religion, including the cognitive and functional approaches
- the development of cultural studies
- concepts in popular culture, such as folk and mass culture, hegemony, encoding and decoding
- the relationships between religion and popular culture

Think of Canada in mid-December: shops and businesses brightly decorated, Santa posing for pictures in the mall, religious groups collecting money for charity, holiday parties and family gatherings filling your time. This is a particularly good time to be thinking of the relationship between religion and popular culture as it is difficult to avoid the multiple, mixed, and highly contentious messages about Christmas. Is it a religious holiday for Christians? Is it a secular holiday to reinforce family connections? Is it a celebration of conspicuous consumption? As people wander the malls, bake gingerbread, and visit light displays in public parks, it is not uncommon to hear Elvis, Bing Crosby, Billy Idol, or even Alvin and the Chipmunks belt out the strains of "Here Comes Santa Claus" with its ironic fourth verse: "Let's give thanks to the Lord above, for Santa Claus comes tonight." Even if there are elements of a Catholic saint figure, Saint Nicholas, embedded into the current Santa Claus myth, Santa is hardly a Christian figure. What parts of the North American Christmas celebration are religious? What parts are popular culture? When do religion and popular culture interact and intermingle in these celebrations?

Defining Religion

Defining religion is no easy matter. Yet, if we are going to study religion and popular culture we must look at the ways religion has been defined and theorized in the past. Many scholars have tried to define the core of what religion is from a range of perspectives. This chapter briefly describes some of the classic theories leading up to a way to think about religion for our current study. To begin, though, I would like to point to religious studies scholar Thomas Tweed's description of theories as itineraries. He writes,

> Drawing on the three primary meanings of the term *itinerary* in the *Oxford English Dictionary*, I suggest that theories are embodied travels ("a line or course of travel; a route"), positioned representations ("a record or journal of travel, an account of a journey"), and proposed routes ("a sketch of a proposed route; a plan or scheme of travel"). Theories are simultaneously proposals for a journey, representations of a journey, and the journey itself (2006, 8–9).

What this essentially means is that no theory of religion can be static—any more than what is theorized is static. All theories, like all religions, are located somewhere, whether that be geographically, philosophically, or emotionally. They also move; they are not stuck to one location. As we look to the various theories of religion and popular culture in this book, we will need to be flexible enough to travel through various times and places, ideas and ideologies, in order to make sense of those who have engaged in this study before us, and in order to move forward.

The academic study of religion began in the Western world as the study of Christianity, with an inclusion, at times, of the perceived flaws of Judaism and Islam. However, things began to change at the beginning of the early modern era (beginning around 1500 CE) largely due to two factors: the Protestant Reformation that resulted in multiple splits of the Christian Church; and the increased global movement of European powers in colonial and missionary endeavours. As the concept of religion lost its coherence as a single, untouchable entity (the catholic/universal Christian Church in Western Europe) scholars become more interested in exploring the beliefs and practices of a variety of peoples, often with the goal of developing an overriding theory of human religion: Where does religion come from? What does it do for human cultures? What is the common element to all religions? To answer these questions, many Western scholars examined what they considered "primitive" religions.

The Cognitive Approach

Some theorists took a **cognitive approach**; that is, they studied how certain beliefs lead to certain practices. This was a common approach in the Victorian era with the development of the field of anthropology and ethnography. One influential figure here was James Frazer (1854–1941), whose theory of **animism**, found in his text *The Golden Bough* (published in numerous volumes over the period of 1890–1915, with an abridged version in 1922), has had continuing influence on public perceptions of religion, though largely rejected by modern scholars. Frazer argued that primitive peoples believed the natural world was animated by spiritual personalities. For example, these primitive people believed the wind and storms must be either an entity possibly attacking them or a sign of anger of a larger divine being. Various practices of petition and appeasement developed due to this belief; these practices form what we call religion. Frazer writes, "By religion, then, I understand a propitiation or conciliation of powers superior to man which are believed to direct and control the course of nature and of human life" (Frazer 1950 [1922], 57–8).

According to Frazer, as cultures develop and gain more sophisticated knowledge, so too their religious practices change. Soon the animated forces of nature develop into complex pantheons of gods and goddesses that operate in similar ways to human society, with a "king god" such as Zeus leading a variety of other influential figures and lower divine or semi-divine beings. As culture progresses further, the powers of all the various gods and goddesses morph into one all powerful deity, such as the God of Judaism and Christianity. Eventually, with the advancements of science, all the "secrets" of the natural world will be known and there will no longer be any need for any divine being or a religion to appease that being. For Frazer and other Victorian anthropologists interested in explaining religion, religion was a natural result of mistaken belief: you think the river is a person; therefore you develop rites to encourage the river to continue to bring your community fish. A more developed society, such as that of Frazer's Victorian England, recognizes that there are not distinct personalities in the natural world, but still relies upon a concept of an overriding personality overseeing the running of the world: hence, the monotheism of Christianity. Frazer believed that someday science would overcome religion as humans discovered the realities behind previous mysteries.

Frazer and other Victorians were clearly influenced by Charles Darwin's (1809–1882) theory of biological evolution and wanted to apply it to religion and culture. By this theory, religion begins as something simple and develops complexity as it evolves. **Monotheism**, a more complex form of religion according to Frazer, is a later stage of civilization than **polytheism**. This theory, of course, held many implications for European contacts around the globe. Most significantly, it reinforced the assumption of European superiority in comparison with a variety of indigenous peoples they "discovered" who still held what the Europeans viewed as a more primitive form of religious belief and practice: animism and polytheism.

The Functional Approach

ÉMILE DURKHEIM'S SACRED AND PROFANE

One response scholars made to theories such as Frazer's was to dismiss the cognitive approach (starting with beliefs) and look to a more functional approach: what does religion do for people and/or society? A good example of this approach is that of Émile Durkheim (1858–1917). Durkheim spent much of his academic life thinking about the way society functions. In many ways, Durkheim is the "father" of the discipline of sociology. Living at the end of the nineteenth century and into the early twentieth century, Durkheim experienced a profound shift in social and cultural ideas. Organized religion was losing some of its influence in Europe as scientific orientation was gaining ground. Industrialization caused major shifts in community formations, leading to greater urbanization and class division. The individual seemed to be more significant than the collective. On some levels this concerned Durkheim: where would moral guidance come from if society were no longer based on communal organizing principles, such as the Church? Would individualism lead to anarchism? Durkheim's concerns with these questions led to a theory about religion that was both unique and conservative. It was unique in its social approach to religion; yet it was conservative in its insistence on the inevitable role of religion in human society.

Durkheim's most influential book, the last one he wrote, was *The Elementary Forms of Religious Life* originally published in 1912. In this text we get his theory of religion based on the specific example of the Aborgines of Australia. Though his methodology is much criticized today (and in fact was criticized in his own day as well), Durkheim believed that by looking at the most simple and "primitive" religion in current existence, he could discover the elements at the base of all religion no matter how sophisticated. His focus was on the division of the sacred from the profane in the practice of **totemism**. The totem, an object representing an animal or plant, was sacred, and thus set apart from the profane. However, Durkheim concluded that the totem was ultimately a symbol of the clan itself; thus the sacred was the collective. This equation put the individual activities of regular eating and working in the realm of the profane. In later religious expressions, said Durkheim, spirits and gods are simply more complex understandings of the totem, and thus are more complex symbols of the collective. For Durkheim, then, "*A religion is a unified system of beliefs and practices relative to sacred things, that is to say, things set apart and forbidden—beliefs and practices which unite into one single moral community called a Church, all those who adhere to them*" (Durkheim 1995, 44, italics original).

As the elementary form of religious life, totemism was a maintenance and celebration of social cohesion, or group identity. Thus, for Durkheim, all religion is fundamentally about social cohesion: he comes to the conclusion that society and religion are irrevocably joined together. So, how to make sense of the changes of his day to what seemed to many an increasingly **secular** world? If, as Durkheim suggests, religion is the formalization of a collective identity, one that provides moral guidance to the individuals involved, then any social good could take the role of the religious symbol. For example, in Durkheim's France, the ideals of freedom, equality, and solidarity take on, for him, the function of religion, even as they challenged the religious organization of the Catholic Church. In Durkheim's definition, religion is not fundamentally about gods, it is about the group and how the group defines its own good. Thus, as long as there is society, there will be religion: the making sacred of a given society's collective good.

MAX WEBER'S PROTESTANT ETHIC AND INNER-WORLDLY ASCETICISM

Another influential sociologist of religion is Max Weber (1864–1920). Unlike Durkheim, who was interested in finding the elementary form of religion and started from what he thought to be the most primitive example, Weber started his study with an economic question: why did **capitalism** develop as it had in the Western world? His deliberation led him to a religious cause (among others) and

Secular

The secular, in a simple definition, is that which is not religious or spiritual. However, in the study of religion and culture, the term secular takes on more significance. A secularized world is one that is not governed by religion. This definition only makes sense if one remembers that for much of Western history the Christian institutions controlled, or attempted to control, much of society. They crowned the monarchs; they collected the taxes; they ran the schools and hospitals; they determined the laws. A secular society is one that does not allow religious institutions to hold this power over other sectors of society. A secular society does not mean that religion has no influence or is absent, but that no single religious institution holds the power to determine laws, leaders, or social programs. In a secular world there is a diffusion of morals and normative worldviews. Durkheim was concerned that allowing for multiple religious (and non-religious) worldviews would diminish the social cohesion he saw as so important to society.

In the mid-twentieth century many scholars believed that with the decrease in the significance of religion for social power, religion itself would begin to disappear. This was called the **secularization thesis**. Much like Frazer, many scholars saw science as becoming so powerful a source of human understanding that religion would be no longer needed. This secularization thesis has largely been proven to be a mistake, at least on a global scale. As Peter Berger (2008), who was once a proponent of the secularization thesis himself, has pointed out, our societies have not become secularized (in the sense of religion disappearing) as much as they have become pluralized. There are more religious options available to the average person, and an increase in both conservative religious belief and practice, as well as an increase in individualized spiritual practice. So while we live in a secular world, where one religion is not dominant over all other social institutions, we also live in a world in which religion and spirituality are continually significant.

so Weber's sociology combines economics, society, and religion. In *The Protestant Ethic and the Spirit of Capitalism* (1904–1905) Weber notes that, in Germany at least, Protestants filled the positions of business leaders and capital investors more frequently than did Catholics. In his explanation of why this was the case, Weber looked to early Protestant reformers, particularly Martin Luther (1483–1546) and John Calvin (1509–1564). Luther challenged the Roman Catholic Church's hierarchy and evaluation of priestly and monastic life as more spiritually significant than secular, worldly life. Luther taught that all believers were equal before God and that everyone, not just priests or monks and nuns, had a vocation (a calling from God). One's secular labour (everyday job) should be understood as a calling from God, and done as if one were doing it for God (i.e., with devotion). John Calvin taught the doctrine of predestination, in which God predetermines who is going to heaven (the elect) and who is not. In this teaching, nothing we do can change the ultimate outcome. While Calvin himself seemed to feel fairly confident in his own salvation, not all his followers were. Due to some significant anxiety about how to know if one were saved or not, Calvinist preachers began to encourage the view that prosperity, if one were properly pious and simple, was a sign of election. Put together, Luther's view that secular labour is a calling from God and the Calvinist view that if you did that job well God would reward you as sign of your election, led to a change of attitude toward the acquisition of wealth. As long as wealth was not squandered, and material pleasures were not indulged, wealth was a sign of godliness. Acquiring wealth without spending it frivolously led to increased capital and increased investment. Weber called this **inner-worldly asceticism**: living simply within the world systems. This inner-worldly asceticism is, according to Weber's theory, the spirit of capitalism; without it capitalism would not have developed as it did. This is not to say that, even in Weber's day, this asceticism was still operative. As Weber writes,

> Since asceticism undertook to remodel the world and to work out its ideals in the world, material goods have gained an increasing and finally inexorable power over the lives of men as at no previous period in history. Today the spirit of religious asceticism—whether finally, who knows?—has escaped from the cage. But victorious capitalism, since it rests on mechanical foundations, needs its support no longer (2003, 181–2).

Capitalism no longer needs the piety of Protestantism to support and keep it going.

KARL MARX'S SUPERSTRUCTURES

Weber was not the only theorist who had attributed a correlation between religion and capitalism. Karl Marx (1818–1883) had already made this claim, although in his view religion was not a *cause* of capitalism but rather an ideological institution, a

superstructure, designed to maintain unequal power relations. For Marx, economic realities determined all human behaviour. Modes of production, how necessities are produced (e.g., food is produced by hunting, agriculture, manufacturing, etc.), determine divisions of labour and power relations. Marx called modes of production the **base** of society. The superstructure was the collection of various institutions that support the base by making it seem natural. Religion, as a superstructure, provided a fantasy for people to keep them in line and unwilling to resist and revolt against capitalism. But rather than resist religion, Marx argued for the need to resist the oppressive base of capitalist modes of production.

WILLIAM JAMES' VARIETIES OF RELIGIONS

Durkheim, Weber, and Marx each approach religion as integrally connected to larger social systems, especially the economy. Other religious studies scholars took a more individualized and psychological approach. Key among these scholars was American psychologist William James (1842–1910). In his *Varieties of Religious Experience* (1902), James moves away from a consideration of the institutional forms of religion and focuses instead on the personal experience rooted in psychological states and types. Thus for him, religion was "*the feelings, acts, and experiences of individual men in their solitude, so far as they apprehend themselves to stand in relation to whatever they may consider the divine*" (1929 [1902], 31–2, italics original).

James believed that religious experiences, particularly those associated with **mysticism**, or feelings of transcendence or union with the divine, were psychological experiences that could be made sense of with psychological theory, outside of any **theological** attachment. This is not to say that James thought these experiences were somehow false or fake. Rather, he was a strong proponent of pragmatism and argued that if a religious experience seemed real and true to the individual, then for them it was. However that does not translate to the individual's experience pointing to any universal truth. Furthermore, James suggested that differing types of personalities found differing types of religious experience profound. An optimistic personality, for example, is more likely to find satisfaction in a world-affirming sense of the balance of nature, while a more pessimistic personality is more likely to find satisfaction in the need to repent of the sins of the material body. Whereas Durkheim thought he could find the elementary forms of all religion in "primitive" society, James thought he could understand the basic varieties of religious experiences by focusing study on what he thought of as the more extreme versions: severe asceticism, martyrdom, mystical experiences of direct interaction with the divine, etc. These were each driven by some psychological need.

MIRCEA ELIADE'S HISTORY OF RELIGIONS

Durkheim and James take both a functionalist and reductive approach to religion. As functionalists, they looked to the role religion plays in society or the individual.

As reductives, though, they argued that their position could explain everything there is to know about religion. Thus, for Durkheim, religion was only about social cohesion; for James it was only about the individual psychological needs. In the middle of the twentieth century, influential religion scholar Mircea Eliade (1907–1986), rejected these type of approaches and called for a study of religion that would look at religion in its own right, not reduced to the function of something else. He believed that "Man becomes aware of the sacred because it manifests itself, shows itself, as something wholly different from the profane" (1959, 11). Eliade was interested in both a historical and a **phenomenological** study of religion. As such, he tried to trace the patterns of the symbolic and mythical in a variety of religious contexts. The major formulation he emphasized was the distinction between the sacred and the profane. Unlike Durkheim, who associated the sacred with society and the profane with the individual, Eliade associated the sacred with the supernatural or extraordinary and the profane with everyday life. According to Eliade, because the sacred is completely other than the profane, it needs a separate language to be expressed; this language is that of symbolism and myth. Eliade's definitions of the sacred and the profane had a huge impact on the way religion was studied in the latter half of the twentieth century. His approach is called "**history of religions**" and attempts to find the patterns of symbolism and mythology throughout world cultures and religions to find the universal patterns underlying all religious and spiritual manifestations.

Return to the Cognitive

PASCAL BOYER, E. THOMAS LAWSON, AND ROBERT N. MCCAULEY

Another twentieth-century approach to looking for patterns of religious and spiritual manifestations reflected the earlier Victorian cognitive approaches to religion, but this time were based in considerably more developed psychological and neurological sciences. According to Pascal Boyer in his book *The Naturalness of Religious Ideas: A Cognitive Theory of Religion* (1994) religious ideas and practices are, in part, dictated by "universal properties of the human mind-brain" (viii). Boyer, and other cognitive scientists of religion, comes to this conclusion based on the recurrence of many features of religions world-wide, such as prayer, veneration of ancestors, funeral rites, symbols, etc. These recurrences occur because our brains are wired similarly and thus various peoples come up with similar content in belief and practice. However, cognitive scientists of religion do not argue that these "universal properties of the human mind-brain" are the only explanation for religions. If that were the case, all religions would be the same. Cognitive scholars E. Thomas Lawson and Robert N. McCauley (2006) argue that we need both interpretive and explanatory methods for exploring religion. The interpretive methods look for meaning within the various beliefs and practices, such as what the totems of various tribes represent culturally. The explanatory methods look for causal relationships, such as what functions in our brain cause humans to give religious symbolism and significance to things that become totems. These methods need not be antagonistic, though they argue that the interpretive method has been heavily favoured over the explanatory method in recent religious studies. Interpretive methods should not ignore the importance of scientific testable theories. As Harvey Whitehouse argues, "The evidence that our minds are composed of numerous specialized tools for handling different types of information is supporting increasingly plausible claims about the shaping and constraining effects of cognition on the invention and spread of culture in general, and religion in particular" (2007, 273).

CLIFFORD GEERTZ'S THICK DESCRIPTION

The cognitive science of religion is typically tied to anthropological approaches. Both are trying to understand patterns in religious belief and practice worldwide. However, another twentieth-century scholar to have a significant impact on the study of religion was anthropologist Clifford Geertz (1926–2006). Like Eliade, Geertz was critical of the reductionist approaches to religion found in earlier scholars. Unlike Eliade or the cognitive scientists, Geertz was uninterested in discovering global patterns of the sacred; instead, he was much more interested in the specifics of particular religious traditions. He advocated a type of **ethnographic** study called "thick description" in which ethnographers recorded not only what was happening, but also its significance. Religion is part of culture, and culture is the shared meaning behind various symbols and actions. Just looking at what people say or do does not necessarily get at the cultural meaning behind those activities, for those within a specific culture. Geertz did not, however, suggest that there was no distinction between religion and other forms of culture. He wrote,

> religion is: (1) a system of symbols which acts to (2) establish powerful, persuasive, and long-lasting moods and motivations in men by (3) formulating conceptions of a general order of existence and (4) clothing these conceptions with such an aura of factuality that (5) the moods and motivations seem uniquely realistic (1993 [1973], 90–1, italics original).

For him, religion was still more than everyday activity. It involved a worldview about the most foundational aspect of life, and an ethos, or way of behaving, based on that worldview.

Geertz's definition warrants some further explanation, as it is used so frequently in current religious studies. First, religion is a system of symbols. Symbols can be visible, aural, literary, or postural representations that point to a specific meaning that can be interpreted in a variety of ways. The way these symbols are interpreted leads to the development of particular moods and motivations in those who find the symbols meaningful. Moods are feelings that draw people together; they create a common worldview. Motivations are ways people act based on those moods; they are the ethos that shapes community actions. For example, we could take the symbol of the creation story in the biblical book of Genesis in which God creates all people in God's image. If this symbol is interpreted as all people are special because they are created in God's image, this could create a mood of relationship and care. The motivation based off this mood could be that if we are all created in God's image and thus are special, then those of us who find this symbol meaningful must treat all people as special, maybe even going so far as to fight for the creation and maintenance of human rights. However, if this symbol is interpreted as all people are created in God's image and thus must live up to that image, then there could be very different moods and motivations. This interpretation could create the mood of conformity and rigid law, which could lead to the motivation that if we are all made in the image of God and must live up to that image, then those of us who find this symbol meaningful must assist all other people to live up to that image, maybe even going so far as to use laws, sanctions, and even violent force against the ungodly. In each of these cases, according to Geertz's definition of religion, the mood and motivation developed will seem completely natural and inevitable based on the symbol.

The "Lived Religion" Approach

ROBERT ORSI AND MEREDITH MCGUIRE

A recent approach to religion, the "lived religion" approach, gives more consideration to the activities of the everyday. This approach is associated with late-twentieth, early twenty-first century studies by scholars like Robert Orsi and Meredith McGuire. The lived religion approach asks what people are doing in their homes, on the street, at work, as well as in specifically religious buildings and contexts. This is not to say these questions were never important before. Other theorists certainly asked them. However, in the lived religion approach the everyday takes centre stage in a way it had not previously. McGuire has found in her research that many people's religious practice does not fit clearly definable categories of the world religions. People claiming to be Roman Catholic may practise Buddhist meditation and attend a Protestant Pentecostal church. People who claim no religious affiliation may still practise a variety of spiritual activities and profess spiritual beliefs. As McGuire writes,

> Because religion-as-lived is based more on such religious practices than on religious ideas or beliefs, it is not necessarily logically coherent. Rather, it requires a practical coherence: It needs to make sense in one's everyday life, and it needs to be effective, to "work," in the sense

of accomplishing some desired end (such as healing, improving one's relationship with a loved one, or harvesting enough food to last the winter). This practical coherence explains the reasoning underlying much popular religion, which may otherwise appear to be irrational and superstitious (McGuire 2008, 15).

THOMAS TWEED

In a similar vein, Thomas Tweed (2006) insists on the non-static state of religions. Religions flow between individual and communal practice, between organic mind-brain activity and cultural constructions, between the movements of migrations and the groundedness of home. While each of the religious studies theorists discussed in this section have something to contribute to a study of religion and popular culture, it is the lived religion approach that is most attuned to a cultural studies approach. For lived religion scholars, all the elements of cultural production and activity, whether professed high culture or mass mediated popular culture, are locations of people's lived experiences.

Issues of Gender, Race, and Class

RANDI R. WARNE

One element of the study of religion that you may have noticed, as we have gone through this short survey, is that until we get to the late twentieth-century scholars, religion is a concern of *men*. In her critical essay "(En)gendering Religious Studies," Randi R. Warne (1998) argues that it was not really until the late 1970s that religious studies scholars, and their theories, began to take into account both the experiences and expertise of women. Scholars were men, and not only men, but white, middle-class men. Race, class, and gender were simply not issues on the radar until the late twentieth century. These issues have become highly significant to the study of religion since then. It is impossible to study people's lived religion without taking into account their socio-economic positioning, their racial and gendered experiences, their sexuality, and their political stance in terms of these concerns. It is equally important to take the scholars' positioning into account as well. These are also concerns of cultural studies, as we will see, and thus crucial elements of the further analyses found in this book.

Applications and Interpretations

If we return to our earlier scenario of Christmas in Canada, we can see that there can be various ways of understanding what is religious about this popular celebration. For the Victorian anthropologists and their concern with belief, the question that must be asked is to what extent people believe in the mythologies they engage with at this time of year. It would seem that children are encouraged to believe in Santa, but as we grow and develop more complex reasoning skills we learn that Santa is not real but a symbol. Christians who believe in the mystical aspects of the birth of Jesus (the virgin birth, the angel declarations, the star in the sky, etc.) are also still in a more "primitive" or childlike state of belief. A more rational approach would be to think of this story as metaphoric, pointing to a larger causation of the world.

Durkheim, however, would counter that position by suggesting that Christmas celebrations are about social cohesion, not belief. Therefore, Christmas celebrations, from nativity plays to visiting Santa at the mall, are religious as they reinforce group status. We are these people who are bound together by a common mythology of salvation and/or consumption.

Weber would emphasize the consumption aspect demonstrating how gift giving at Christmas represents the celebration of wealth and capitalism that flows from a specifically Protestant Christian history, though now typically divorced from the specific theology of piety and calling.

The psychological approach of James would suggest that if a person feels spiritually connected to the mythology and practices of the season, then this is real religion, whether the connection be to the baby Jesus or to Santa Claus.

Cognitive scientists would look to brain functions to determine the way we physiologically need festivals and demonstrate how Christmas, in its various forms, might fulfill this need, in a similar way that Eid ul-Fitr (the ending feast of Ramadan) may fulfill that need for those in Muslim-majority countries.

Geertz would ask us to think about what the symbols of Christmas make real for those who celebrate: generosity, family, salvation, consumerism. These become religious symbols as they shape people's sense of ultimate reality.

Furthermore, the lived religion approach would caution us from associating strictly dogmatic and/or institutional religious practice with religion. The Christian churches may say only the celebration of Jesus is truly religion, but individuals put their devotion in many different places. Some may actually thank the Lord above that Santa Claus comes tonight, and who are we, as scholars, to say that is a less valid religious sentiment than singing the Hallelujah Chorus (a popular chorus of Handel's *Messiah*, written in 1741, and frequently sung in Christian churches on Christmas Eve or morning). As we can see, there are many different ways religious studies scholars think and talk about religion.

But what about popular culture?

Defining Popular Culture

If the study of religion is complicated by disagreements and debates amongst scholars on what religion actually is, so too popular culture resists clear definition.

However, it is helpful to look at some of the ways popular culture has been defined as a starting point. This section will introduce some of the theorists we will explore in further depth throughout the book. Again, like in the study of religion, these theories are not static, nor is popular culture. We must continue with Thomas Tweed's insistence that theory be about movement rather than static statements.

The idea of "popular" culture is a relatively new one developing out of a specific upper- and upper-middle class concern with industrialization, urbanization, and class consciousness. In the late eighteenth century and into the early nineteenth century "popular culture" began to be used to refer to two major areas of cultural concern: **folk culture** and **mass culture**. For those scholars and cultural connoisseurs who looked into the past with a romantic vision, the preservation of folk culture, largely rural and ideal, was a necessity born to an urban industrial world. Popular culture, in this sense, was the cultural production of a simpler society that was lost, or dying, in modernity. For others, popular culture became the term used to deride a developing mass culture associated with the new urban working class. An influential proponent of this position was the British cultural critic Matthew Arnold (1822–1888).

Popular Culture Theorists

MATTHEW ARNOLD AND THE LEAVISITES

In *Culture and Anarchy* (1869), Arnold clearly articulates a position in which Culture (note the capital "C") was something which refined the human. However, society had taken a turn toward degraded popular culture, such as the proliferation of music halls with their rowdy and degenerate songs and activities. This position was further reinforced by the work of F.R. (Frank Raymond) Leavis (1895–1978) and Q.D. (Queenie Dorothy) Leavis (1906–1981), along with their following, the Leavisites. Writing in the 1930s, F.R. Leavis and Q.D. Leavis saw the twentieth century as marked by cultural decline, tied to the twin evils of capitalism and Marxism. In their writing, the Leavises and their followers both critiqued mass culture as depraved *and* looked with longing to the folk culture of their imagined rural English past. F.R. Leavis, for example, argued that films "involve surrender, under conditions of hypnotic receptivity, to the cheapest emotional appeals, appeals the more insidious because they are associated with a compellingly vivid illusion of actual life" (Leavis 1933, 10). The popularity of working-class cultural activities (not recognized as capital "C" Culture) was in many ways a threat to the cultural authority of the upper classes. The emphasis on Culture, or "**high culture**," was a way to maintain social difference. One significant difference that developed is the relationship to commercialism; "high culture" was non-profit, needing the sponsorship of the wealthy, while popular culture was commercial and thus driven not by "pure" artistic vision, but consumer market demands.

THEODOR ADORNO AND MAX HORKHEIMER AND CULTURE INDUSTRY

In the late 1940s another version of the concern with mass culture arrived in the work of the Frankfurt School, particularly that of Theodor Adorno (1903–1969) and Max Horkheimer (1895–1973). Together Adorno and Horkheimer coined the term the "**culture industry**." However, rather than seeing mass culture as a product of a depraved working class, trying to gain cultural authority over the upper classes, Adorno and Horkheimer took a decidedly Marxist turn, arguing that the culture industry was produced by those in power as a way to maintain cultural authority and economic privilege. The working-class consumers were simply duped into thinking popular culture was "theirs." A more in-depth discussion of the Frankfort School is found in Chapter 2.

ANTONIO GRAMSCI AND NEO-MARXISM

Not all cultural theorists informed by Marxism took the pessimistic view of the Frankfurt School. Some preferred the **neo-Marxist** approach of Antonio Gramsci (1891–1937). Gramsci was imprisoned by the fascist government in Italy from 1926–1932 during which he wrote more than 30 notebooks, now called the *Prison Notebooks*. These notebooks outline many ideas that shaped a twentieth-century neo-Marxism, particularly Gramsci's theory of **hegemony**.

Hegemony involves taking the interests of those in power and making them seem universal, and natural. However, hegemony is not domination through physical force; it relies on skills of negotiation in which the powerful need to convince the masses. Gramsci writes in his *Prison Notebooks*, "the attempt is always made to ensure that force will appear to be based on the consent of the majority, expressed by the so-called organs of public opinion—newspapers and associations—which, therefore, in certain situations, are artificially multiplied" (Gramsci 1971, 80). Gramsci argues that while popular culture is still often perceived as a structure imposed by those in power (as the Frankfurt School argues), it is also a site of struggle for meaning. Consumers (the masses) are not just cultural dupes (even if some of them are some of the time). This approach to popular culture, sometimes termed "culturalism," coalesced into the field of cultural studies in the 1970s and 1980s, thanks largely to the work of scholars such as Raymond Williams (1921–1988) and Stuart Hall (1932–).

RAYMOND WILLIAMS

Raymond Williams rejected the Leavisite disdain of working-class culture, perhaps because he came from a working-class background himself. Rather than the focus on a "high culture" that would reinforce middle- and upper-class values as normative, Williams had a wider definition of culture that included the everyday and ordinary lives of all people. For him, culture was a way of life in which meanings and values were expressed through the various cultural products created and consumed. The job of cultural analysis was to study these recorded or documentary cultural products to clarify the meanings and values of the given culture. These meanings and values, however, are not only found within commodities themselves, but in how people use and interact with them.

STUART HALL

Stuart Hall further explored the differences in meanings given to a commodity by its producer—encoding—and those given by the consumer—decoding. While the producer encoded meanings in a product, not every consumer would decode the meanings in the way the producer intended. While recognizing the often hegemonic values encoded in most popular culture, Hall was more interested in what people did with those cultural products: how they were decoded. For him, popular culture is a site of power struggle between those trying to impose hegemonic values and those resisting. In this sense, popular culture becomes the prime site of the negotiations needed to both maintain and resist hegemony. A more in-depth discussion of "culturalism" is found in Chapter 3.

The cultural studies approach to popular culture puts a heavier focus on consumer decoding, though it does not neglect questions about producer encoding. The relationships between the various meanings of any given popular cultural product or process have much to tell us about the social and political climate of a given society. Questions about race, gender, class, and post-colonialism are at the forefront of cultural studies. Increasingly, questions about globalization and the effects of both homogenizing and diversification are addressed in studies of popular culture. For some, the spread of Western, and particularly American, culture around the globe has lead to a homogenizing of culture, making everything the same. Some refer to this as "airport culture" or the "McDonaldization" of the world. Other scholars, however, see this "Americanization" thesis as too reductive. It does not allow for the **agency** of other peoples to resist and negotiate, that is to decode, cultural products in a variety of ways. In many ways, though American popular culture is available globally, it is consumed in very different ways; many people around the world blend their indigenous traditions and values with Western popular culture to create new **hybrid** cultural practices. Furthermore, while American, or more generally Western, culture is available globally, so too are a vast array of cultural products and practices from around the globe available in the West, leading to a diversity of culture that counters the argument that all culture is becoming one (American) global culture.

A cultural studies approach to Christmas celebrations in Canada would focus on how people understand their use of various products, services, and celebrations, much in the same way a lived religion approach would. However, cultural studies does not solely look to individual preferences, but also puts heavy emphasis on social groupings (e.g., race, class, gender, sexuality, etc.). So, while it is interesting to think about how any individual understands her or his annual contribution to the Salvation Army toy drive, it is even more significant to think about how her or his social positioning may influence that understanding and practice. These questions push us to think about power dynamics in society, in a way a simple study of individual practice may not.

Religion and Popular Culture

The relationship between religion and popular culture can be quite complicated. Religion, on the one hand, seems to be about the sacred, that which is set apart from the everyday, and concerns that which is of highest value or meaning in any given culture or society. Popular culture, on the other hand, seems to be about entertainment and the everyday world. What do these two things have to do with each other? In his book *Authentic Fakes: Religion and American Popular Culture* (2005) David Chidester asks this very question. He answers it by arguing that popular culture should not be viewed as superficial, but concerned with the very serious work of identity construction and meaning making, much like religion. Thus there will be overlaps, parallels, contrasts, and other relationships between what we understand as popular culture and religion.

Bruce David Forbes and Jeffrey H. Mahan, in their book *Religion and Popular Culture in America* (2000), give us four categories to help us think about the relationships between religion and popular culture:

1. religion in popular culture
2. popular culture in religion
3. popular culture as religion
4. religion and popular culture in dialogue

This section briefly outlines these four relationships before we move into the more detailed study of the rest of the book.

Religion in Popular Culture

The most obvious relationship between religion and popular culture is that religious themes and stories are widely used in a variety of popular cultural products. We do not need to look far to find examples: Mel Gibson's movie *The Passion of the Christ*; Dan Brown's novel *The Da Vinci Code*; Kayne West's song "Jesus Walks"; the display of yoga in advertising campaigns; a water bottle with the image of a Buddha on it. There are a number of ways scholars have approached the study of religion in popular culture. Many take a humanities approach that addresses the aesthetic and narrative aspects of any given product or "text." One example of this approach can be found in the collection of essays compiled by B.J. Oropeza in *The Gospel According to Superheroes* (2005). These essays look to the narratives of superheroes in comics, television and film, focusing on perceived universal myths. Ken Schenk's essay "Superman: A Popular Culture Messiah" not only explains the seemingly obvious Messianic symbolism of the classic Superman story, he also explores this Messianic story as a story of human heroism. Schenk concludes his essay with the observation that Superman

> represents all that is best in human value. He embodies our desire to overcome evil with good. His origin and character indirectly raise classic questions about what a god or human might be. If reality is measured in part by the effect something has on the world, then Superman is real. He has inspired and impacted countless lives and continues to do so. He calls us to follow his example and fight for truth and justice in the world (44).

This analysis of the Messianic Hero draws on the understanding of myth proposed by Mircea Eliade: myth as a symbolic language to speak of the sacred. While there may be culturally specific ways of telling these stories, for Eliade, Oropeza, and Schenk the basic ideas underlying the stories are universal. Our cultural studies approach is less interested in the aesthetic concerns (Is this a well-written story? Does the technology adequately represent the underlying theme of the story? Does the narrative fit within larger mythic structures?) and more interested in questions about what kinds of messages are encoded and decoded in this product. Forbes and Mahan include in their collection Jane Naomi Iwamura's discussion of the way western film has used the image of the Buddhist monk. She draws on Edward Said's theory about **Orientalism** and shows how the Buddhist monk becomes a stereotype of a spiritual exotic in contrast to a disenchanted western world. We explore this argument in more detail in Chapter 7.

A cultural studies approach, like Iwamura's, asks questions such as, how does this product reflect an understanding of the religious imagery, story, symbolism, and where does that understanding come from? How is this particular use of this imagery, story and symbolism implicated in gender, class, race and/or colonial **discourses**? How do people use these products? Is it different for a person of South Asian Hindu background to take a yoga class at the local health club than it is for a person of European Christian background? Is Dan Brown's version of feminine spirituality informed by his gender and is it read differently by people of different genders? While the questions asked of these products are complicated, the

Discourse

The concept of discourse in cultural theory is much more than simply conversation or communication. Discourses are ways of talking about the world that do not only communicate, but shape, knowledge. Discourses provide limits to what is communicable. Michel Foucault (1926–1984) in his influential book *Discipline and Punish* (1975) talks of discourse as constructing "regimes of truth," which block any language for thinking of alternate truths. For example, the discourse of gender in Western culture has constructed gender as dualistic, feminine and masculine, such that it is very difficult to discuss alternative understandings of gender in any way. Even attempts to do so can only do so within the confines of the discourse (i.e., masculine women or feminine men or transgender as a crossing from one gender to the other). The very structure of the English language disallows a reference to a non-masculine, non-feminine person (as "it" is presumed to be non-personal). Though it is almost impossible to break away from discourses, they can be challenged and negotiated, as the very language of feminism, queer theory, and transgender/transsexuality attempt to do.

recognition of the relationships between religion and popular culture here is not particularly complicated. Religion is used by those creating popular culture.

Popular Culture in Religion

The second relationship is that of popular culture in religion. Many of the genres, technologies, and media of popular culture have been adopted by religious organizations in some way or another. Prominent in this research is the use of television, and now the Internet, for the use of Christian evangelism, in televangelism, although the use of these media for preaching purposes is not limited to Christians. Likewise a variety of religious organizations have used rock music or rap, the romance novel genre, or video and board games to promote religious messages. Forbes and Mahan include in their collection a discussion by William D. Romanowski on the way the Contemporary Christian Music (CCM) industry has used popular musical genres to **evangelize** youth, though their success seems more in providing music for those youth already committed to an evangelical Christian life. Interestingly, Romanowski sees that the more popular Contemporary Christian Music became, the less evangelical it became. He writes, "The intent may have been to save souls and minister to young Christians, but the Christian music industry brought evangelical religion even further into the free-for-all competition of the consumer marketplace" (2000, 109). This quote highlights that many of the questions asked of this relationship between religion and popular culture have to do with the kinds of modifications religious messages must make to be appealing to the mass audience drawn to the popular genre. Neil Postman, in his famous book *Amusing Ourselves to Death* (1985), argued that the switch from print-based to television-based religious teaching required a significant shift in message, not only medium, leading to, in his opinion, a diminished sense of religiosity. We will explore Postman's concerns more fully in Chapter 9. Regardless of the potential to become more consumer oriented, it is becoming increasingly obvious that a religious organization unwilling to engage in more popular forms of information sharing and experience will lose its influence on practitioners.

Popular Culture as Religion

A more controversial approach to religion and popular culture is to look at instances when popular culture seems to function like religion. A lot of the scholarship on fandom and sports fits within this category. For example, the way fans revere superstars such as Elvis or Lady Gaga looks very similar, in some cases, to how Catholics revere saints. Forbes and Mahan include in their collection the discussion by Michael Jindra of *Star Trek* fandom and the appeal of the worldview created by Gene Roddenbery of a humanist optimistic future. This worldview, says Jindra, operates like a civil religion. In fact, he concludes, that "*Star Trek* fandom expresses Americans' idealism, and offers fans reasons for hope in the future" (2000, 177). This is a hope they have not found in traditional religion. Forbes and Mahan also include David Chidester's discussion of the Church of Baseball. The way some sports enthusiasts attend games looks very similar to the way some religious practitioners attend worship services. Fans of superstars and sports teams often find a kind of social cohesion that can look very much like the social cohesion brought by religious affiliation. In *Film as Religion*, John C. Lyden argues that film itself operates like religion, providing viewers with myths, morals, and rituals. As such, he suggests an approach to religion and film that looks more like inter-religious dialogue rather than finding Christian or Muslim or Hindu messages within film. These myths, morals, and rituals may look "secular" to the casual observer, but, like religion, they shape viewers sense of the world and provide, what Clifford Geertz would call moods and motivations for daily behaviour.

Religion and Popular Culture in Dialogue

The fourth category Forbes and Mahan give us is religion and popular culture in dialogue. This dialogue may, in many cases, actually be conflict as many of the questions raised in this dialogue are questions of ethics. To what extent does popular culture provide opposing ethical guidelines than those found in traditional religions? To what extent do popular cultural products reflect similar ethics without the "spiritual" component? Can religious practitioners learn from popular culture how to be better Christians or Jews or Muslims? One issue coming out of some of these questions is that of the influence of violent imagery in music, film, and gaming. While some religious figures have denounced such popular culture as morally degenerate, others have looked to the context the violence reflects and suggests a more justice-focused response. In his discussion of rap music in the Forbes and Mahan collection, Anthony Pinn suggests that a negative response to the violence found particularly in gangsta rap is only one possible religious response. He also sees possibility in a "nitty gritty" **hermeneutic** that expresses the realities of life that call for response. We engage in this discussion in more detail in Chapter 6. Another example of a conflict and/or dialogue between religion and popular culture comes in the religious responses to J.K. Rowling's Harry Potter series. In Amanda Cockrell's (2006) study of the Christian right response to Harry Potter she suggests that not only is the concern about the way that the occult is deemed normal and even potentially positive, but the Harry Potter world is too close to the real world. Unlike the magic in stories like Tolkien's *Lord of the Rings*, which are set in a different world, Harry makes his way through today's Britain to enter into a magical world that overlaps with the "muggle" or non-magical world. This becomes too much of a temptation for children to think they can access occult magic in the real world, according to some Christians.

Our earlier example of Canadian Christmas celebrations actually fits into each of these categories. We clearly see traditional Christian messages in popular culture, whether it be Beyoncé singing "Silent Night" or the biblical Christmas story recited in "A Charlie Brown Christmas." We also see religious groups utilizing popular culture to promote their message. A good example of this is the Salvation Army Santas. Popular culture often operates as religion, as we have already discussed, when we think of the symbolism of Santa and gift giving as representing a sacralizing of generosity and even consumption. The dialogue between religion and popular culture takes many forms at Christmas. On one hand it can be Christians critical of the conspicuous consumption prevalent in North American Christmas celebrations. On the other hand it can be thanking the Lord above that Santa Claus comes tonight. In each of these cases it becomes very clear that to separate the religious from the popular cultural aspects of Christmas celebrations is a difficult task indeed.

Summary

This chapter has introduced you to a variety of theories about religion. We have looked at cognitive theories based on belief in the form of Victorian anthropology, and ones based on more recent cognitive science. In contrast, a variety of functional approaches, such as Durkheim's sociological theory and James' psychological theory have looked to what religion offers us, rather than how we construct religions based on our beliefs and/or mind-brain requirements. Many religious studies theorists are interested in looking for patterns, whether they be phenomenological patterns proving an actual sacred/divine force, or the behavioural patterns of cognitive science. Religion is often associated with the development of capitalism, as seen in Weber and Marx. A number of scholars are less interested in overarching patterns and more concerned with specific cultural symbols and how they work in those cultural locations. Geertz argues for the need of thick description that focuses on the local rather than the universal. In some ways the "lived religion" approach localizes this thick description even further to the individual and/or small scale community. In all these approaches, religion is difficult to pin down. To theorize something this dynamic requires movement and flexibility.

We also need this flexibility in theorizing popular culture. There have been scholars in the past that have insisted popular culture was a degenerate form of entertainment for the lower classes that needed to be resisted and/or eradicated. By the middle of the twentieth century, however, we begin to see more serious consideration given to popular culture. The theory of the culture industry still sees popular culture in largely negative terms as a form of keeping the masses from revolting. Culturalism counters with the possibility of resistance in meaning making, seeing popular culture as a site of negotiation of power. Both theories rely on the suspicion of hegemony as a force to keep a small group in power and a larger mass compliant. The study of popular culture further requires a full-fledged jump into the political realms of race, gender, class, post-colonialism, and globalization. In this, though, popular culture is no different from religion. Theorizing both can be a highly political activity.

Review Questions

1. What does it mean to take a cognitive approach to religion?
2. How does Émile Durkheim define the sacred and the profane? How does this compare with the way Mircea Eliade defines the sacred and the profane?
3. According to Max Weber, how do Protestant ideas contribute to the development of capitalism?
4. What does it mean to take a functionalist approach to religion?
5. How is the lived religion approach similar to the cultural studies approach to popular culture?
6. What is the difference between thinking of popular culture as folk culture versus mass culture?
7. What is hegemony and how is it related to popular culture?

8. What is the difference between encoding and decoding popular culture?
9. What are the different relationships between religion and popular culture?
10. How does Christmas in Canada reflect the interactions and intersections between religion and popular culture?

Useful Resources

Print

Chidester, David. 2005. *Authentic Fakes: Religion and American Popular Culture*. Berkeley: University of California Press.

Forbes, Bruce David and Jeffrey H. Mahan. 2005 [2000]. *Religion and Popular Culture in America*. Revised Edition. Berkeley: University of California Press.

McGuire, Meredith B. 2008. *Lived Religion: Faith and Practice in Everyday Life*. Oxford University Press.

Pals, Daniel L. 2006. *Eight Theories of Religion*. Second Edition. Oxford University Press.

Pals, Daniel L. 2009. *Introducing Religion: Readings from the Classic Theorists*. Oxford University Press.

Storey, John. 2006. *Cultural Theory and Popular Culture: A Reader*. Third Edition. Harlow, England: Pearson Education Limited.

Storey, John. 2009. *Cultural Theory and Popular Culture: An Introduction*. Fifth Edition. Harlow, England: Pearson Education Limited.

Tweed, Thomas. 2006. *Crossing and Dwelling: A Theory of Religion*. Cambridge: Harvard University Press.

Online

Beyoncé singing "Silent Night" on *Regis and Kelly*: www.examiner.com/christian-education-in-richmond/beyonce-sings-silent-night-video

Lyrics for "Here Comes Santa Claus": www.41051.com/xmaslyrics/herecomes.html

Hallelujah Chorus flash mob: www.youtube.com/watch?v=SXh7JR9oKVE

2

Marxist Approaches

OBJECTIVES

This chapter will help you develop an understanding of

- the basic ideas of Marxist and neo-Marxist thought
- the approach of the Frankfurt School to popular culture
- the neo-Marxist argument against self-help spirituality
- the commodification of religion

In 2006 Rhonda Byrne produced a video and book, both called *The Secret*, in which she shares her journey from desperation to enlightenment through the discovery of an ancient and well hidden "secret." Drawing on the writings of historical figures from Abraham Lincoln to the Buddha, and featuring modern-day self-help gurus, *The Secret* reveals to viewers and readers the "law of attraction." Whatever we are thinking of is what we will attract. If we are pessimistic and think only of our hardships, we will attract more hardships. If we are optimistic and think of what we truly want, we will manifest those goals. *The Secret* promises that whatever we want, we can get. Whatever our life is, we have attracted to ourselves with our thoughts. As examples of the kinds of things we can attract to ourselves, the movie shows a woman looking at a beautiful necklace in a store window and "projecting" the desire for that necklace. Later she is given it as a gift by, presumably, her significant other. Another scene has a man driving in his car thinking of how he cannot be late for work, only to be stopped by a construction crew and bumper to bumper traffic. Even though he clearly does not want to be late, because he is thinking about being late, he attracts the circumstances to make him late.

The Secret is representative of a kind of mind-body-spirit movement of the twenty-first century that focuses on, first of all, positive thinking, and second, manifesting any desire. Participants in the film tell us that this secret has been known by a small few for thousands of years, who have wanted to keep it to themselves, and keep us working to maintain their desires. Luckily for us, Rhonda Byrne and the other self-help teachers have discovered it and are willing to share it with everyone. They are here to help us bring a revolution to our lives. In some ways, Byrne and company present *The Secret* as a tool to improve our lot in a similar way to other revolutionaries who argue that the working classes are under the thumb of those in political and economic power. Of course the most famous of these revolutionaries is Karl Marx (1818–1883).

Marx is well known for his economic theories about capitalism. He is also known for naming religion as the "opium of the people" (Marx and Engels 1975, 175). Marx's concern about religion is tied to his economic theory and his concept of ideology. While it may seem that a Marxist approach to religion and popular culture would be simply a rejection of religion, this is not the case. A number of revisions and reformulations of Marxist thought have developed in such a way that scholars can use his ideas to think through the place of popular culture in Marxist economic theory as well as analyze religious ideas, ideologies, structures, and limits in ways Marx himself may not have done. This chapter explores Marxist approaches to studying religion and popular culture. To do so, we first give an overview of the relevant Marxists theories, as first formulated by Marx and then reformulated by later thinkers, particularly those who made up the Frankfurt School. We then look at a more contemporary example of using Marxist thought to analyze the development of popular spirituality from self-help teachings such as *The Secret*, to adoption of tai chi and yoga by Westerners, to the selling of spiritual kitsch, to the incorporation of mind-body-spirit concerns in corporate contexts.

Marxist Theory and Political Application

Marx argued that the most fundamental element of society, the element that shaped all other elements, was the mode of production of the necessities of life. This argument is called **historical materialism**. In *The German Ideology*, originally written in 1846, Marx and his collaborator, Frederick Engels, write,

> Morality, religion, metaphysics, all the rest of ideology and their corresponding forms of consciousness, thus no longer retain the semblance of independence. They have no history, no development; but men, developing their material production and their material intercourse, alter, along with this their real existence, their thinking and the products of their thinking. Life is not determined by consciousness, but consciousness by life (Marx and Engels 1964, 38).

What they meant by this is that the way any society goes about making or getting food, clothing, shelter, etc., dictates what kinds of other social systems would be in place. The mode of production (hunting and gathering, feudal agriculture, industrial capitalism) is the **base** of society. All other institutions are **superstructures** designed to maintain a given mode of production. So the government, education, religion, the arts, etc., all operate in specific ways that maintain the mode of production. In Marx's time, mid-nineteenth century Europe, he saw the developing industrial capitalism as fortified by other institutions. For Marx, capitalism was a mode of production that was particularly problematic as it created **alienation** for most people from their labour and from each other. The working classes, which Marx called the **proletariat**, worked for the benefit of those who owned the factories, corporations, and other businesses. Marx called the owners the **bourgeoisie**. The proletariat worked for money but had no ownership of what they made, thus they were alienated from these products. The bourgeoisie owned the products of the proletariat labour and could, thus, make a profit. In this system, the proletariat was required to become more and more efficient so their labour would make more products, so the bourgeoisie could make more profit; however, the income given to the workers did not match the profit gained by the factory owners. The owners got increasingly wealthy while the workers were required to work harder for less.

This system, says Marx, is bolstered by the superstructure, which creates, sustains, and circulates **ideology** designed to keep the proletariat from revolting. Marx argued that those who controlled material production, the bourgeoisie, also controlled mental production. He writes in *The German Ideology*,

> The class, which is the ruling *material* force of society, is at the same time its ruling *intellectual* force. [. . .] The individuals composing the ruling class possess among other things consciousness, and therefore think. Insofar, therefore, as they rule as a class and determine the extent and compass of an epoch, it is self-evident that they do this in its whole range, hence among other things rule also as thinkers, as producers of ideas, and regulate the production and distribution of the ideas of their age: thus their ideas are the ruling ideas of the epoch. For instance, in an age and in a country where royal power, aristocracy and bourgeoisie are contending for mastery and where, therefore, mastery is shared, the doctrine of the separation of powers proves to be the dominant idea and is expressed as an "eternal law" (Marx and Engels 1964, 60–1, italics original).

The ideologies that were produced and spread by those in power worked to make the system seem natural. Religion (Christianity in Europe) taught people to submit to the state and work diligently for a future reward in heaven. The legal system labelled anyone trying to make change as criminal and lacking in morals.

Capitalism

Capitalism is an economic system based on private ownership of means of production and distribution geared toward the generation of profit. The term "capital" comes from the Latin and refers to chattel or cattle as movable property. Early forms of capitalism, such as mercantilism, developed through contact with other peoples in distant lands. In the sixteenth to eighteenth centuries, mercantilism involved the trade of, largely, raw materials not available in the home country. Mercantilism was intimately tied to European colonialism and expansionism. In the eighteenth and early nineteenth centuries, capitalism radically intensified due to the Industrial Revolution. Industrialization involved the removal of the connection between labour and product. As factories developed and increased production with decreased investment of time and money, there was a decline of the artisan and guild. People increasingly participated in a fraction of the production process, through assembly-line labour, rather than producing a whole product as a form of art. The factory-produced goods, which could be made en masse, were cheaper than the artisan-produced goods, and thus the market for artisans began to decline. Due to the profit available with the increased production of goods, the factory owners began to replace the merchants and landowners as economic leaders. The factory owners owned the capital, the tools and materials of production, and thus claimed all the profit from selling the product. They were able to pay relatively cheap wages because there

Popular culture told stories and produced images in which capitalism was presented as a natural backdrop to everyday life. Each of these superstructures contributed to ideology that hid the realities of power relations and possible change from those that derived the least benefit from the capitalist system. Marx firmly argued that the role of the philosopher or cultural theorist was not just to observe this system, but to change it. Thus Marxism has an inherent political agenda: to disrupt the capitalist superstructures and encourage the proletariat to take control of their own labour. Once they had done this, they could institute a truly **communist** society where everyone shared resources and there was no need for government.

Vladimir Lenin and Mao Zedong

A number of revolutionaries took Marx's ideas and embedded them into political movements, most notably Vladimir Lenin (1870–1924; Soviet Union) and Mao Zedong (1893–1976; China). The creation of communist states drew on Marx's critique of capitalism and emphasized the uplift of the proletariat, but, in most cases, tended toward totalitarian governmental systems rather than the utopia of Marx's vision of no need for government. In a totalitarian state, the government controls was a large population of the working class, or proletariat in Marx's terms, who needed employment. Population numbers were rising and there were limited resources in rural settings to support that population. Many people from rural areas moved into the cities that developed around the factories. The competition for work became fierce, and workers were encouraged to look out for themselves (and their families) rather than thinking about the good of the community. This shift from rural agricultural living, and its communal responsibility, to wage-labour, emphasized the importance of the individual; an emphasis that was also key to the rising liberal philosophy of the age.

With the development of urban centres around factories came an increased working-class consciousness. Marx hoped to motivate this working-class consciousness to resist capitalism overall. While his revolutionary charge was not taken up successfully in many places, the push for improved conditions in the factories did eventually lead to laws restricting working hours and gradual increases in wages. What this accomplished was the formalization of "free" or leisure time and increased disposable income. As factories became more efficient and pushed out greater numbers of goods, and workers gained in economic stability, the workers were increasingly encouraged to use their disposable income to purchase non-necessary goods, often goods they had themselves made. This led to the development of a commodity culture of capitalism whereby "novelties" became the way to pleasure and prestige.

everything, both public and private life. In both the Soviet Union and China, the so-called communist governments forced all people to comply with their version of proletarian control, and heavily punished all bourgeoisie. While Marx may have advocated the overthrow of the bourgeoisie, he believed there would be no need for government control over the people; all people would treat each other well and fairly because of their good will and love of society. Thus Leninist and Maoist communism is not really Marxist communism. Marx's influence, even if misinterpreted, is not limited to these state formations. His critique of capitalism, and particularly his formulation of base and superstructure have prompted further questioning on the part of cultural theorists, and much of academic scholarship in the humanities and social sciences owes something to Marxist thought.

Antonio Gramsci and Hegemony

One influential Marxist thinker was Antonio Gramsci. Gramsci was an Italian intellectual who was involved with the formation of the Communist Party of Italy. He was imprisoned by the Fascist government of Mussolini in the 1920s. While he was in prison he wrote more than 30 notebooks in which he outlines his Marxist-inspired theories of culture and social systems. A significant concept he develops in these notebooks is the idea of **hegemony**. Hegemony is the system of coercing the working class masses to accept the dominant ideology of the ruling classes. Hegemony operates not through physical force or threat, but by convincing people that the dominant ideas are the only possible truths available. This idea was certainly already present within Marx's discussion of ideology, but Gramsci supplied further nuance. He writes,

> Undoubtedly the fact of hegemony presupposes that account be taken of the interests and the tendencies of the groups over which hegemony is to be exercised, and that a certain compromise equilibrium should be formed—in other words, that the leading group should make sacrifices of an economic-corporate kind. But there is also no doubt that such sacrifices and such a compromise cannot touch the essential; for though hegemony is ethical-political, it must also be economic, must necessarily be based on the decisive function exercised by the leading group in the decisive nucleus of economic activity (1971, 161).

Hegemony works through negotiation and the promise of pleasure. For example, as a way to reinforce the necessity and naturalness of a capitalist system, workers are bombarded with messages that they need to buy products or services to be happy. They can only buy these products or services if they have money, and they can only get money by working a wage-job, that is selling their labour in the capitalist market. Thus the superstructures present "truths" that maintain the base economic system. But these "truths" are coated in "benefits." Another example that Gramsci points out is the hegemony of the Catholic Church (in Italy): people are told that if they are good they will receive eternal reward in heaven. Being good means following the rules of church and state. Revolting against these institutions will result in eternal damnation. The idea of hegemony is that the people are convinced that if they do not follow the dominant norm of living they will be even more unhappy than what they may be in the current system.

The Frankfurt School and Neo-Marxism

A group of German scholars took this idea of hegemony and developed a **neo-Marxist** critique of cultural and social development. These scholars were generally associated with the Institute for Social Research in Frankfurt, originally set up in 1923, and as such have come to be known as the Frankfurt School of thought. The Frankfurt School was both critical of capitalism and dismayed with the direction taken by Marxist-influenced communist states. They used Marxist theory in conjunction with other theories such as psychoanalysis and existential philosophy to create what they called "**critical theory**" as a means of adequately understanding the capitalism of the twentieth century. Primarily they were critical of the Enlightenment idea of progress through scientific and technological advancement. They argued that we as a species were not becoming freer with these advancements, but actually more constrained. However, they did not see a Marxist revolution as solving the problems, largely because this revolution did not seem to be successful in Marxist states in creating a better world, and was never able to unify workers successfully in most of the world. It is important to note that the Frankfurt School was in operation at a time of growing **fascism** in Europe both in Italy and Germany. Many of the members fled Germany just prior to World War II and did much of their writing in the United States. Their construction of critical theory was based on this experience of fascism as well as their observations of American life during this time.

Theodor Adorno, Max Horkheimer, and the Culture Industry Thesis

Two key contributors to the Frankfurt School were Theodor Adorno (1903–1969) and Max Horkheimer (1895–1973). Together they developed the "**culture industry thesis**." This thesis suggests that rather than progressing into greater freedoms in the industrialized world of the twentieth century, we had been plunged into greater restrictions. Adorno and Horkeimer focused their critique on the production of popular culture and concluded that popular culture held severe ideological constraints. This means that popular culture is produced by those who have power to keep those who do not have power in line. In other words, popular culture is a tool to enforce hegemony by entertaining people into passivity. Furthermore, what we are entertained by is predictable and standardized, even when seeming to provide multiple options and critique of the dominant ideology. As Adorno and Horkheimer write in their *Dialectic of Enlightenment*, originally written in 1947, "Culture today is infecting everything with sameness" (2002, 94). We may think that we have individual choice in the kinds of popular cultural forms we enjoy and participate in, but, says Adorno in a scathing critique of popular music, it is a **pseudo-individuality**. In reality we have the same stories told over and over again, and the same music played in standard formats. These popular cultural products are designed to distract us from recognizing there are other options than just capitalism. Adorno and Horkheimer write, "Entertainment is the prolongation of work under late capitalism. It is sought by those who want to escape the mechanized labor process so that they can cope with it again" (2002, 109). We sit back, enjoy our iPod playlist while we sell our labour; we unwind after a hard week's work at the movie theatre or night club. None of these activities, however, motivate us to challenge the system; rather, they reinforce the necessity of capitalism and other hegemonic ideals. Any opposition that attempts to resist this culture industry eventually gets co-opted into the system, as can be evidenced by the mainstreaming and commercialization of punk or rap music. Ultimately, say Adorno and Horkheimer, popular culture maintains social control by creating a compliant population as consumers conform to hegemonic values.

Key to the culture industry thesis is the idea of commodity fetishism. In commodity fetishism, exchange value dominates over use value, and thus it contributes to the creation of "false" needs, luxuries, trinkets, and things we want but don't necessarily need. Exchange value is what people are willing to pay for any given commodity; use value is the practical way the commodity supplies a need. If we think about the commodity of Hollywood film, we can see that the exchange value becomes more significant than the use value. How much we are willing to pay to see a film in the theatre dictates the entire Hollywood industry, yet what is the actual use value of a film? Is a film a real or a false need? Adorno and Horkheim would argue the latter.

Walter Benjamin and Consumer Meaning-making

While Adorno and Horkheimer's "culture industry" thesis represents the general position of the Frankfurt School, there was some dissension within the school. Walter Benjamin, also associated with the Frankfurt School, directed some of his media studies on the technological reproduction of art, with a particular focus on film. What interested Benjamin was the way that reproduction removes art from its aura, that is, art's authentic, singular, original existence. The reproduction of a painting, for example, is something different than the original. However, in media such as film and photography, there is only the reproduction, without an authentic, singular original. As Benjamin writes in his 1936 essay "The Work of Art in the Age of its Mechanical Reproduction," "*The technological reproducibility of the artwork changes the relation of the masses to art*" (2008, 36, italics original). This meant, to Benjamin, that technological reproduction allowed for a shattering of tradition and the opening up of plural interpretations. These interpretations are developed not only by the producer, but by the consumer of the art. Thus, unlike Adorno and Horkheimer, who put the emphasis on the production of popular culture (culture industry)—giving power to the producer to coerce the consumer—Benjamin puts emphasis on the meaning-making available to the consumer. His concept allows for a more active and political consumption of popular culture, rather than the culture industry's passive duped masses. In this way, Benjamin lays a path for the development of culturalism, which will be explored in more detail in Chapter 3.

Applying Marxist Theory

Selling Spirituality: Jeremy Carrette and Richard King

If we think of Marxist theory as antagonistic towards religion, which Marx certainly was himself, it can be difficult to see how a Marxist approach to religion and popular culture can take the religious side seriously. For Marx, religion is a drug that clouds the minds of the masses so they accept the hegemonic ideology. However, some scholars have utilized Marxist and neo-Marxist theory to challenge the assumption that religion is antithetical to revolution. A good example of this approach is that of Jeremy Carrette and Richard King in their book *Selling Spirituality* (2005). In this book, Carrette and King argue that the "secularist critique of religion, most famously represented by Marx's claim that religion is the opiate of the masses, now urgently needs to be applied to the ideological institutions and practices of corporate capitalism itself" (23). While, they suggest, religion and **spirituality** can be sites of resistance to the hegemonic ideals of neo-liberal corporate capitalism, unfortunately, they continue, "the term 'spirituality' is in the process of being appropriated by business culture to serve the interests of corporate capitalism and worship at the altar of neoliberal ideology" (28). Allowing corporate capitalism to usurp the language and practices of spirituality will lead to further entrenchment of the "god" of the market, while reclaiming religious heritage will challenge the supremacy of that "god." This section will explore this argument as an example of using neo-Marxist theory to explore popular cultural renditions of spirituality.

NEO-LIBERAL CAPITALISM

To begin, it is important to contrast the capitalism of Marx's day with that of the late twentieth and early twenty-first centuries. Capitalism in the nineteenth century was largely a matter of industrialization and the shift from rural existence and artisan control over manufacturing to that of the urban factory. Marx's concern was with the selling of labour instead of using one's labour to create one's own subsistence. This selling of labour required a dependence on those who had capital and, thus, those who had capital held social, economic, and political power over those who only had labour to sell. The capitalism of the twentieth and twenty-first centuries has evolved from this early industrial form to what is called **neo-liberalism**. Liberalism is a philosophical and political perspective that focuses on the individual and the individual's rights and responsibility to use rationality to better society.

Spirituality

It has become commonplace to make a strong distinction between religion and spirituality, whereby religion is the institutional practice and set of beliefs, while spirituality is one's personal, individualized beliefs and practices. This distinction is often associated with a difference between external roles and subjective concerns. In religion, people follow the rules dictated by someone else (for example, a god or a set of priests). In spirituality, one turns inward to one's own authentic interactions with the world around oneself. Spirituality is, then, understood as individualistic rather than communal. There have been increasing numbers of people thus identifying themselves as "spiritual but not religious": those who have concerns with personal spirituality and holistic living but do not affiliate with any religious organization. While this distinction between religion and spirituality has become very common it is sometimes misleading. Many people who participate in religious organizations would also see their participation as spiritual; their interaction with a religious community and devotion to a particular deity or set of deities provides them with spiritual strength and personal validation of their worldview. So, a Catholic participating in mass is not just doing a religious ritual but may also be spiritually nourished in the process. That said, in the context of Carrette and King's concerns with corporate spirituality, we are looking at a form of spirituality that has been often labelled **New Age** spirituality and that exists primarily outside of traditional religious organizations. This New Age spirituality includes a conglomeration of various practices and ideas from Eastern religious traditions (Hinduism, Buddhism and Taoism in particular), indigenous traditions, and marginalized Western magical and metaphysical traditions, such as Wicca. In this type of spirituality one does not convert to Hinduism, for example, just because one finds yoga to be spiritually significant. One is able to draw on a number of different traditions to create one's own unique, individualized spiritual system.

Neo-liberalism puts this focus of individualism, rationality, and utilitarianism to the service of the capitalist economy.

The most significant aspect of neo-liberalism is the rule of the market. Neo-liberalism asserts that the market, if allowed to operate without constraints, will benefit all individuals. The more goods flow and the greater the profits made, the more money will trickle down to all levels of society. However, this will only work if there are minimal, or no, impediments to profits, such as governmental regulations, or unionization, that limit the way a company can do business. Regulations, such as minimum wages, tariffs, and environmental and/or safety protocols, reduce the ability of a company to operate freely and with maximum profit. The market should regulate these issues, rather than the government implementing seemingly arbitrary rules. For example, if people want to be paid more, they need to prove themselves worthy with a higher level of skill and determination than their neighbours. Competition will allow for those who deserve higher wages to receive them and those who are incompetent and/or less determined to succeed to feel the sting of deprivation that will motivate them to work harder. To assist in this motivation, neo-liberalism calls for cuts in public expenditures for social services. The government should not be providing safety nets for people, such as unemployment benefits or welfare, as these programs only allow people to sit back and opt out of the market economy and become a drain on the productive population in the form of taxes. Another goal to motivate people to dedicate themselves to their employment is to privatize necessary services, such as health care, education, utilities, etc. This would lead, according to neo-liberalism, to a more effective output and further drive for people to engage skillfully in the market economy so as to be able to afford these services. In all of this deregulation and privatization, neo-liberalism eliminates the concept of the "public good" and replaces it with the ideals of individual responsibility. Individuals who are poor are responsible for finding their way out of their situation, by working harder. Society as a whole is not responsible, in neo-liberalism, for addressing systemic issues of poverty, as the market—if allowed to operate without restriction—will eventually benefit all individuals who participate.

PERSONALIZING OF SPIRITUALITY

With the emphasis on individualism and privatization, neo-liberal capitalism has tended to diminish the influence of religious organizations. Religious institutions tend to promote a "public good" and tend to require members to support one another. This does not fit well with the neo-liberal agenda. This is not to say some religious people or institutions have not promoted neo-liberalism. However, neo-liberalism does not depend upon the support of religious institutions. That said, the individual experiences of spirituality have become useful tools in the development, maintenance, and furthering of neo-liberalism. At least, so argue Carrette and King. The focus on the individual has led to an individualization of spirituality, loosening the tie between spirituality and religion. Carrette and King see this focus as largely a result of the psychologization of spirituality. Psychology as the science of the human self focuses on the individual and thus authorizes individuality as a "natural" thing, rather than a political construct. Carrette and King are quite critical of many forms of psychology that they perceive as isolating the self from the community. They point to such popular psychologists as M. Scott Peck who, in his 1978 book *The Road Less Travelled*, presents religion as a personal worldview and spirituality as about self-discovery. In this personalizing of spirituality, Carrette and King see a resonance with neo-liberal individualism. They suggest, "*psychology as a modern discipline of the self is a political apparatus of modern society to develop and sustain consumers"* (56, italics original).

A personalized spirituality becomes a private concern that does not address a public good. In neo-liberalism, this personalized spirituality also connects with the market in two ways. First, individuals, who are accustomed to the choice of market goods, see religion and spirituality as another commodity that should be available to all who may choose to participate. Thus, we want to pick and choose our own ideas, practices, and resources to create our own personal sense of spiritual well-being: we want to have full access to a spiritual marketplace without the limits of religious institutions telling us what rules to follow. Second, these various ideas, practices, and resources become part of the economic market in that they are available for a fee. Those who participate fully in neo-liberal capitalism, presumably, have access to disposable income, and thus, can afford to pay for quality spiritual teaching in the form of books, workshops, CDs, DVDs, retreats, etc. The exchange value of these commodities can overwhelm the use value, particularly when a well-known teacher is seen as a spiritual guru because of the high cost of his or her workshops. The spirituality that is sold in these forms is neo-liberal in its participation in the market economy as well as its continued support and maintenance of the ideology of individualism, privatization, and personal achievement.

Let us return to our earlier discussion of *The Secret*. Carrette and King do not address *The Secret* in their book as they were writing prior to *The Secret*'s release. However, by looking at some of their critique, specifically of the Barefoot Doctor Stephen Russell, we can see how they might respond to *The Secret*. The Barefoot Doctor is an alternative health therapist with a particular interest in the practices of Taoism. He has appeared regularly on British TV and newspapers and has written a number of New Age spirituality books. In his book *Liberation: The Perfect Holistic Antidote to Stress, Depression and other Unhealthy States of Mind* (2002) he writes,

> People treat you according to what you unconsciously project from within. If you're feeling oppressed by others, someone in particular, a group or the world in general, it is because you're oppressing yourself and projecting the resulting oppressive energy on to them. As soon as you stop oppressing yourself, others will stop oppressing or stop appearing to oppress you. When you stop oppressing yourself, no matter how oppressive the situation you may currently find yourself in, you will no longer feel oppressed by it (158; quoted in Carrette and King 2005, 105–6).

This position seems quite similar to that of *The Secret* whereby we attract to ourselves what we are thinking about. This is the law of attraction. In *The Secret* video we are given a scenario where therapist Bill Harris tells us of a gay student who was continually harassed by homophobic people around him. Harris tells us that this client is thinking about his oppression and thus attracting it to himself. Once he was able to accept the law of attraction he was able to change his thought. With positive thinking he attracted positive interactions. This change in outlook resulted in him no longer being harassed by homophobic people.

A NEO-MARXIST CRITIQUE

The fundamental concern that Carrette and King have with this kind of spirituality, a concern developed directly from a neo-Marxist critique, is the heavy influence on individuality and personal desires rather than group/class consciousness. This idea that we can attract wealth or happiness through our thoughts implies that there is no need for "public good," nor governmental safety system for those disadvantaged (we only need to positively think our way out of poverty), nor critique of any systemic problems in our society. Carrette and King say of the Barefoot Doctor, "Russell's is a rallying call for the heroic individualist of western society to 'make it happen' in a world where individual self-expression takes precedence over social justice and concern for the other. [. . .] the arising of any state of mind that is disturbed by the status quo is immediately dismissed as 'negative' and reduced to the level of an individual health problem" (106–7). While The Secret does tells us that those in economic and political power have kept us in the dark so as to maintain their power, an idea similar to the neo-Marxist concern with hegemony, the ultimate solution for Rhonda Byrne and the other self-help teachers she collaborates with, as with the Barefoot Doctor, is individual positive thinking to create a better world for the individual within the capitalist market. The Secret does not advocate positive thinking to bring about the downfall of oppressive power structures; it suggests the power of positive thinking to bring oneself into the company of the rulers of the power structures. The Secret and the Barefoot Doctor promote neo-liberalism rather than challenge it.

Carrette and King are concerned not only with the buying and selling of religious commodities in the spiritual marketplace, but also with the use of spirituality by corporate capitalism to increase profit. What this means is that corporations are increasingly using the language and tools of mind-body-spirit holism to encourage higher productivity in their employees. By providing employees with benefits such as yoga classes, spiritual awareness seminars and the like, corporations are utilizing spirituality to maintain and even further develop corporate capitalism. Thus corporations convince their employees to take care of their mind-body-spirit balance in order to allow them to work more efficiently. How do they do this? Carrette and King suggest that the use of spirituality language in the workplace allows employees to believe the corporation takes them seriously as individuals, mitigating the depersonalization of neo-liberal economics. Using spirituality also provides "the all-important "feel-good" factor that is so important for improving worker efficiency and loyalty" (Carrette and King 2005, 134). Thirdly, using spirituality in corporate settings allows employees to think their corporation is "alternative" and less oppressive than other corporations out there, even as it maintains its position within the neo-liberal marketplace.

In Carrette and King's critique of the selling of spirituality we can see a number of Marxist, and more specifically neo-Marxist, strands. Carrette and King seem to be following in the footsteps of the Frankfurt School. Just as Adorno and Horkheimer saw a culture industry in popular cultural entertainment, which utilized our desire for pleasure to placate us and keep us from resisting and/or rejecting hegemonic values, so Carrette and King see the spiritual marketplace and corporate spirituality as utilizing our desire for authenticity to keep maintaining the capitalist system. What is important in both cases is the emphasis on popular culture/spirituality as a tool for coercing us into accepting the hegemony.

Commodified Religion: Jeffery A. Smith and Hollywood

Spirituality and the New Age are not the only locations of the **commodification** of religion. Jeffery A. Smith (2001) provides an extensive analysis of the commodification of religion, largely Christianity, in Hollywood films. While commodification means the transformation of relationships, formerly untainted by commerce, into commercial relationships of exchange—buying, and selling—according to Smith these commodities are not devoid of moral values. It is possible to see, though, how these moral values also play into the prevailing hegemonic value system of the day. While Smith is not making a specific Marxist argument in his paper, his discussion can be used to show how neo-Marxists might interpret these commodifications. Smith sees four trends throughout the twentieth century that shift from an American landscape that was decidedly Christian through to a more religiously and spirituality diverse and eclectic context. Exploring his four trends will allow us to see that the selling of religion is not limited to New Age spirituality.

THE DIVINE INTERVENTION OF CLASSICAL THEISM IN FILM

While Smith does not see his four trends as isolated from each other, that is, there is overlap in their influence, he does associate them with the time periods of their peak influence. The first two trends, then, are found most significantly in the first half of the twentieth century. Right at the beginnings of the Hollywood enterprise, says Smith, there is a strong trend toward a divine intervention of classical theism. Early cinema, though sometimes controversial, was also a medium for selling moral instruction through biblical stories. A strong example of this is Cecil B. DeMille's film *The Ten Commandments*. Both the original 1923 silent film and the

1956 remake sell the biblical story as sensational entertainment, but maintained the Christian belief that God existed and intervened in human history. Even in films that were not specifically religious stories this understanding of theism and God's intervention shows up. Smith notes that D.W. Griffin's 1915 film *The Birth of a Nation* "end[s] with Jesus pacifying conflict" (Smith 2001, 194). Classic theism does not disappear in Hollywood films, though its significance and specific imagery of divine intervention do not maintain quite the popularity of the early Hollywood days. We could think of films such as Mel Gibson's 2004 film *The Passion of the Christ* for a good example of this classic theism in current filmic entertainment. All of these examples sell the Christian God as a being who punishes evil and blesses good, and tie that image to a compelling and entertaining story.

GOD AS A GUIDE TO PERSONAL TRANSFORMATION IN FILM

Co-existing with the divine intervention model of classical theism, early twentieth-century Hollywood film provides us with the commodification of a more liberal God who provides inspiration but leaves it up to humans to make their own choices. These are stories where God is a guide, helping people achieve personal transformation. A popular example of this trend can be found in Frank Capra's 1946 film *It's a Wonderful Life*. In this delightful Christmas story, George Bailey, after giving in to despair and contemplating suicide, is given the opportunity to see the world without his influence, thanks to an angel sent to guide him back to hope. Smith suggests that this shift to a more liberal, guiding God was partially a response to the catastrophic events of the early twentieth century (e.g., two world wars and a depression). If God was the classic intervener, as seen in the earlier trend, then why had he not more clearly intervened in these cases? As Smith writes, "The Creator, it seemed, should not be held responsible for repressions, genocide, and a host of other ancient or modern ills" (2001, 207). God may guide us, but we humans have to make our own choices. This image of God began to sell more successfully than the wrathful God of classical theism.

THE SELLING OF EVIL IN FILM

Smith sees a shift in the commodity of Hollywood religion in the middle of the twentieth century, as **existentialism** became more common in the 1950s and 1960s. Existentialism is a philosophical movement which begins roughly with the writings of Soren Kierkegaard (1813–1855), though he would not have used the term "existentialism" to refer to his philosophy and theology. Existentialism focuses on subjectivity—the importance of the individual experience. Popularized by Jean-Paul Sartre's (1905–1980) formulation that existence is prior to essence—that is, the individual's experiences and character are more important than the "universal" characteristics individuals share with other humans—existentialism attacked complacency to authority, particularly religious authority. Existentialists call for personal responsibility and moral choice. However, there is no morality embedded in nature or tied to a universally truthful religious doctrine. If there was a clear moral "right" then it would not be a choice to follow it; it would not reflect on the individual who did what everyone knows to be right. The same can be said for religion. If it is clear to everyone that God exists (proven) then it is not faith. One should make the choice to believe (or not believe) in an unprovable God, not because that is what "the Church" or "science" may tell you is true, but because you have made that choice as an individual. This choice is a private and unjustifiable act, validated only by what happens after the leap is taken. Existentialists argue that no evidence of God's existence can be sought. Thus to sell God in Hollywood would not be popular with the rising generation of existentialists.

Interestingly enough, what was popular was the selling of evil without a God to counter it. Smith describes a heightened interest in the satanic and corruption of authority in the middle of the twentieth century. We can see this in such films as Roman Polanski's 1968 film *Rosemary's Baby*, which features Satan, and Satan's child, with no corresponding God figure, and William Friedkin's 1973 film *The Exorcist*, which certainly includes a demon even as the Catholic priest Father Karras struggles with his belief in God. In films like these we are sold the idea that there is no all-powerful God though there still are supernatural forces which interact with humanity, often for evil purposes, and humans are on their own in combating these forces. That these films were made during the Vietnam War (1959–1975) is not coincidental. Little evidence of an intervening God, or even one who provided guidance, was credited to this time period of brutal military action and heightened protest at home. However, much evil was to be experienced. This existentialist trend in Hollywood films sold viewers the idea that evil was real and we can only fight it on our own terms, as individuals, rather than rely on God (or in many cases even the group mentality of "America").

DIVINE AS HUMAN AND THE SUPERNATURAL AS SCIENCE

By the end of the twentieth century, Smith sees a shift to a disintegration of any rigid categories of right and wrong. Rather than focus on strong moral issues, many of these films looked to elevate sensuality and life. Smith suggests this is a reflection of the American baby-boomer concern with mortality and immortality rather than morality and immorality. What feels good must therefore be good, at least for the individual. When we get religious motifs in late twentieth century films they often have to do with the desire of the divine to experience the senses of humanity. Nora Ephron's 1996 film *Michael*, with John Travolta, shows an angel revelling in earthly pleasures such as drinking, smoking, and sex. Similarly Brad Silberling's 1998 film *City of Angels* tells the story of an angel, played by Nicholas Cage, who chooses a human life in order to fall in love.

While Smith focuses solely on the twentieth century, we can also see another trend that moves us into the twenty-first century. I call this the trend toward scientific supernaturalism, or spiritual science. In a number of films in this trend we see an integration of concerns of scientific exploration with spirituality, trying to find the soul or prove (or disprove) the supernatural using scientific means. An early version of this can be seen in Robert Zemeckis' 1997 adaptation of Carl Sagan's novel *Contact*. This is a film that debates the role of religion or faith and science, showing them to be less different than most perceive, at least when science moves far enough away from the known. Another interesting example of this trend is the shift in the way the Force is understood in the prequel trilogy of George Lucas' *Star Wars* (1999; 2002; 2005) from what was presented in the earlier films. In the original films (1977; 1980; 1983), the Force is clearly something spiritual that emanates from all life forms. However in the 1999 *Star Wars: The Phantom Menace*, the Force is tied to midichlorians, which are microscopic symbiotic life forms found in high quantities in Jedis. The spiritual has been explained through science.

So, what do all these trends in representations of God or morality or the spiritual have to do with Marxist or neo-Marxist theory? In each case we see religion being sold as commodities to the masses through the Hollywood industry, a key component of what Adorno and Horkheimer called the culture industry. One could use a neo-Marxist argument to say that the particular kinds of God or spirituality sold in these films maintains a particular kind of hegemony. In the early twentieth century, Hollywood was suspected of degenerate morals and values. In selling a classical theism, viewers could justify their interest in the Hollywood entertainment while still upholding the mainstream affiliation with Christian traditions, whether these are traditions of God intervening directly in human life or providing inspiration to help us make right choices. In both cases neo-Marxists could argue that the audience was both entertained and sold a set of moral values that suited the powers holding control of the American government, economy, and religious institutions: doing good will be rewarded and the laws of the land dictate what doing good is. However, by the middle of the twentieth century this message did not sell as well. People were beginning to rebel, to counter the hegemony. The Vietnam War was a catalyst of this rebellion, but not the only one. In time of upheaval, one could argue that the shift to a more existentialist imagery was deliberately designed to sell an image of evil afoot in the land. This evil, however, was not the government, nor war, nor racism, sexism, and classism. It was the devil himself. While people were fascinated by images of Rosemary being raped by Satan in *Rosemary's Baby*, or the child Regan twisting her head fully around while possessed by a demon in *The Exorcist*, they were not thinking about revolution. The shift to a celebration of sensationalism, or even hedonism, simply shifted viewers' thinking to their own pleasures, again away from politics. As Smith points out, "Religious doctrine was reformulated into carefully marketed morsels of highly sweetened pleasure available in suburban mall multiplexes and megaplexes. Spirituality was being reduced to a self-regarding satisfaction suitable for a consumer culture" (2001, 192). Even though Smith, himself, is not doing a fully neo-Marxist analysis in his essay, the theories of the Frankfurt School can be applied, particularly the ways in which the culture industry reinforces hegemonic ideology.

Critique of Neo-Marxism: A Culturalist Position

In following from the neo-Marxism of the Frankfurt School, Carrette and King are seeing capitalism as a hegemonic norm whereby those in economic power are determined to use the resources of popular culture to keep us passive and happy with our current circumstances. One of the most significant critiques of this approach comes from the culturalism position, which will be discussed in more detail in the next chapter. Simply stated, this critique questions the passivity of consumers and the abiding dominance of hegemonic values. Yes, many people sit back and absorb what is given in popular culture, but that does not mean everybody does. Some people resist popular culture. Some people reform popular culture. Some people negotiate the meaning of popular culture. Applied to Carrette and King's thesis about "selling spirituality," then, culturalists may suggest that there are many different kinds of consuming possible within the spiritual marketplace.

Paul Heelas

Paul Heelas, in his book *Spiritualities of Life: New Age Romanticism and Consumptive Capitalism* (2008), argues that it is not enough to assume spiritualities that utilize consumer culture are simply bolstering capitalism and keeping people happy within their allotted positions of the capitalist market. Drawing on ethnographic work—interviews, observations and surveys—with people involved in New Age spirituality, Heelas shows that many people involved in alternative spiritualities are trying to push away from consumerist culture. They may not always be successful, but their intentions and self-identifications must be taken into account when trying to analyze the phenomenon of New Age spirituality, says Heelas. Furthermore, consumption itself can mean a number of things: yes, it can be passive absorption of the hegemonic values dictated by a culture industry, but it can also mean choice, agency and even, more simply, life, as we all must consume to live.

As the examples provided by Jeffrey Smith in the trend of Hollywood representations of God and the divine show, there are also, at times multiple hegemonies in competition with one another. While we can see that many films have the same plot and same message—just with different cast, context, and clothing style—a more complex interaction is happening, even in Hollywood. Furthermore, what Smith's article does not highlight is the increased influence of independent filmmakers countering the hegemony of Hollywood. The tools of neo-Marxism are not insignificant. However, it seems they are being used less in the forms found in the Frankfurt School as more scholars are insisting on increased complexity, both in the context of religion and popular culture, and the available theories to study it.

Summary

Marxism involves the critique of capitalism as a system that requires some people to remain alienated from their own labour in order for others to increase their wealth and power. Marxist theory suggests that it is through ideology or hegemony that the superstructures, such as religion, the state, the legal system, popular culture, etc., convince the workers that the capitalist system is the only possible, even natural, way of structuring society. This theory has been applied to popular culture by the Frankfurt School to see a singular culture industry as producing popular culture to entertain and distract us from understanding the realities of our oppression by the capitalist system. Scholars such as Carrette and King use this argument to analyze the role and effect of popular spiritualities in maintaining and even furthering neo-liberal capitalism. In the self-help spiritualities offered by such products as *The Secret* and the teachings of the Barefoot Doctor, a neo-Marxist critique sees further entrenchment of neo-liberal individualism at the cost of any group solidarity or concern with social justice. Similarly one could look at commodified versions of Christianity and other forms of spirituality as maintaining a hegemonic moral value while entertaining people in order to keep them from addressing very real political concerns outside the theatre. However, this neo-Marxist approach has been highly criticized for not considering the role of the consumer and our further chapters will work to show the complex relationship between producer, commodity, and consumer.

Review Questions

1. What is the relationship between the base and superstructure?
2. How does ideology make capitalism seem natural?
3. How does hegemony coerce compliance?
4. What is the culture industry thesis?
5. According to Walter Benjamin, what is the significance of technological reproduction of art?
6. What is the common distinction made between religion and spirituality?

7. What is neo-liberalism and what is its relationship to the concept of the "public good"?
8. Why are Carrette and King critical of psychology?
9. How does *The Secret* promote neo-liberal ideas?
10. How does Carrette and King's analysis of popular spirituality compare to Adorno and Horkheimer's analysis of popular culture?
11. What are Jeffrey Smith's four trends in Hollywood representations of the divine?
12. How did the Vietnam War influence the shift in representations of God and the supernatural in Hollywood films?

Useful Resources

Print

Adorno, Theodor and Max Horkheimer. 2002. *Dialectic of Enlightenment: Philosophical Fragments*. Trans., Edmund Jephcott. Stanford, CA: Stanford University Press.

Byrne, Rhonda. 2006. *The Secret*. New York: Atria Books.

Carrette, Jeremy and Richard King. 2005. *Selling Spirituality: The Silent Takeover of Religion*. London: Routledge.

Heelas, Paul. 2008. *Spiritualities of Life: New Age Romanticism and Consumptive Capitalism*. Oxford: Blackwell Publishing.

Marx, Karl and Friedrich Engels. 1964. *The German Ideology*. Moscow: Progress Publishers.

Peck, M. Scott. 1978. *The Road Less Travelled*. Touchstone.

Russell, Stephen. 2002. *Liberation: The Perfect Holistic Antidote to Stress, Depression and other Unhealthy States of Mind*. HarperCollins.

Smith, Jeffery A. 2001. "Hollywood Theology: The Commodification of Religion in Twentieth Century Films." *Religion and American Culture*. Vol. 11, No. 2: 191–231.

Video

Byrne, Rhonda. 2006. *The Secret*. TS Production.

Capra, Frank. 1946. *It's a Wonderful Life*. Liberty Films.

DeMille, Cecile B. 1923; 1956. *The Ten Commandments*. Paramount Pictures.

Ephron, Nora. 1996. *Michael*. Turner Pictures and Alphaville.

Friedkin, William. 1973. *The Exorcist*. Warner Bros.

Gibson, Mel. 2004. *The Passion of the Christ*. Newmarket Films.

Griffin, D.W. 1915. *The Birth of a Nation*. Epoch Producing Inc.

Lucas, George. 1977. *Star Wars*. Lucasfilm

Lucas, George. 1980. *The Empire Strikes Back*. Lucasfilm.

Lucas, George. 1983. *Return of the Jedi*. Lucasfilm.

Lucas, George. 1999. *The Phantom Menace*. Lucasfilm

Lucas, George. 2002. *Attack of the Clones*. Lucasfilm

Lucas, George. 2005. *Revenge of the Sith*. Lucasfilm.

Polanski, Roman. 1968. *Rosemary's Baby*. Paramount Pictures

Silberling, Brad. 1998. *City of Angels*. Regency Enterprises and Atlas Entertainment

Taylor, Steve. 2004. *Capitalism and Modern Social Theory*. Insight Media.

Zemeckis, Robert. 1997. *Contact*. Warner Bros.

Online

Official Website of *The Secret* and *The Power*. http://thesecret.tv/index.html

The Barefoot Doctor. www.barefootdoctorglobal.com

3

Culturalism

OBJECTIVES

This chapter will help you develop an understanding of

- the importance of structures of feeling in culturalism
- the relationships between encoding and decoding meanings in documentary culture
- the various structures of feeling tied to differing representations of zombies
- the multiple meanings given to vampires, including the *Twilight* series
- the evangelical Christian responses to the occult, including the *Harry Potter* series

The neo-Marxist approach utilized by Carrette and King suggests that the New Age movement, as discussed in Chapter 2, may be furthering a neo-liberal, capitalist agenda. However, this position often assumes passivity on the part of consumers. How do people actually engage with what Paul Heelas calls "spiritualities of life"? In this chapter, we explore alternative spiritualities that emphasize the growing interest in the occult in religious and popular cultural products. Raymond Williams and Stuart Hall provide a counter-argument to that of Adorno and Horkheimer. They argue that cultural analysis is about clarifying the meanings and values of particular ways of life through what Williams terms "documentary" culture. Hall, in particular, calls for seeing popular culture as a site of power struggle where meaning is created in the interpretation and articulation by the consumer. These theories work well with Clifford Geertz's suggestion that religion is a set of symbols which provide moods and motivations for people and with Meredith McGuire's lived religions approach. When popular culture utilizes religious symbolism we get a particularly poignant site of power struggle in the determination of religious authenticity. As a way of exploring these theories more practically, this chapter looks to popular portrayals of the occult, particularly focusing on zombies and vampires.

Zombies and vampires are supernatural beings derived from religious lore. They are also core characters in popular horror genres. Additionally, small segments of the population have taken on the roles and/or identities of these supernatural beings, particularly vampires, to create their own spiritual worldviews. The multiple meanings given to zombies and vampires illustrate the importance of culturalism in the study of religion and popular culture. We end the chapter with a final discussion on evangelical Christian responses to the occult.

Raymond Williams

As a response to the Frankfurt School, and their insistence on the culture industry thesis, a group of scholars, including Richard Hoggart, Raymond Williams, and E.P. Thompson, began to push for a more nuanced understanding of the interaction between production and consumption of popular culture. These scholars developed what is known as **culturalism**, eventually formalizing that study in the creation of the Birmingham Centre for Contemporary Cultural Studies. While each of these scholars stressed the importance of agency in both producer and consumer, we will focus specifically on Raymond Williams' articulation of this position, for its clarity and significance in cultural studies as a field.

Williams was interested in a complete study of culture and as such looked to the various ways that culture is defined and used in the English language. He distinguished three definitions of culture: the social, the ideal, and the **documentary**. Social culture is a way of life. When we talk about Canadian culture or university culture, we are talking about a sense of how people in that group live and define themselves as a group. Ideal culture is the notion of the elite, perfected products created by a social culture; in this sense ideal culture is the same as high culture, such as highly valued art, music, literature, etc. Documentary culture is all the cultural products created by any given social culture, whether perceived to be ideal or not. This would include the most base tabloids and sitcoms along with the most praised literature and opera. What Williams was interested in studying was social culture and determining what he called "the structure of feeling" of any given culture. The **structure of feeling** is basically the whole of a culture that is created by all the various parts. To discern the structure of feeling was to chart the patterns found in all the cultural productions and consumptions. To do so, however, Williams insisted that scholars must take seriously the documentary culture, not solely the ideal culture. In his essay "The Analysis of Culture" published in *The Long Revolution* (1961) Williams writes,

> The significance of documentary culture is that, more clearly than anything else, it expresses that life to us in direct terms, when the living witnesses are silent. At the same time, if we reflect on the nature

of a structure of feeling, and see how it can fail to be fully understood even by living people in close contact with it, with ample material at their disposal, including the contemporary arts, we shall not suppose that we can ever do more than make an approach, an approximation, using any channels (49).

Williams recognizes that even in looking to all the documentary culture we may not get a full picture or understanding of any given culture, even if we are living within it, but especially if we are looking in from outside. However, it is only by examining all cultural products, not just the ideal, that we can get the closest to a full picture of the structure of feeling as is possible. Cultural studies, for Williams, is about clarifying as much as possible the meanings and values in a particular way of life by analyzing the construction and consumption of any and all forms of cultural production.

In understanding what documentary culture is trying to express as meaning and value of a particular way of life, Williams pointed out the need to distinguish between the **commodity** itself and what people make of that commodity. Thus, in contrast to the Frankfurt School, who were largely interested in the hegemonic values embedded into popular culture by the producers, Williams, and the other scholars taking the culturalism approach in the newly formed discipline of cultural studies, were interested in the interactions between the producers' intended meaning and the way consumers actually consumed and interpreted cultural products.

Stuart Hall

Stuart Hall continues in the approach initiated by Williams. He argues that popular culture is a site of power struggle. The documentary culture studied by cultural theorists is not inscribed with meaning, but the meaning is created in the interpretation and **articulation** by the consumer. Producers may try to generate hegemonic truths, in the manner suggested by Adorno and Horkheimer, but consumers are not always cultural dupes (even if they sometimes are). Cultural products have a meaning given them by producers, but consumers also have an active role in the interpretation of products. Hall articulates a system of **encoding** (by producers) and **decoding** (by consumers) of meaning in any cultural product. Hall, in his study of television media, argues that "production and reception of the television message are not, therefore, identical, but they are related: they are differentiated moments within the totality formed by the social relations of the communicative process as a whole" (1980, 119). A producer encodes a meaning in a product, such as a television program. Viewers watching the program do not necessarily decode that program in the way it was intended by the producer. The viewers/consumers may articulate an alternative meaning. However, that alternative meaning always has a relationship to the intended meaning. They are not the same but they are tied together by the limits of genre, imagery, cultural understandings, etc.

For Hall all communication is code; no communication is inherent. Some codes become so ingrained in certain societies, or segments of societies, that they may seem natural or unconstructed; they may become **naturalized**. Hall says, "what naturalized codes demonstrate is the degree of habituation produced when there is a fundamental alignment and reciprocity—an achieved equivalence—between the encoding and decoding sides of an exchange of meanings" (1980, 121). What this means is that in some cases the meaning tied to any given image or code has become so culturally expected that the decoding matches the encoding not because the meaning is necessary but because it is culturally accepted. This cultural acceptance leads insiders of the culture to presume it *is* a necessary or natural meaning. This is particularly evident when using **denotative** meanings of codes, that is, the most literal meaning. When I say the word "cross," the denotative meaning is the intersection of two straight lines. It is a code, as the letters "c-r-o-s-s" do not inherently point to the intersection of two straight lines, but it is a naturalized code to English speakers. As we move into **connotative** meanings of code, moving away from literal meanings, we are faced with more diversions of interpretations. The most naturalized connotative meaning of the word "cross" in a Western context, of course, is Christianity and Jesus Christ. However, even with this code there are different meanings. For some the cross could be decoded as a symbol of salvation (Jesus dying to save people from their sins); for others it is a symbol of suffering (either Jesus' suffering on the cross or the suffering of various people in the name of the cross).

While a message is always encoded in any production, in the decoding process, Hall argues that consumers have three types of readings available: dominant, negotiated, and oppositional. The **dominant reading** is the "preferred reading" (preferred by the producer). This is where the consumer decodes the message in the product in the same way the producer encoded it. For example, James Cameron talks of his film *Avatar* as a statement about both environmental conservation and the rights of indigenous peoples (see Adams 2010). To accept it as such would be to decode this film as intended. The **negotiated reading** happens when consumers understand the message encoded by the producer, but chose to adapt the meaning differently than intended for specific local contexts or conditions. For example, the *Star Trek* series was originally designed by Gene Roddenberry as a way to express a **humanist** vision of future human ability to create a peaceful, scientific, and technologically advanced world without prejudice. Since its original airing, multitudes of fans have taken Roddenberry's message and implemented elements into their own lives to the extent of joining Starfleet Federation crews (fan clubs) and developing religious ideology and ritual around the Vulcans, Klingons, and other non-human life forms encountered throughout the various renditions of the series. Roddenberry certainly did not intend to create new religious communities, but the fans have adapted the *Star Trek* world to their own context, for their own purposes. An **oppositional reading** is when one chooses to decode a message in a contrary way to the intention. An example here could be the way some evangelical Christians decode the *Harry Potter* series as a guidebook to the Satanic and occult, completely contrary to J.K. Rowling's intention to write a coming-of-age story in a fantastical setting. These three readings—dominant, negotiated, and oppositional—could be seen as points on a continuum, between accepting the producers intended meaning to rejecting it outright. Between these two options are a myriad of negotiated positions and possibilities. How one decodes any given cultural product is directly related to the identification, or non-identification, with the encoded message.

Culturalism and Religion: Encoding and Decoding

If we think of culturalism, very generally, as the study of documentary culture to attempt to discern the structures of feeling of a given culture—recognizing the importance of both encoding and decoding practices in the construction and consumption of that documentary culture—it soon becomes very clear that we need to think through the place of religion and spirituality, as part of that documentary culture, in this set of processes. Two of the approaches to religious studies discussed in Chapter 1 are particularly useful for us here: Clifford Geertz's social anthropology and Meredith McGuire's lived religion.

Clifford Geertz

Clifford Geertz (1926–2006) argues for the importance of making sense of symbol sets to understand the **ethos** and **worldview** of a given culture. This is similar to what Williams calls the structure of feeling. Geertz is concerned that anthropologists are so focused on what people are doing and what those actions do for a community and individual, that they forget to think about the symbols used and the meanings understood by practitioners. How can one understand the importance of celebrating the mass within Catholicism if one is not deciphering the symbolic meanings of the wafer and the wine? While this is a simplistic example based on a very commonly understood rite, as one engages in the less familiar, the importance of the symbolic meanings becomes even more significant. What Geertz explains in his essay "Religion as a Cultural System" (originally published in 1973) is that the meanings encoded in religious products and images are important to understand, just as Hall insists that the meanings encoded in popular cultural products are important to understand. This does not mean that all consumers or practitioners will decode those symbols in the same way, but a cultural understanding of how they are *intended* to be decoded is necessary for a full interpretation of how they *actually are* decoded. If we do not know what the preferred reading is, we cannot make any sense of the negotiated or oppositional readings.

Meredith McGuire

Culturalism, of course, does not let us stop with the analysis of the preferred reading, nor would Geertz advocate such a limited view. It is in later religious studies theorists though, that we get a stronger articulation of the importance of exploring and, in some cases validating, the multiple readings available for any given religious symbol set. In particular, the push towards a study of lived religion, clearly articulated by Meredith McGuire, focuses on the way individuals engage with religious documentary culture in ways that maintain, challenge, and resist dominant structures of feeling. She writes, "The term 'lived religion' is useful for distinguishing the actual experience of religious persons from the prescribed religion of institutionally defined beliefs and practices" (2008, 12). However, religion is, McGuire argues, "fundamentally social. Its building blocks are shared meanings and experiences, learned practices, borrowed imagery, and imparted insights" (2008, 13). Taking McGuire's method of listening to the multiple readings of religious culture alongside Geertz's deciphering of the dominant encodings allows us to engage in a study of religion and popular culture within the culturalism approach.

Christopher Partridge

One scholar who has attempted to do just this, in relation to contemporary Western alternative spiritualities, is Christopher Partridge. In his two-volume book set, *The Re-Enchantment of the West* (2004; 2005), Partridge explores the development of alternative spiritualities, including spiritualities of life as discussed in Chapter 2. Partridge's exploration looks not only to those committed to **New Age** or other alternative spiritual practices, but a larger structure of feeling found in Western popular culture and spirituality. He calls this growing structure of feeling, "occulture." The **occult**, as characterized by things hidden or concealed and "enriched with new meaning related to ancient knowledge and the secrets of antiquity" (Partridge 2004, 68-9), is an increasingly important strand of religious and cultural symbol sets found in popular culture. For Partridge,

> Consumers of occulture may be witting or unwitting; they may engage with it at a relatively superficial level or they may have strong religious commitments; they may themselves contribute to

the pool of occultural knowledge or they may simply drink from it. Occulture is the spiritual *bricoleur*'s Internet from which to download whatever appeals or inspires; it is the sacralising air that many of our contemporaries breathe; it is the well from which the serious occultist draws; it is the varied landscape the New Age nomad explores; it is the cluttered warehouse frequently plundered by producers of popular culture searching for ideas, images and symbols (2004, 84–5).

In his study, Partridge looks to film, literature, music, the Internet, alternative health movements, and extraterrestrial conspiracies; he interrogates New Age spirituality, modern Satanism, eco-Paganism, and apocalyptic movements. Each of these both contributes to and is shaped by Western occulture. To adequately understand these movements and cultural products one must recognize that "cultural artifacts come with interpretation or 'preferred meaning' attached" (2004, 124). However, one must also explore how "ideas and themes are detached from their original contexts and invested with new meanings in order to serve the personal interests of the individual self" (2004, 121). Both the encoding and decoding are important. So, as we will explore further below, to fully understand the significance and understanding of occult figures such as zombies and vampires—that is, figures that come from ancient worldviews about the hidden supernatural—we must think about their cultural meanings and how these meanings have shifted through time and migration. We need to explore how contemporary producers draw on traditional understandings while reinvesting these characters with new meanings. And we need to examine how consumers are decoding these multiple background meanings for their own purposes.

Applying Culturalism: Reading Zombies

In his book *The Lust for Blood: Why We are Fascinated by Death, Murder, Horror, and Violence* (2011), psychologist Jeffery A. Kottler suggests that

[a]lthough science fiction horror remains popular, it is vampires and zombies who enjoy unprecedented popularity in all their manifestations. What both vampires and zombies share is immortality; they are members of the undead club. We are fascinated with them as much for their ability to cheat death as for their monstrous predation. They literally feast off the energy and spirit of the living, a perfect metaphor for anyone who seeks wealth, power, and status at the expense of others' misfortune (104).

Zombies are a staple of Western popular cultural horror films. Whether the early classic, *White Zombie* (1932), the later George A. Romero films, *The Night of the Living Dead* (1968) and its sequels, or the comedic *Shaun of the Dead* (2004), the undead have thrilled millions. However, when we examine what these zombies represent, and how they are read by audiences, it becomes clear very quickly that there are a variety of structures of feeling that interact with the symbol of the zombie. Exploring a couple of these different symbol sets will show how it is significant to understand what a culture's preferred reading (coding) of the zombie is, in order to understand how that zombie is used and consumed (decoded).

The documentary film *Zombies: When the Dead Walk* (2008) takes us through two distinct cultural contexts in which zombies have held power. Though these contexts are distinct, they are also interrelated in a number of ways. The first context is that of Haitian vodou (commonly referred to as voodoo), a religious movement developed through the interaction of European Christianity and West African traditional religions in the context of slavery, and the subsequent resistance to that slavery. The second context is that of Hollywood horror films. While the zombie can be central to both contexts, it represents very different things and thus is interpreted, or read, in different ways. While in each case there can be dominant, negotiated, and oppositional readings, because the preferred reading is different, the way audiences and/or practitioners interact with the dominant reading is different.

Vodou Zombies

Wade Davis, in his book *The Serpent and the Rainbow* (1985), documents his travels to Haiti to discover the process of zombification. He argues that in the Haitian context, zombies are a part of the system of maintaining social cohesion. Those who violate social and community rules and values are at risk of being turned into a zombie. In this context, a zombie is someone who has been ritually killed, whose soul is ritually stolen and enslaved. Davis argues that he discovered a formula of local medicine that could induce a death-like state (paralysis and such low heart rate that doctors are fooled into proclaiming death). A *bokor*, a vodou sorcerer, administers this poison as part of the ritual process of creating a zombie. A physical zombie then has his or her body magically/medically revived and put to work serving the sorcerer who enslaved him or her. Haitians also believe in an astral zombie which is created when the soul is stolen and the body remains dead. The soul is captured in a ritual container and made to bring blessings or curses on whomever the sorcerer wishes. In Haitian vodou, zombies are very much real, and not entertaining. Haitians do not fear the zombie itself. They fear becoming a zombie. This fear of becoming a zombie contributes to the maintenance of social rules, hierarchies and value systems. Zombification is also tied to the fears of slavery—a slavery

Vodou

Vodou is a syncretic religious tradition that originates in the French slave colony of Saint-Domingue in the eighteenth century. Saint-Domingue was a very wealthy plantation colony that brought in many enslaved Africans. As the slaves were forced to practise Christianity (Catholicism) and repress their African traditions, unique integrations of traditional African, particularly the West African vodun of the Fon and Ewe peoples, and Catholic practices and symbols developed. Vodou posits a supreme God, called Bondye (bon dieu), who is the creator of all things. However, Bondye is a distant God, and thus other, lesser deities or spirits are revered. These are called *lwa*. There are many *lwa* and each is associated with a corresponding Catholic saint.

Vodou rituals typical happen in a temple called a *Hounfour*. Here songs are sung for the *lwa* and practitioners believe the *lwa* join in the celebrations through possessing the bodies of participants. When a given *lwa* possesses someone's body that person acts like and speaks for the *lwa*. Ceremonies are led by priests (*Houngans*) or priestesses (*Mambos*). In addition to the priest and priestesses, there are sorcerers, the *bokor*, who may practice either "light" or "dark" magic which includes the creation and control of zombies.

In 1804, the slaves of Saint-Domingue successfully revolted against their French masters, creating the second republic in the new world, after the United States of America. This republic, Haiti, was the first black republic and successful slave revolt. The response to this revolt involved the isolation of Haiti by other American and European governments leading to mass poverty for a people unable to trade, or positively interact, with its neighbours. Due to the role vodou played in uniting the enslaved Africans together, it was given a particularly negative image by other surrounding slave-owning nations and colonies. As Christopher Moreman (2010) observes, "Depictions of Haiti as a Caribbean version of the 'Dark Continent' heightened cultural anxieties towards the former slave colony, and eventually facilitated an American takeover of Haiti in 1915" (266). Haiti returned to self-rule in 1934, but not before a slew of publications by American military personnel reinforced a connection between Haitian vodou and demonic black magic, with an emphasis on the figure of the zombie.

that extends into death. A zombie contributes to a structure of feeling that values religious/ritual community and the importance of freedom.[1]

---

1. Interestingly, Wade Davis' book, *The Serpent and the Rainbow*, was itself turned into a Hollywood horror film, staring Bill Pullman, about an anthropologist who goes to Haiti to find the drug used to create zombies and is left unsure of what is fantasy and what is reality.

Hollywood Zombies

In the American Hollywood tradition, there have been a number of different uses of the zombie figure. First introduced as a sign of the primitive and demonic nature of Haitian religious culture, the zombie operates in an atmosphere of racial and colonial fear. Zombies represent the evils of "blackness," or Africanness, and the fear of colonial and slave resistance. The victims of zombies, or of Haitian *bokor*, were typically young, white women who were at risk of being polluted by a black evil. One example is *White Zombie* (1932), the first full-length Hollywood zombie film. Though the voodoo master in this film, Murder Legendre, is white (played by the horror screen giant, Bela Lugosi), he is a master of the Haitian "voodoo" religion, and thus a representative of the demonic black magic. In this story, Madeleine travels to Haiti to meet up with her fiancé. She is turned into a zombie by Murder Legendre, at the request of another man who wants to seduce her away from her fiancé. Much struggle ensues and eventually Murder is killed thus releasing Madelaine back into the saving arms of her man. Ultimately in early Hollywood zombie films the young, white women are saved by white men who triumph over the primitive, demonic cults of the Haitian/African people. This movie was made while the American military still held control over Haiti and reflects the common fears of Haiti and zombies found in the literature coming out of that occupation.

When George A. Romero re-introduced the zombie to a large audience in the late 1960s we see a radically different vision. In *Night of the Living Dead* (1968) we have the struggle of a few people to save themselves from a horde of zombies. These zombies have not been created through voodoo/vodou ritual, but rather possibly through some sort of radioactive contamination in the atmosphere. Though the zombies in this film are relatively easy to destroy, their sheer numbers make them near impossible to escape from. In the end, all the human resisters are dead, either consumed by or become a zombie. Zombies in these later films can be anyone, are characterized by mindless group mentality, and are virtually unavoidable. They are rarely associated with specific religious ritual anymore; more likely they are associated with horrifying viruses or chemical warfare. In fact, as Christopher Moreman (2010) points out, these new zombies are distinct from the Haitian version as well as the early Hollywood version in their complete lack of a living master. They are neither controlled by a vodou *bokor* nor any other creator and thus they represent a diminishing of religious (or other) authority. Without a master, the new zombies roam aimlessly, completely controlled by their own hunger. Those resisting the zombies are largely trying to maintain their own individuality against the horde, rather than maintaining social cohesion, as in the Haitian context. These two different Hollywood versions of the zombie point to differing structures of feeling. In the early twentieth century, America was dominated by racial tensions, particularly culminating in a fear of blackness associated with demonic ritual. The zombie is the threat to the white, Christian majority and must be resisted to maintain the social cohesion of the dominant classes. In the middle- to late-twentieth century we begin to see a challenge to that desire to maintain the rigid distinctions between classes and racial groups, as well as a decrease in the power of religious and political authority. In many sectors of American society, including Hollywood, dominant society is increasingly critiqued for its mindless following of the trends and acceptance of military and corporate guidance. This was the era of the Vietnam War and much like in the existentialist trend of images of the divine, which we saw in Chapter 2, Hollywood tended toward a valorization of the individual over the authorities and a threat of evil without the corresponding good God to save us. The zombie here points to the fear of becoming one of the masses, rather than a unique and authentic individual. Unlike in the earlier zombie movies where the heroine was always saved, in Romero's *Night of the Living Dead*, there is really little hope of survival. In the end, the zombies, as representatives of the evils of consumption, are all that survive.

Moreman suggests an alternative, negotiated, reading to these late twentieth-century zombies. In his essay "Dharma of the Living Dead: A Meditation of the Meaning of the Hollywood Zombie," (2010) Moreman draws on Buddhist ideas of **nonattachment** to suggest that the zombies in, particularly, Romero's films can be understood as representing the suffering resulting from attachment to hungers and desires. Buddhism posits attachment to desires of the world as the thing that keeps us from ultimate **enlightenment**, the end goal of Buddhism. When we are attached to desires, including the desire to remain alive, we are consigned to a continual cycle of death and rebirth. Enlightenment results in the escape of this cycle. The zombies are reborn as mindless consumers. They are a warning to give up our attachments. The trick is in the representation of those resisting the zombies. As they (or we) fight to maintain our lives, we are in fact, living out our attachment to life and the inevitability of becoming the zombie. Moreman writes,

> The modern zombie-craze, then, can be seen as growing out of a 1960s countercultural depiction of life in the face of impending death without the sacred canopy of a formerly Christian authority. In its place, the risen corpses force the living to recognize their own mortality and in so doing recognize the impermanence of the self. The modern zombie as zombie illustrates an enslavement to attachment and cravings. [. . .] By confronting the zombie, and so confronting our own mortality, we can come to accept finitude and thus become authentically individuated Beings unconcerned with selfish but impossible yearnings (278).

Bringing a Buddhist structure of feeling to the Hollywood zombie results in a decoding of the popular symbol in a negotiated way that aligns with the critique of consumption but suggests a specifically Buddhist ultimate message of unattachment. Let's move to an exploration of the symbol of the vampire to further highlight the complex relationships between encoding and decoding.

Applying Culturalism: Reading Vampires

Like the zombie, vampire stories have developed in a number of different contexts over place and time, implicating a variety of structures of feeling. The classic story of Dracula, constructed by Bram Stoker (1847–1912) in 1897, has provided a template for the aristocratic, mysterious, dangerous vampire, as well as the insatiable and sexualized female vampire. However in recent renditions, such as in *Buffy the Vampire Slayer*, *Twilight*, and *True Blood*, for example, the evilness of the vampire is reduced, or even removed, for an alternative interpretation of vampires as isolated, misunderstood, romantic figures. Partridge argues that some of these changes are direct results of the changing religious worldviews available within Western culture. In the earliest vampire stories, and still evident in Stoker's version, Christianity is dominant and thus the battle between good and evil is primary. Tied to this battle is the use of Christian symbols to repel or destroy the vampires (crosses, holy water, etc.). However, as we see alternatives to Christianity being embraced in Western culture, particularly the developing occulture, Partridge argues that we see significant changes to the vampire stories. Francis Ford Coppola's 1992 version of Stoker's story, *Bram Stoker's Dracula*, while including significant Christian symbolism, also includes the concept of reincarnation, thus shifting away from the traditional religious symbol set. In the TV series, *Buffy the Vampire Slayer*, we see an increasing devaluing of Christian symbols. Partridge points out specifically the episode "Doppelgängland" (first aired on the WB Television Network on February 23, 1999) in which a vampire looks at the Christian symbols—cross and holy water—and walks away with a snarky, "whatever." What Partridge notices about the most recent vampire stories, is that, much in line with the increasing importance of a re-enchanted nature and even nature religion, the most common weapons against vampires are "the products of the natural world such as silver, sunlight and garlic" (2004, 130). Regardless of the preferred reading, though, we have multiple decodings of these various stories.

Milly Williamson and the Victorian Vampire

Milly Williamson (2005) argues that the way early vampire stories, such as the highly influential *Dracula*, are interpreted has everything to do with audience positioning;

however, much of the discourse around these stories has been based on dominant readings tied to authorial position. In the case of Stoker's *Dracula* literary analyses have focused on the discourse of masculinity and sexual repression, drawing heavily on psychoanalytical theory and the position of Stoker as a middle-class white male in Victorian England. This analysis sees the vampire, Count Dracula, as a threat to the moral order of Victorian England because he seduces and corrupts innocent women, specifically the characters Lucy and Mina. As these women become vampires through Dracula's intervention, they become increasingly sexualized. Lucy, who becomes a full vampire, transitions from innocent to immoral seducer of children. The male heroes in the story both need to resist the sexualized woman, even as they are drawn to her, as well as save her from her immorality. For Lucy, this means she needs to be killed to save her soul; for Mina, she is saved before she becomes a full vampire. The female vampires in *Dracula* represent temptation to immorality and the fears of aggressive female sexuality. However, Williamson challenges the assumption that there is only one possible reading of this novel and suggests that women, the working class and the poor of this time period and place would have had very different responses to the narrative. In making this argument, Williamson focuses heavily on the important scene within *Dracula* where the vampire Lucy is destroyed by the Crew of Light, the middle-class, educated men, including Lucy's fiancé. The lead up to this scene sees a progression in the men thinking of Lucy as an innocent victim to seeing her as a wanton monster. The actual staking of her with a large wooden stake by her fiancé has often been interpreted as the male destruction of female sexuality through symbolic penetration and control. For the middle-class male Victorian reader, then, this scene shows the dangers and titillation of female sexuality that needs controlling and destroying by the male.

Williamson, while not denying that this is certainly one possible reading of the Dracula story, suggests that contextualizing the story further into Victorian treatments of dead bodies, particularly those of the poor and the morally unaccepted, leads to some alternative readings. The era when *Dracula* was published was a time of increasing medical development, including the practice of anatomy, which consisted of exploring cadavers to uncover the secrets of the human body. There was a booming trade in dead bodies, often stolen out of graves by grave robbers and given crude and even perverted treatment, particularly women's bodies. As laws were set in place to limit the acceptability of grave robbing, the state provided doctors and anatomists with the bodies of the poor from the workhouses and those whose families could not afford to properly bury them. The working class and poor were in constant fear of the treatment of their bodies and those of loved ones, deeming the dissection involved in the study of anatomy to be unnatural and morally problematic. Thus, Williamson suggest, when these groups of people read about the staking of Lucy, with its attendant gruesome mutilation, they are not necessarily placing the scene within the discourse of dangerous female sexuality as much as the discourse of the mutilated corpse. "It is possible to suppose," says Williamson, "given the distrust of surgeons and anatomists generally, that readers may have been more suspicious of the Crew of Light than Stoker intended, and not at all reassured by their triumph" (24). Their fear becomes that of the male vampire slayers, rather than the vampire herself. In this oppositional reading, the vampire slayers, who are intended to be the figures of moral responsibility, become the figures of fear and loathing, the threat to avoid; they are the immoral beings.

Of course, Williamson was unable to directly ask women and working-class Victorians about their interpretations of *Dracula* and scholars of the day did not think to do so themselves. Williamson is speculating given a variety of conditions we do know about that historical period to determine as much as possible the structure of feeling of the Victorian working classes. When looking to more recent versions of the vampire, it is easier to get first-hand representations of a variety of interpretations through interactions with audiences, both fans and critics. For example, the *Twilight* series provides another example of multiple readings.

The *Twilight* Series

Utilizing vampire narratives to construct a romantic fairy tale, Stephanie Meyer blends her own Mormon understanding of love relationships with the traditional gendered assumptions found in the long history of vampire stories. In the *Twilight* series, the relationship between vampire Edward Cullen and human Bella Swan highlights Mormon morality and gender norms even as it draws on occult fascinations. Edward is strong; Bella is clumsy and weak. Edward is protective; Bella is vulnerable. Edward is morally conservative; Bella wants to be more sexually experimental. Edward keeps Bella from straying into sexual temptation, thus showing the male role in controlling the behaviour of women. As Melissa Ames (2010) points out, not only is Bella "consistently depicted as the damsel in distress forever in need of rescue by a male, [. . .] the underlying message present is that sex is sinful and off limits" (40), at least prior to marriage. Further to this conservative sexual morality, the idea of eternal marriage, foundational to Mormon doctrine, is idealized in the marriage of Edward and Bella and Bella's eventual "conversion" into a vampire. Their love will last forever.

The *Twilight* series is targeted towards teen girls. However, as Elizabeth Behm-Morawitz, Melissa A. Click, and Jennifer Stevens Aubrey (2010) point out, a large number of adult women are also fascinated by both the books and movies. Interestingly, in their analysis of how these various ages of women engage with the romance and sexual morality of the stories, Behm-Morawitz *et al.* found variations in readings. For example, they used survey and focus-group methods to determine female fans' interpretation of the love relationships of the film and found that only

Mormons

The Mormons, more accurately referred to as the Church of Jesus Christ of Latter-day Saints (LDS), is an American religion first developed in the 1800s under the leadership of Joseph Smith (1805–1844). Smith claimed to have received a revelation from the angel, Moroni, who led him to a buried text written on golden plates. This text is known as the Book of Mormon and tells the story of the tribe of Joseph (one of the lost tribes of Israel) who came to America after leaving Jerusalem in 600 BCE. This story established a Hebrew origin of American Indians, and his revelation cast Smith himself as a living prophet. Smith's goal in the formation of the LDS was to restore the lost tribe of Israel and restore the original Christian church in a purified community.

For Mormons, God is a finite being who is part of space and time. Human beings are literally the children of God, in the same way Jesus was the son of God. The goal of Mormons is to worship God faithfully so as to eventually enter the celestial kingdom where they will also become gods. To enable this celestial existence, Mormons must be baptized, follow the rules of the Church, and become sealed to one another through eternal marriage. As Catherine Albanese writes, "Marriage, they held, would continue in the life to come, and full salvation could not be reached for either man or woman without it" (227). Temple rites even include baptism and marriage for those who had died prior to the new revelation, so they too could join the celestial kingdom community. The need for sealing to reach the celestial kingdom was motivation for the practice of polygamy in a context with more females than males. However, due to public pressure against polygamy, the Church of Jesus Christ of Latter-day Saints officially stopped polygamy in 1890, ostensibly due to a new revelation. The practice of polygamy continues to be upheld by small groups who broke away from the LDS and are called, by the LDS, fundamentalist Mormons. There are approximately 14 million members of the LDS worldwide.

55 per cent of adult women and 49 per cent of teen girls "most strongly desired Edward and Bella's relationship" (144) in comparison with other, more equal, relationships portrayed in the series. These are high numbers, but not high enough to assume that all fans (never mind all viewers) are identifying strongly with Meyer's message of what an ideal relationship should be. Behm-Morowitz *et al.* found that those who identified with some element of feminist identity were least likely to idealize the Edward-Bella relationship, even while being drawn into the story. Critics of the *Twilight* series often argue that the romantic relationship between Edward and Bella is teaching young women a problematic and unrealistic reliance on conservative romance. Behm-Morowitz *et al.*'s study shows that amongst fans, the acceptance of this message is heavily mixed.

A Negotiated Reading of Vampires

We have been exploring a number of readings of vampires by fans and critics. However, another reading has developed in the late twentieth to early twenty-first century that must be acknowledged. In this negotiated reading, not only are vampires read as mysterious, romantic figures, as in the *Twilight* series, they are also identified as real. The development of a vampire subculture takes the stories of vampires to a new level where the vampire is not only desirable, but where one identifies *as* a vampire. Lynne Hume explores the vampire subculture in her essay "Liminal Beings and the Undead: Vampires in the 21st Century" (2006), where she looks at the move from interest in the fantasy genre of vampire literature and role-playing games, to the claim of being a "real" vampire. She suggests that "the luminal figure of the vampire, neither truly living nor truly dead, suspended between life and death, human-like but not human, provides a niche for young people who feel they are on the fringe of society" (9). Many of these self-identified vampires, inspired by the vampires in the fiction of Anne Rice (author of *Interview with a Vampire* and its sequels) and other stories, engage in the drinking of blood (either human or animal) as a perceived necessity for their spiritual and physical well-being. Some believe themselves to be something other than human. Hume insists that "people seem to want to do more than merely read about enchantment, they want to actively engage with their fantasies, extend their imagination, and live enchanted lives" (13). The individuals and groups she explores in her study, such as the Temple of the Vampire, do this through embracing and becoming the vampire. We will discuss the construction of hyper-real, or invented, religions more fully in Chapter 9.

Applying Culturalism in an Evangelical Christian Structure of Feeling

The examples outlined in this chapter address some expressions of occulture in popular culture and some religious foundations and engagements specific to zombies and vampires. When addressing the occult in popular culture, though, it is also prudent to look to a specifically evangelical Christian understanding of the occult as this understanding has permeated much of common culture in North America.

Though there is considerable diversity within evangelical Christianity, there is also considerable consistency. Evangelical Christians are conservative Protestants who believe in the **inerrancy** of the Christian Bible. This means that they believe it is the literal Truth. Some evangelicals believe every word of the Bible is true, and thus if science disputes the biblical version, for example, where evolutionary theory disputes the creation story, then science is wrong. Inerrancy means the Bible is always true. However, some evangelicals will allow that the Bible is inerrant only in matters of religion and ethics. The cosmology and historical accounts of the Bible can be interpreted more liberally or metaphorically.

Born Again

All evangelicals believe in the necessity of being "born again." They believe all humans are sinful; however, Jesus, the son of God, died on the cross to take on the sins of the world. He took those sins into hell, where he conquered death and Satan. He then rose from the dead and ascended back into Heaven to re-join with God the Father. All people who believe in Jesus and specifically "ask him into their hearts,"—accept his sacrifice—become new people in the eyes of God: they are born again as Christians. All evangelicals must make their own choice to be a Christian; it is insufficient to simply be raised in a Christian home.

Evangelical Christians are conservative in their moral values. Though there is considerable variety, they are typically strict and traditional in regards to pre-marital sex and gender roles, alcohol and recreational drugs, and other issues, such as gambling, dancing, rock music, etc. Anything that is presumed to take one away from the holiness dictated by God in the Bible is prohibited. Many evangelicals take this conservatism into the political realm as well. This is particularly evident in the United States with the development of the Christian Right, which tries to bring conservative Protestant values into the larger political system to create (or preserve) a "Christian America." Here we will focus more on the way evangelical Christians integrate the occult with a concept of evil.

Associations with Evil: Lynn Schofield Clark

Due to their strong belief in the powers of good and evil, associated with God and Satan respectively, evangelical Christians typically associate the occult with the satanic. In an interesting study of youth conceptions of the supernatural in secular media, Lynn Schofield Clark has suggested that the evangelical Christian concern with evil has actually fueled the popular imagination for supernatural forces associated with the occult, such as zombies and vampires, along with ghosts, witches, demons, and extraterrestrials. This is not to say that these popular representations are encoded, or decoded, in evangelical Christian ways. Clark writes, "But even as concerns about evil and the realm beyond become more widespread, evangelicals are not in control of how these concerns will be understood or addressed" (2003, 26). In her study, Clark showed five distinct ways that youth responded to the supernatural in popular culture, including Christian youth. While some were Traditionalists that were committed to a conservative religion and made a strict divide between religion and media, actually avoiding much secular media, many others were more willing to blur the lines between "reality" and media. Those Clark calls the Intrigued separated institutional religion from alternative beliefs: thus they could both believe in Christianity and various church doctrines, while also believing in ghosts or other supernatural beings not explicitly tied to their religious ideologies. Those of a Mystical bent were more likely to have had direct experiences with the supernatural and thus saw popular cultural versions as more authentic, though for many of these Clark indicates that their experience promoted fear and ambivalence. The Experimenters tried out various rituals and beliefs as found in television or movies. The Resisters rejected any form of organized religion but were still willing to consider the possibilities of other supernatural forces as seen in popular culture (Clark 2002).

While certainly not all of Clark's sources were evangelical Christians, the point she is trying to make is that the way the supernatural and occult were understood by many was founded on the original evangelical Christian association of the occult with something evil, or at least possibly evil. Not everyone decoded occult activity as evil; but there was the underlying understanding that cultural norms, or a certain structure of feeling, were being resisted by allowing the occult a positive image.

The *Harry Potter* Series

Though most evangelical Christians associate the occult with the satanic, and thus evil, this does not mean they all decode popular cultural representations of occulture in the same way. A clear example of this can be found in the evangelical Christian response to the *Harry Potter* series by J.K. Rowling. Though it seemed to many in the mainstream press that all evangelical Christians were anti-Harry Potter— doing such extreme things as burning the books—in fact, evangelical Christians were divided on this issue. Danielle M. Soulliere, in her essay "Much Ado about Harry: *Harry Potter* and the Creation of a Moral Panic" (2010), argues that there was a significant division between Christians, for sure, but even between evangelical Christians on the way the Harry Potter series should be understood and used.

Some evangelical Christians feel the series promotes the occult and thus is evil. This association comes from a literal reading of Christian biblical texts, a foundational tenet of evangelical Christianity. Exodus 22:18 says "Thou shalt not suffer a witch to live"; Deuteronomy 18:10–12 says "There shall not be found among you any one that maketh his son or his daughter to pass through the fire, or that useth divination, or an observer of times, or an enchanter, or a witch. Or a charmer, of a consulter with familiar spirits, or a wizard, or a necromancer. For all that do these things are an abomination unto the LORD." These are harsh indictments against the occult in the Christian Old Testament. The biblical case against the occult, though, is not limited to the Old Testament. The New Testament carries such indictments as well. Galatians 5:20–21 gives a list of sins including,

> Idolatry, witchcraft, hatred, variance, emulations, wrath, strife, sedi-
> tions, heresies, Envyings, murders, drunkenness, revellings, and such
> like: of the which I tell you before, as I have also told you in time past,
> that they which do such things shall not inherit the kingdom of God.

Finally, in Revelation 21:8 we can read "But the fearful, and unbelieving, and the abominable, and murderers, and whoremongers, and sorcerers, and idolaters, and all liars, shall have their part in the lake which burneth with fire and brimstone: which is the second death" (all biblical passages are from the King James Version). Given these biblical statements it is not surprising that evangelical Christians, who hold the Christian Bible to be inerrant, would be concerned with their children reading books that normalize witchcraft and wizardry.

Soulliere points out, however, that other evangelical Christians feel the Harry Potter series promotes Christian values of redemption and thus was usable to teach Christian children. For them the witchcraft in the series was merely fantastical and not to be associated with real-life occult practices. A good example is a 2005 essay found in the evangelical Christian journal *Christianity Today* in which Russ Breimeier suggests that

> Throughout the series, Rowling uses her heroes to champion the fruit
> of the Spirit: love, joy, peace, patience, kindness, goodness, faithful-
> ness, gentleness and self-control. And conversely, evil is characterized
> by common sins like pride, wrath, and selfishness—all things that
> Harry faces and learns to overcome. Harry's growth in character from
> an uncertain boy into a man of virtue is central to the books and films.

He further suggests that parents need to help their children understand the differ-ence between fantasy witchcraft and real occult practices in the world. The themes of the Harry Potter series are positive, according to Breimeier, and the magic simply a plot device. What this example shows is that even within a specific subculture, such as evangelical Christianity, with the same symbol sets, we can find multiple readings (decodings) of a give popular cultural product.

Summary

Partridge points to the desire for a re-enchanted world and the exploration of occulture in forming that re-enchanted world. Drawing on Raymond Williams we can see occulture as a structure of feeling. To understand it fully, we must engage in the popular cultural versions of occulture, such as stories about zombies and vampires. However, these stories, and their central symbols, speak to multiple structures of feeling varied by time and place. A vampire is never just a vampire: it is always encoded in culturally specific ways. Stuart Hall, however, reminds us that just because it is encoded in a particular way, it does not mean everyone reads it in that way. For some, the vampire is desirable; for others, evil; and for others, self-identifiable. Culturalism is the study of the multiple readings available of documentary culture in order to try to understand, as best as is possible, a specific structure of feeling, by way of dominant, negotiated, and oppositional readings. These decodings, however, must maintain a relationship of some sort with the encoding determined by the producer. Cultural products are never arbitrary; they are always complex codes calling for deciphering.

Review Questions

1. How is culturalism different from the culture industry thesis of the Frankfurt School?
2. Why is documentary culture important to Raymond Williams?
3. What is the relationship between the encoding and decoding of meanings in any given cultural product?
4. What is "occulture"? Why is it significant for the study of religion and popular culture?
5. How are Haitian zombies and Hollywood zombies different?
6. What might a Buddhist perspective on the late twentieth-century Hollywood zombie look like?
7. How might Victorian working-class women decode Bram Stoker's *Dracula*?
8. What elements of Mormon belief are represented in the *Twilight* series?
9. What is the relationship between vampire stories and the development of a vampire subculture?
10. Why do some evangelical Christians oppose occult images?

Useful Resources

Print

Click, Melissa A., Jennifer Stevens Aubrey, and Elizabeth Behm-Morawitz, eds. 2010. *Bitten by Twilight: Youth Culture, Media, and the Vampire Franchise*. New York: Peter Lang.

Davis, Wade. 1985. *The Serpent and the Rainbow*. Toronto: Stoddart.

Meyer, Stephanie. 2005. *Twilight*. Little, Brown and Company.

Meyer, Stephanie. 2006. *New Moon*. Little, Brown and Company.

Meyer, Stephanie. 2007. *Eclipse*. Little, Brown and Company.

Meyer, Stephanie. 2008. *Breaking Dawn*. Little, Brown and Company.

Partridge, Christopher. 2004. *The Re-Enchantment of the West*. Vol. 1. London: T & T Clark.

Partridge, Christopher. 2005. *The Re-Enchantment of the West*. Vol. 2. London: T & T Clark.

Rowling, J.K. 1997. *Harry Potter and the Philosopher's Stone*. Bloomsbury Children's Books.

Rowling, J.K. 1998. *Harry Potter and the Chamber of Secrets*. Bloomsbury Children's Books.

Rowling, J.K. 1999. *Harry Potter and the Prisoner of Azkeban*. Bloomsbury Children's Books.

Rowling, J.K. 2000. *Harry Potter and the Goblet of Fire*. Bloomsbury Children's Books.

Rowling, J.K. 2003. *Harry Potter and the Order of the Phoenix*. Bloomsbury Children's Books.

Rowling, J.K. 2005. *Harry Potter and the Half-Blood Prince*. Bloomsbury Children's Books.

Rowling, J.K. 2007. *Harry Potter and the Deathly Hallows*. Bloomsbury Children's Books.

Stoker, Bram. 1897. *Dracula*. Archibald Constable and Company.

Video

Ball, Allen. 2008–present. *True Blood*. HBO.

Craven, Wes. 1988. *The Serpent and the Rainbow*. Universal Pictures.

Halperin, Victor. 1932. *White Zombie*. United Artists.

Romero, George A. 1968. *Night of the Living Dead*. Image Ten, Laurel Group, and Market Square Productions.

Weedon, Joss. 1997–2003. *Buffy the Vampire Slayer*. The WB/UPN.

Wright, Edgar. 2004. *Shaun of the Dead*. Universal Pictures.

Zuckerbrot, Donna. 2008. *Zombies: When the Dead Walk*. Reel Time Images and Vision TV.

Online

The Temple of the Vampire, www.vampiretemple.com

Vampires, www.vampires.com/

Performativity

OBJECTIVES

This chapter will help you develop an understanding of

- the concept of ritual as performative utterance
- Judith Butler's theory of performativity
- the construction and performance of gender and religion by Madonna and Lady Gaga
- the performance of gender in ritualized professional hockey

You are at a Madonna concert. The stage is dark in anticipation of the next number. Mournful organ music begins to play as a large cross is raised up. As an orange backlight begins to grow, you realize that Madonna herself is "hanging" on the cross. She begins to sing, "I have a tale to tell ..." Does the performance of this song mark a religious moment? Can ritual happen in a concert hall or auditorium? What is happening when the secular and female Madonna is playing the sacred and male Jesus? What does this potentially blasphemous, potentially transformative act do or communicate?

One of the biggest hits of 2011, Lady Gaga's "Born this Way," is a dance song with a message that has inspired millions, and even spawned the "Born this Way" Foundation, which fosters safe, empowering communities for young people. Lady Gaga's elaborate seven-minute video for a five-minute song begins with a creation story in which Mother Monster (Lady Gaga) gives birth to "a new race within the race of humanity, a race which bears no prejudice, no judgment, but boundless freedom"; at the same time, she gives birth to "evil." Is this creation story a religious moment? Can ritual happen in a music video? What is happening when Lady Gaga is playing Mother Goddess? Is this a deliberate move away from Father God? What does this potentially blasphemous, potentially transformative act do or communicate?

You are at an NHL game. You watch or attend hockey games religiously, never missing a game. Hockey is your life. In this particular game, the star player of your favourite team, the Montreal Canadiens, has been injured by the opposing team. This is a normal state of events, as any hockey fan knows: hockey is a violent game and that's what makes it so entertaining. However, rather than sitting out the rest of the game, the star player takes some pain killers, has his ankle wrapped, and goes back out on the rink to eventually score the winning goal. The crowds go wild. Fighting, suffering for the sake of the game, toughness: these are all part of the expectations of the ritual of hockey. Does his willingness to suffer in this way make this player a "real man"? Is this a necessary sacrifice for the ritual of hockey playing? Can men's hockey be entertaining without the fighting?

This chapter explores these questions in the contexts of pop icons and sport stars performative presentations of both gender and religion. Drawing on ritual studies and Judith Butler's performativity, we will think through what is happening in these moments of the performance of religion and how both Madonna and Lady Gaga have tied religion to sexuality, femininity, and androgyny in interesting, sometimes subversive, ways. We also look to hockey as a less subversive and more normative performance of gender, particularly masculinity, through ritualized violence and suffering. The theories of performativity are notoriously dense and complicated. This chapter will try to make them understandable without simplifying them. Keep in mind, though, multiple readings of this chapter in particular may be necessary to get all the nuances of these theories.

Ritual Studies and Performance Theory

The work of the culturalists and Clifford Geertz as discussed in Chapter 3 is about discerning the multiple meanings or readings of any given cultural product; however, scholars interested in **performance theory** move toward a concern with the specific acts of cultural interactions. They ask about what these acts *do*, not just what they *mean*. In the field of religious studies, this concern is found in certain forms of ritual studies.

Ritual studies has a long history beginning with the early religious studies theorists we met in Chapter 1. Scholars such as James Frazer were interested in the role **ritual** had in the development of religion overall. Debates over the primacy of ritual over mythology were heated in the late nineteenth century. Did ritual develop to act out pre-existing myths? Or did myths develop to make sense of pre-existing ritual? By the twentieth century, scholars had mostly put aside the questions of origins and began to ask questions of meaning, process, and effect. Drawing on Durkheim's theory (Chapter 1) that religion was about social cohesion, ritual studies scholars began to talk of ritual as that which brings individuals together into the collective.

Victor Turner

In the mid-twentieth century, Victor Turner (1920–1983) developed a theory of ritual as social drama, wherein the tensions of society could be worked out. Here ritual is part of the process of community redefinition: ritual marks a transition within the social order. Turner was drawing on Arnold van Gennep's (1873–1957) construction of rites of passage as including "preliminal rites (rites of separation), liminal rites (rites of transition), and postliminal rites (rites of incorporation)" (van Gennep 1960, 11). Turner took this structure and saw that through ritual, individuals enter a **liminal stage**—that is they are no longer part of the social order, but in a space that can at times defy the social order. At the end of the ritual, the individuals involved re-emerge into the social order, thus reaffirming it. For example, in a Protestant Christian immersion baptism, an individual starts off as outside of the community—a non-member. The liminal state is being in the water, where one is in the process of being cleansed of sin—ritually drowned or killed with Jesus. Although killing goes against the community values, and places the participant, for a short moment, in a state of un-being—a liminal state. Coming out of the water is a transformation into a member of the community—a new birth. Thus the sinner dies and a community member is born. A culturalist may ask the questions: What does the cleansing mean to the minister? What does it mean to the person being baptized? What does it mean to the congregation? A ritual studies scholar, particularly one interested in performance theory, will more likely ask the questions: What did this ritual *do*? How is the individual changed in the context of the community? Was it effective?

Ronald Grimes

In *Ritual Criticism* (1990), Ronald Grimes talks about ritual as a concept that has been created by scholars. This concept allows us to think about specific rites. But it also allows us to think about the processes of ritualizing and ritualization. Thus when we talk about ritual, we are talking about something quite large and often diffuse. A **rite** is a specific, patterned event, such as the Catholic mass or Muslim daily prayers. These rites are differentiated from ordinary, everyday activities. Grimes encourages us not to use the term *rituals* to refer to specific rites; ritual is a much broader term. Grimes wants to include the concept of **ritualizing** which is the process of inventing or cultivating rites. An example of this might be the development of rites for newly experienced events, such as the marking of transition through sexual reassignment surgery. This transition can be ritualized, either within a specific religious context or not, through the creation of a new rite. Grimes also includes in ritual the concept of **ritualization** which involves activities not usually thought of as rites, such as watching TV. In ritualization we do various activities *as if* they were ritual even if they have no specific religious content or intention. Fans who "religiously" watch *True Blood* or attend Toronto Maple Leafs games do not necessarily see these activities as *actually* religious. But their activities can *do* some similar things as religious rituals—they can create or maintain community and/or give further meaning to individual lives.

Grimes highlights the difficulty in creating a singular definition of ritual that would cover all elements of rite, ritualizing, and ritualization, in all cultures. Thus, he suggests using a system of ritual family characteristics that includes: performed; formalized; repetitive; collective; patterned; traditional; highly valued; multilayered; symbolic; idealized; dramatic; paradigmatic; mystical; adaptive; and conscious. With this list he suggests that "just as no two family members have *all* the pool of family characteristics, so no ritual action is likely to display all of these" (1990, 13). Furthermore, Grimes argues, "no single quality is unique to ritual. [. . .] When these qualities begin to multiply, when an activity becomes dense with them, it becomes increasingly proper to speak of it as ritualized" (1990, 14). Of course this then makes it difficult to discern what actually is ritual and what is not. Ritual scholars do not always agree. Some argue that it is perfectly acceptable to approach activities like housecleaning as ritual. Others would limit ritual to something outside of everyday activity. For Grimes, the more ritual characteristics an activity has, the more we are justified in calling it ritual.

Catherine Bell

In *Ritual Theory, Ritual Practice* (1992), ritual studies scholar Catherine Bell also takes up the concept of ritualization. She suggests that ritualization can be thought of as circular, involving the "production of a ritualized body which in turn, produces ritualized practices" (93). Bell sees ritualization as a social communication. As we engage in ritualization—which is a practice that involves our bodies—we are placed within a social relationship. At the same time, our social relationships dictate our participation in ritualization. For example, attending a concert of our favorite pop icon could be ritualized. It could be seen as an act outside of our ordinary life (the profane) and involving an engagement with what we see as of ultimate value (the sacred). We participate in this ritualization from the position as "fan." Our participation would be altered if we were involved in the performance, for example. Our participation also creates our fandom, even as it is motivated by our fandom. We want to go to the concert because we are fans; but we understand our fandom as increasing in value and degree by putting the time and expense into going to the concert. Thus ritualization can be seen to shape and be shaped by identity.

Ritual and Performance

Many ritual studies scholars see ritual as operating like language: that is, it is a communication. The difference between culturalists and performance theorists is that culturalists focus more on the **semiotics**—interpretation of the meaning of the language—whereas performance theorists focus more on the **syntactical**—the concern with structure and grammatical rules. Many of these scholars look to the work of J.L. Austin (1911–1960), who developed the concept of "**performative utterance**" in his lecture "How to Do Things with Words" given at Harvard University in 1955 (Austin 1975). Performative utterance is speech that *does* something, rather than just describe something. For example, if I say "my friend is getting married today," this is a description of something that is intended to occur. If a priest says "I now pronounce you husband and wife," this is a performative utterance, because in saying the words, the couple literally become husband and wife. Though Austin focused solely on speech acts, ritual studies scholars see the symbolic acts of ritual as operating like language. Thus they are interested in the performative "utterance" of the acts, that is, how symbolic acts *do* something, not just *mean* something.

If ritual is a performative utterance or act, a symbolic act that *does* something, then it is also possible to think about the effectiveness of the act. Was it successful (i.e., did it actually do something)? Austin acknowledged that some utterances did not succeed, that is they were, in his language, "infelicitous." Grimes takes up this notion of the **infelicitous** performance and applies it to ritual. Austin proposes two categories of infelicitous, or ineffective, performances: misfires and abuses. Misfires happen when the structure of the "utterance" is faulty. For example, if I, as someone who does not have the legal or religious authority necessary, say "I pronounce you husband and wife," this is a misfire. The ritual doesn't *do* anything, because I am not authorized to make that performative utterance: the ritual/utterance misfires. An abuse happens when the intention is lacking. For example I could say "I do" in a wedding ceremony with absolutely no intention of honouring the marriage commitment. Thus, the ceremony might seem like it did something—joined two people into one—but because I did not have the correct intention for that ritual, it is infelicitous: it is an abuse of the ritual performance.

Grimes, in his text *Ritual Criticism* (1990), adds to these two categories, providing nine types of infelicitious performance that go beyond just the speech act. Not only are there misfires and abuses, says Grimes, but there are ineffectualities ("act fails to precipitate anticipated empirical change"), violations ("act effective but demeaning"), contagions ("act leaps beyond proper boundaries"), opacities ("act unrecognizable or unintelligible"), defeats ("act discredits or invalidates acts of others"), omissions ("act not performed"), and misframes ("genre of act misconstrued") (Grimes 1990, 205). Say I go through a wedding ceremony with a stranger and then never interact with my "spouse" again. This rite has then been ineffectual as the relationship has not changed. We are still strangers. Or perhaps I am wed against my will to someone and forced to live with him. Yes, we are married but the rite was demeaning to at least one of the participants (me). It is a violation and thus not truly effective. In some contexts if I wed another woman this would be seen as infelicitous because the rite has moved out of the proper boundaries (of marriage between a man and a woman only). This could be seen as a contagion rather than an effective rite. What if I get married in China and I neither understand the words nor the ritual process? Am I truly married? This could be an example of opacity rather than effective ritual. Of course I could always refuse to have a wedding ceremony and just live with my partner *as if* I were married. Here we have an omission of the rite. Finally, a misframe could happen if I choose to wed someone I've only met in the Second Life virtual world without thinking the rite has any real-world implications. We explore this scenario more fully in Chapter 9. Grimes shows that there are many ways that rituals can fail to perform what they are intended to perform. However, when they are successful, transformations happen.

Judith Butler and *Bodies That Matter*

Ritual studies theorists draw on Austin's concept of performative utterance to make sense of both religious and non-religious ritual. Other scholars, though, are also interested in the performativity of cultural practices; this is evident in the work of influential scholar Judith Butler. Butler was foundational in the development of feminist cultural studies. Her theories on performance provided a new way of thinking of gender and sexuality along with the cultural implications of these.

While some feminist theory had already largely accepted and promoted gender as a social construction (see more on feminist theories in Chapter 5), Butler, also drawing on Austin's notions of performative utterance, brought the notion of performance into the discussion of the construction of gender beginning in her 1990 book *Gender Trouble*. This book, written at a point of transition in feminist theory (when feminist theory began to think less of "the woman" and more about the diversity of "women's" lives), takes the feminist concern with gender and shows how gender is integrally related to sexuality. This move was at the forefront of a new discipline called **queer theory,** in which the naturalization of gender, sex, and sexuality is continually disrupted. Butler argued that not only is gender constructed, but it is constructed through the very **anticipation** of gender. This anticipation is related to **compulsory heterosexuality**. Because humans have prioritized reproduction, they have anticipated a natural connection between two types of humans necessary for reproduction—a male and a female. This anticipation creates the need to type all humans into one of two categories and assign them cultural and

Queer Theory

Queer theory developed in the 1990s as scholars began to critique an essentialist understanding of gender and sexuality. The term "queer," originally used to indicate something strange or odd, and used as a derogatory slang for gays and lesbians, has been reclaimed to represent a disruption of sexual essentialism. First reclaimed by gay and lesbian activists and street kids in the 1980s, "queer" was used by Teresa de Lauretis to title a conference in 1990 at University of California, Santa Cruz. This use, says David Halperin, was "scandalously offensive" to the academic community (2003, 340). However, de Lauretis

> hoped both to make theory queer (that is, to challenge the heterosexist underpinnings and assumptions of what conventionally passed for "theory" in academic circles) and to queer theory (to call attention to everything that is perverse about the project of theorizing sexual desire and sexual pleasure) (Halperin 2003, 340).

Other scholars, such as Judith Butler, soon began to use this term for their own work as well.

Queer theory deconstructs **heteronormativity** and works to show how the discourse of compulsory heterosexuality developed and the influence it has had on various cultures. In utilizing the concept of queerness, queer theory challenges identity politics that reinforce essentialized identities. For example, rather than positing the "naturalness" of homosexual identity within individuals, as those involved in gay and lesbian studies do, queer theorists are more likely to argue that all sexuality is constructed in various ways; none of it is natural. Sexuality is a discourse, and like all discourse, it is shaped by social and cultural conventions that have little to nothing to do with "nature" or "biology." Queer theorists, like Butler, also deconstruct the assumptions of sex as a biological given, at least in the two-sex model we presume in Western science. They suggest that there is more variety than strictly two sexes. For example, Anne Fausto-Sterling (1993), a feminist biologist, argues that there are at least five sexes, based on the biology of genitalia and chromosomes. Even people who "look" male, for example, may have higher levels of female secondary sex characteristics (developed breasts, limited body hair, etc.) and/or a Y chromosome. Queer theory questions the need to continue to fit a person such as this into either a male or female category and suggests opening up the sexual categories to allow for more diversity.

social characteristics—masculine and feminine. In this sense gender is constructed through the presumed need to have two genders tied to two sexes for the purposes of reproduction. However, Butler does not stop there. Not only is gender anticipated by compulsory heterosexuality and thus constructed in this dual way, it is performed daily: the performance of gender is something that continues indefinitely;

one is never done constructing themselves as a man or a woman. Performing gender is something we all *do*; we don't *have* a gender, as if it is something attained once and then held onto as a possession. The acts of being masculine or feminine are repetitive and ritualized. They are repetitive culturally in that many people continually act them out reinforcing their "naturalness." They are also repetitive individually in that no given individual *becomes* masculine or feminine and then is done with their performance. We always need to continue performing in order to maintain our gendered identity. In this way gender becomes **naturalized**. We think it is natural because we see everyone else doing it and we continue to do it ourselves every time we sit in a chair or walk down the street or speak to another person. We are largely unaware of our actions as performance.

Butler famously appealed to **drag** as an example that showed the performativity of gender in very clear ways. Drag, when males dress up as women or females dress up as men and then act in those gender roles, reveals gender to be contingent upon actions—the truth of gender is displayed as contextual. This discussion of drag continues in Butler's second major text, *Bodies That Matter* (1993) where she points out that drag is ambivalent; it both defies and reiterates gender norms. However, its subversiveness lies in its ability to show the imitative structure of hegemonic gender and heterosexuality: drag imitates the performance of heterosexual gender in a way that both idealizes that dual-gender system and also de-naturalizes the appropriate players. Yes, women are supposed to wear make-up, dresses with high heels, act coy and at times seductive and sexy; they walk in a certain way, sit in a certain way, speak in a certain way. But it is females, not males, who are supposed to be these women. Drag challenges that and thus challenges that femininity is natural to femaleness and shows that this femininity is a performance. If it is a performance for these males, it is also a performance for the females who take on this kind of femininity.

In *Bodies That Matter* Butler also takes a step further in her discussion of the performativity of gender. She argues that not only is gender constructed by its own anticipation, but sex is also anticipated and thus our very bodies are understood within a dual-sex system anticipated by compulsory heterosexuality and reproduction in ways that appear natural. Not only do we perform our gender—masculine or feminine—we also perform our sex—male or female. Butler asks, "Through what regulatory norms is sex itself materialized?" (1993, 10). Butler is not suggesting that bodies do not exist as biological matter, but that our discourse about our bodies is shaped by our anticipations; in this case, the anticipation that we must have two sexes for reproduction. This anticipation requires us to place everybody within one of two categories that are constructed to make sure we have a heterosexual system leading to reproduction. But why do we need all humans to fit into a reproductive role? If it is true that we need males and females to reproduce, that does not necessarily make it true that we all need to fit within those categories, as we do not all need to reproduce.

Many readers have suggested what Butler is saying is that since gender and sex are not natural, they are constructed through discourse and anticipation leading to a continual performance to maintain the sense of gender and sex being natural, that we can just set them aside: if we perform our gender, we can just choose what gender we want and how we want to act independent of cultural or social norms. Butler, however, refutes these interpretations. She is not saying that gender and sex are voluntary performances: we cannot just decide to act one way one day and another a different day; we cannot step outside of the discourse completely. However, resistance can happen to a certain extent. Butler argues, drawing on Michel Foucault, that agency is found only in the possibilities opened up by the constraints themselves (see the section on Discourse in Chapter 1). Meaning, yes, we can resist the norms, but only as the norms enable us to resist: we can exaggerate gender (as is sometimes the case with drag); we can try to blur the lines between gender. But we cannot escape gender. We are bound by the constraints of the heterosexist gender system. All our resistance can only happen within and in relation to that system.

Unlike the ritual studies performance scholars, Butler's concern with performativity is not a concern with efficacy. In fact, she is more interested in the disruptions of the intended outcome, when performance makes obvious the constructed nature of gender, rather than hides it in naturalized activity. However, both Butler's interest in denaturalizing performance and Grimes' interest in determining efficacy of ritual performance can be used to analyze the performances of pop music stars Madonna and Lady Gaga, both of whom integrate sex/gender performance with religious ritual.

Applying Performance Theory: From Madonna to Hockey

Pop Icons: Madonna

The pop icon Madonna is well known not only for her musical talent, but also for her theatrical performances in music videos and on concert tours. She is famous for her play with image and impersonation, re-creating her image frequently over her 30-plus year career, with a particular focus on redefining her own relationship to gender and sexuality. Numerous academic scholars have analyzed Madonna's performance and identity (for some examples see Hulsether [2000]; Guilbert [2002]; Fouz-Hernández and Jarman-Ivens [2004]). José I. Prieto-Arranz suggests that

Madonna "remains as controversial today as when she first gained notoriety three decades ago" (2012, 173). Many have noted how difficult Madonna's image is to pin down. Patricia Pisters, in her analysis of Madonna's performance of femininity suggests that

> Madonna deliberately complicates the possible readings that can be made of her work. She can rarely be consigned to a stable category: when one thinks she is pleading for equality, she foregrounds hyper-femininity and difference; when one thinks she is relying on binaristic or stable representations of sexuality, she simultaneously deconstructs those binarisms. In short, she is semantically slippery (Pisters 2004, 26).

Corinna Herr (2004) and Stan Hawkins (2004) both highlight the **masquerade**, or role-playing, activity of Madonna. Both, however, point to a Butlerian notion of performance. Madonna is not performing a pre-existing essential identity; she is impersonating a fantasy, and through her performance she shows the fantasy to be exactly that—a fantasy. As Herr suggest, the masquerade is not a representation of the real; the mask itself is the only real there is. This is a similar notion to Jean Baudrillard's concept of the hyperreal, which we will discuss further in Chapter 9.

Let us take a closer look at some specific moments in Madonna's immense career to explore the ideas of performativity more carefully. These moments come from the performance of a few well-known hits in both video and tour format. First we will explore Madonna's performance and juxtaposition of the two of her biggest hits in her early career, "Like a Virgin" and "Like a Prayer" in her 1990 *Blond Ambition* tour, as well as the original videos created for each of these songs. The second moment is Madonna's later controversial performance of the song "Live to Tell" in her 2006 tour, *Confessions*.

"Like a Virgin" was Madonna's first international number one hit, released in 1983. The original video came at the beginning of the music video craze, coinciding with the success of MTV, which had been launched in 1981. The video is tame by current standards, including Madonna's own later repertoire. In the video Madonna appears as her early iconic self—teased blond hair, heavy eye make-up, abundance of inexpensive jewelry including a crucifix hanging at her waist—dancing in a boat travelling along the canals of Venice looking directly into the camera. Alternately, we see a coifed Madonna in a white wedding dress waiting for, and eventually being swept up by, her groom. Already in this early video Madonna performs contradicting practices of femininity. She is the aggressive woman who looks us in the eye; she knows what she wants and shows it. She is also the blushing bride waiting to be carried away into the fantasy of conventional heterosexual bliss. Throughout the video we also see periodic glimpses of a tiger; perhaps a sign of the dangers of performing femininity?

A more controversial video released in 1989, "Like a Prayer" is much more explicitly a theatrical performance ending with a curtain call. This video tells a story in a more or less linear fashion: Madonna is a young woman who witnesses an attack by a group of white men on another white woman. She then sees a "good Samaritan" figure trying to help the injured/dead woman. When the police arrive, they arrest the "good Samaritan," who is a black man. The Madonna character is uncertain what to do, as she is afraid of the attacking men. She runs to a church and finds solace in a black saint/Jesus figure (who is the same actor as the accused black man) and a black gospel choir. At the end she goes to the jail and tells her account of the events, thus saving the accused black man. All the while, Madonna is singing about the prayer-like quality of her romantic love.

From a religious studies perspective, Mark Hulsether argues that Madonna's "Like a Prayer" video is an example of **liberation theology**; what the video *does*, more than what the lyrics might mean, is call out the racism of American society and ritualize anti-racist responses. Liberation theology is an interpretation of Christian texts and doctrines through the experiences of the poor and oppressed. Liberation theologians focus on Jesus' life as ministry among the poor and oppressed and, also, focus on the struggle to end poverty and oppression. Thus liberation theology includes a critique of the economic and social structures and activities of churches in maintaining power structures. A particular form of liberation theology is **Black theology** which articulates the religious struggles of Black communities in a hostile White supremacist world. Jesus, in Black liberation theology, is signified as the oppressed man *par excellence* and liberator of all who suffer and are exploited. Since Jesus represents the oppressed, and since in a White supremacist context oppression is equated with Blackness, Jesus is identified with the Black community: Jesus is Black. Hulsether argues that the Black Jesus/saint figure in Madonna's video aligns the video with Black liberation theology, as does Madonna's message of white racism and the challenge to that racism through the narrative.

However, the narrative is not the only significance of this video. Through the depiction of rituals of gospel singing and praying, "Like a Prayer" takes on the aura of ritual more directly. As viewers observe the Madonna character engaging in a familiar ritual process, they are invited to enter that process themselves. To do so requires that they adopt, for the moment at least, elements of black theology. As a statement against white supremacy, the viewing of "Like a Prayer" can also be a practice of transforming that white supremacist society. If it is effective, that is. If effective, watching this video could bring one into a liminal state of identification with the fictional characters. At the end, when the curtain closes, one is transformed into an anti-racist activist.

Gospel Music

The gospel music featured in Madonna's performance of "Like a Prayer" is a style of music that developed out of the Protestant Black Church experience in North America. Gospel music emerged in the early twentieth century through an integration of spirituals and blues, both of which develop from the contexts of African enslavement in America and continuing racial tensions after emancipation. The spirituals were songs sung by enslaved Africans in the American south. They contain themes of freedom from slavery drawing on the stories of the Israelites found in the Christian Old Testament. These songs were both about spiritual messages as well as tools to help the illiterate slaves communicate. Blues developed in secular contexts in African American communities as a music that expressed the pain of living in oppression and focused on the daily experiences of sex, violence, and poverty. The spirituals were sacred; the blues was secular. In a sense, both were ritualized practices. The singing, and listening, became a liminal state in which one was no longer bound by the racism and oppression of slavery. Going through this liminal stage took one into a transformed social identity. While this new, or renewed, identity may not have always involved physical and legal freedom, it did involve spiritual or emotional freedom.

In the 1930s, a former blues musician, Thomas Dorsey, dedicated his life to the Church. He took on the mission of putting the religious message of the spirituals to the musical style of the blues, creating the new genre of gospel music (see Boyer 1992). This music has since become a significant element of the Black Church experience, as well as developing a successful commercial music industry. Bernice Johnston Reagon describes gospel music as having "high-powered spiritual force, with increased emphasis on vocal rhythms and calculated use of vocal textures to create greater intensity" (1992, 5). Gospel music often takes the form of a soloist with a choir singing backup. There is frequently a call and response relationship between soloist and choir, or with soloist and congregation. Singing is typically accompanied by a swaying dance and clapping, with intermittent raising of hands to the heavens. Gospel music is a central part of the regular ritual practice of many African-American Christian churches. For more on African-American musical traditions see Chapter 6.

Of even more significance for theories of performativity are the live performances of the above two singles, particularly in the 1990 *Blond Ambition* tour. This tour occurred around the same time as Butler began working on queer theory. While Madonna is unlikely to have specifically read Butler's work, her performance does reflect many of the issues with which queer theorists were engaging. In this tour Madonna chose to perform "Like a Virgin" immediately followed by "Like a Prayer." This juxtaposition brings the performance of sexuality and religion into close connection. "Like a Virgin" is transformed in this performance context with the addition of Middle Eastern sounding musical themes and erotic dancing far racier than in the original video. Madonna is dressed in a gold bustier lying on a red-draped bed for the entire performance of this song. She is accompanied by two male dancers who are wearing exaggerated cone-shaped bras. Thus in this song's performance we have an obvious performance of gender and sexuality as hyper-constructed. The male dancers do sex and gender in an ambiguous way—male bodies with large breasts—making sex and gender, as categories, ambiguous. Madonna's sexual cavorting, with the ambiguous dancers and in self-arousing activities, also makes sexuality ambiguous, bringing in the question of how to categorize a female/feminine sexual relationship with androgynous or at least ambiguous bodies as well as with her own self.

As the tones of the song fade, Madonna's voice resounds with a single word: "God." We are then brought into the first chords of "Like a Prayer." José I. Prieto-Arranz argues that "this is beyond any doubt the moment when sex and religion, two constants in Madonna's career, achieve their most perfect union" (2012, 186). The "God" could be the final statement of "Like a Virgin"—the declaration following orgasm. Or, it could be the initial prayerful statement of "Like a Prayer," indicating a shift in focus. Prieto-Arranz suggests it is both. And in the statement, Madonna is "confirming a conception of sex as God-given pleasure" (Prieto-Arranz 2012, 187). Or perhaps we could say that Madonna is making sex a religious ritual. We will see this theme of integrating the sexual and the sacred again in our discussion of Wonder Woman in Chapter 5.

As the performers transition to "Like a Prayer," Madonna is cloaked with a priest-like black robe and joined by more dancers dressed as priests and background singers dressed as nuns. As a group these performers engage in "Like a Prayer" without the liberation theology markers of the video. Instead we have an almost conventional engagement with prayer postures and gospel singing—though one is not usually accustomed to seeing nuns sing gospel.

In "Like a Virgin" Madonna performs sex; in "Like a Prayer" Madonna performs religion. In both contexts, if we take a Butlerian approach, these performances are anticipatory as well as subversive. Madonna is operating within a cultural system of heterosexual normativity. Inherent to that system is a focus on sex and sexuality. Though Madonna's performance in "Like a Virgin" pushes the boundaries of what is acceptable, she is still maintaining the needed focus on sex. However in complicating the gendered representations and showing the very constructedness of maleness, femaleness, and heterosexuality, Madonna and her dancers perform a subversive challenge to the heteronormative system; it is a queer performance. In "Like a Prayer" Madonna anticipates the Christian understanding of the divine and religious ritual which is part of the cultural system in which she is performing.

Within this context, she subverts this normative Christianity by using Christian imagery of prayer and the figures of priests and nuns while singing about sex. Her performance of prayer, and the Catholic wardrobe alongside the Protestant Black gospel singing, shows the constructedness of Christianity in North America, denaturalizing Christianity as the anticipated norm of American religion. For Madonna, Christianity is performed like gender or sex.

A certain denaturalizing of Christianity comes again in a later tour performance. In the 2006 *Confessions* tour, Madonna shocked some by performing her 1986 hit "Live to Tell" while "hanging" on a cross, wearing a crown of thorns. The cross itself was glitzy with a disco ball finish. Through most of the song, Madonna stood on a small platform with arms extended resting on supports to give the appearance of hanging on the cross. While she sang, a counter ran above her head; when the count reached 12,000,000, Madonna came off the cross while images of African children orphaned by the AIDS epidemic were projected behind her. At the end of the song, a voice spoke a passage from the gospel of Matthew: "For I was hungry and you gave me food; [. . .] I was naked and you gave me clothing; I was sick and you took care of me. [. . .] And God replied, whatever you did for the least of my brothers, you did it to me" (Matthew 25:35–40).

Named blasphemous by both the Roman Catholic Church and the Russian Orthodox Church and condemned by many others, this performance draws upon Christian imagery and ideology to make a political statement. Madonna responded to this controversy by explaining that she was trying "to bring attention to the millions of children in Africa who are dying every day (or) are living without care, without medicine and without hope. I am asking people to open their hearts and minds to get involved in whatever way they can" (Madonna quoted in Reuters 2006). By performing on the cross, Madonna becomes a Jesus figure. This ritualized performance thus portrays the need to help AIDS orphans as a Christian message. The biblical passage used re-emphasizes this. However, as it is Madonna taking up this cross—the female, sexually explicit, pop icon—her performance also wreaks havoc with the assumptions of Christian identity. The Christianity here is not about living a "pure" life according to any traditional Christian doctrines, but about helping the poor and oppressed—again a liberation theology message. By performing Jesus, Madonna strips Christianity of its sexual and gender norms and expresses, in some sense, the gospel.

A question we still have not addressed with these examples is the efficacy of these ritual performances. Do they work? Have they created the transformation ritual studies scholars, such as Grimes, argue is necessary? Or are they infelicitous? As Christian ritual we could argue that each of these performances is both misfired and abused. Madonna neither has the authority of a priest, as she performs in "Like a Prayer" nor the reputation of a Christ-like figure as she performs in "Live to Tell."

Thus the rituals misfire, as she cannot take on the necessary roles to make these truly Christian rituals. Nor, one might presume by drawing on Madonna's larger corpus, and her performance in "Like a Virgin," are her intentions that of promoting and furthering Christian values. Thus the rituals are abuses. However, if we argue that these rituals are never intended to be authoritative Christian ritual, perhaps they "work" after all. In *Blond Ambition* Madonna successfully blends sexuality and religiosity: she effectively makes "sex a God-given pleasure" as Prieto-Arranz suggested. In *Confessions* she got attention and focused it onto the plight of African children orphaned by the AIDS epidemic. In both cases she contributes a type of liberation theology as suggested by Hultheser. That organized Christian churches do not like it does not necessarily make it infelicitous. In fact, perhaps *because* the organized Christian churches do not like it, it is effective.

Pop Icons: Lady Gaga

Following closely in the footsteps of Madonna is the twenty-first–century pop icon Lady Gaga. Like Madonna, Lady Gaga plays with image and performance in ways that show the ultimate constructedness of identity. Lady Gaga also plays with Christian, particularly Catholic, images and performance in ways that are reminiscent of Madonna. Though we could examine a number of Lady Gaga's songs and videos, one particularly good example of playing with gender and religion performance comes in the video for her 2011 song "Born this Way."

The lyrics of the song "Born this Way" suggest an **essentialist** position on identity. We are all good and beautiful, regardless of race, sexuality or ability, because God made us that way. The video version, however, challenges the very notions of essentialist identity and performs a construction of gender, sexuality, and religion. Before the song begins, Lady Gaga tells, and shows, us a creation story in which Mother Monster (Lady Gaga) gives birth to a "perfect race without prejudice." Alongside this birthing, however, is the birth of evil. Good and evil are brought into being by two sides of the same Mother, and continue to interact throughout the video.

Naming this Mother a *Monster* Mother fits with Lady Gaga's use of the term "my little monsters" to refer to her fans. Victor P. Corona suggests that "Monster becomes a metaphor for the maddening swirl of images, anxieties, and fads in hypermodernity" (2011, 10). Drawing on Gilles Lipovestky description of **hyper-modernity** as "the culture of the fastest" (Lipovestky quoted in Corona 2011, 2), Corona sees Lady Gaga's hypermodernity in "her elaborate performances and sartorial experimentation" (2011, 2). She is the most audacious, the wildest, the strangest of all pop stars. The video "Born this Way" certainly plays out this hypermodernity. After the prelude, the song begins with Lady Gaga walking through the lines of her dancers, wearing relatively plain underwear and, for Lady Gaga, muted make-up and hairstyle. Most noticeable are Lady Gaga's cheek bones, amplified through prosthetic augmentation. So, while she is singing, "I was born this way," she is clearly presenting a constructed self. Does this contradict the message of the song? What is happening in this performance? What does it do?

In a Butlerian perspective we could argue that "Born this Way" anticipates a notion of equality: the lyrics seem to be especially drawing on the discourse of anti-homophobia. Being gay or straight, cisgendered (masculine gender in a male body or feminine gender in a female body), or transgendered are essential categories—we are born this way and should not be required to change. Elements of the video which show androgynous dancers in orgy-like settings as reflections of the "goodness" born by Mother Monster reinforce this message. But the play in the performance of this song, while sporting facial augmentation, following a fictionalized creation story, adds another dimension. We are born this way. What way? A fictionalized, constructed way. We are constructions. The performance does the construction and encourages viewers to continue to construct themselves. To be true to oneself, it seems, is to play with identity and performance. Richard J. Gray II suggests that "Lady Gaga *is* performance" (2012, 8). Furthermore, "When Gaga performs, she performs life scenes that we are too afraid to address ourselves" (Gray 2012, 8). Gray has edited one of the first academic texts on Lady Gaga; his anthology has a focus on performative theory. Most of the essays in this collection note that Lady Gaga is a performance artist. However, she is something more than that. Her performance does not really end. Lady Gaga herself has claimed that she is always performing; she is always Lady Gaga. Again, when the always constructed, performative artist sings about being "born this way," we are again challenged to rethink an essentialist interpretation of that phrase.

Not only are we constructions in this video, so is God. The lyrics indicate that it is perhaps God, "capital H-i-m" who made us this way. However, the performance of the creation story indicates that it was Mother Monster who gave birth to us or at least her little monsters (both good and evil). So who is God? Is Mother Monster God? The ritual performance of creation, casts human existence in the hands of a Goddess figure who is responsible for both good and evil. This performance challenges both the patriarchal and moral understandings of the Christian God, even as directly engaging in this understanding with the reference to "capital H-i-m." By implication, just as Mother Monster is a construction of Lady Gaga's artistic performance, so "God" is a construction of the culture(s) she is addressing. Lady Gaga's video anticipates a creation God, but shows that creator to be a creation itself. If God is a construction, then the idea that "He" made us in an essentialist way is further complicated. We are born this way, as a construction, by a construction: What we perceive to be natural is not. It is all performance.

Sports

While our discussion of pop icons Madonna and Lady Gaga have addressed the performance of gender and sexuality in video and live concert, this has largely been a focus on femininity, androgyny, and queer theory. A brief exploration of the performance of masculinity in the ritual of sports adds another dimension to our discussion. A number of religious studies theorists have focused on the ritual aspects of sports, both the playing and the fandom (see Price 2000; Evans and Herzog 2002; Caterine 2004; Scholes 2004; Chidester 2005; and Andrews 2011). In these studies, we are told that attending sporting events can function in a similar way to attending church services by providing community and common values.

For example, David Chidester in *Authentic Fakes* (2005) quotes Buck O'Neil, baseball player and first African American coach in major league baseball, "It is a religion" (quoted in Chidester 2005, 32). O'Neil clarifies this by explaining that it is governed by set rules. Chidester suggests that it is not only the rules that characterize baseball as religious, but offers four reasons for arguing that baseball is, in fact, a church. First, it provides a heritage and collective memory in the midst of a continually changing America. Second, it provides a commonality amongst players and fans, "a sense of belonging to a vast, extended American family that attends the same church" (2005, 36). Third, it relies on a sacred space: both home and stadium. Fourth is the importance of sacred time of ritual:

> The entire proceedings of the game are coordinated through a ritualization of time. But baseball also affords those extraordinary moments of ecstasy and enthusiasm, revelation and inspiration, that seem to stand outside the ordinary temporal flow (2005, 37).

HOCKEY

In thinking about the performative ritual of playing sports itself, some theorists have focused on the seemingly inherent violence involved, particularly in professional sports. Tracy Trothen does this in her study of professional hockey, which incorporates the themes of "violence, embodiment, and sexuality" (Trothen 2009) in a similar way to Christian atonement theology. In both professional hockey and Jesus' death and resurrection in atonement theology, suffering and violence are a given, but not necessarily an evil. For Christian theology, atonement requires the violence of Jesus' death, but that leads to salvation. In professional hockey "the greater the suffering, the greater the commitment" (Trothen 2009). To be clear here, Trothen is not suggesting that the violence of professional hockey brings salvation in the way Christians believe Jesus' death and resurrection brings salvation; however, she is suggesting that the performance of a professional hockey player emphasizes the need for violence, the moral ambiguity, and even moral good of that violence for particularly male players. This, in turn, performs a particular kind of masculinity tied to the ritual of suffering and commitment, in what she calls the liminal space of the game. Those who are willing to be tough enough to play through injury become heroic figures. As Trothen remarks, "The glorification of self-sacrifice and pain and suffering is certainly found in traditional atonement theories, as well as in hockey" (2009).

Feminist theorist on masculinities, Raewyn Connell, points to the importance of suffering and commitment in sports. She sees this emphasis, particularly in professional sports, as working to construct and maintain a hegemonic masculinity. Though it is clear through various cultural studies that there are multiple kinds of masculinities throughout the world, hegemonic masculinity is that pattern of masculinity that is most desired and associated with authority and power. Sport becomes an important source of the imagery of hegemonic masculinity whereby the performance of toughness and violence is a performance of manhood. For Connell this does not only happen in professional sports, but also, and perhaps more importantly, in the school system. Connell suggests that physical education has become "part of the regulation and disciplining of bodies" (2008, 140). That is, through physical education and the teaching of sport, which is the most gender-segregated aspect of public education, gender is constructed. Sport then becomes a performance of gender, and for men, specifically, a performance of hegemonic masculinity.

This glorification of toughness and violence is involved in a performance of hegemonic masculinity becomes clearer when Trothen compares the NHL hockey to women's hockey. Though she notes that women's athletics are becoming more popular, and also "disrupt the normative identification of sport with men," women's hockey "is not noted for physical violence" (Trothen 2009). Women players seem to show more respect for the other players, rather than the male hockey where fights are seemingly about honour and proving oneself as tougher than the opponents. This performance of masculinity reinforces the normative gender roles of a compulsory heterosexuality. Similarly, the women's hockey players are performing a more gentle game implying, perhaps, a feminine style. Thus, unlike with the pop icons who use performance to disrupt these gendered assumptions, hockey players reinforce them.

Summary

Both Madonna and Lady Gaga provide us with ample examples of denaturalizing gender, sexuality, and religion, through performativity. Professional male hockey players provide examples of reinforcing gendered assumptions with their performance of violence and suffering. While this is certainly not the only way to analyze these pop icons or sports stars and their productions and performances, performativity does allow us to engage with the work that popular culture can do. In its most ritualized form, popular culture can transform us, moving us from one state, through the liminal, to another state. We can become little monsters as Lady Gaga ritually gives birth to our conception of ourselves as born this way. We are also made highly aware of the constructedness of gender, sexuality, and religion through the work of these performers, in ways that can affect our own perceptions of our gender, sexuality, and religion. Importantly, though, neither Madonna nor Lady Gaga, the disrupters, takes us out of the discourses of gender and religion; their subversions can only happen within the discourses available. In ritualizing creation, Lady Gaga must engage with Christianity; in ritualizing sexuality, Madonna must engage with heterosexuality. As Butler argues, they can only resist within the limits allowed by the discourse. But resistance is possible. Furthermore, resistance is not desirable to all. Many sports players, and, according to Connell, school systems, are still highly invested in the concepts of masculinity and femininity and continue the performance to regularly construct and reinforce these hegemonic gender identities as natural.

Review Questions

1. What does ritual do, according to Victor Turner?
2. What is the difference between ritualizing and ritualization?
3. What is a performative utterance?
4. How might a speech act be infelicitous, according to J.L. Austin?
5. What does Judith Butler believe the performance of gender anticipates?
6. How is gender naturalized?
7. Why does Mark Hulsether believe Madonna's video "Like a Prayer" is an example of liberation theology?
8. How does Madonna's performance of her song "Live to Tell" during the *Confessions* tour construct Christianity?
9. How does Lady Gaga's performance in the video "Born This Way" challenge a surface understanding of the lyrics of the song?
10. Are Madonna's and Lady Gaga's performances in the examples shown in this chapter effective ritual?
11. How does the violence and suffering in hockey perform a heteronormative masculinity?

Useful Resources

Print

Bell, Catherine. 1997. *Ritual: Perspectives and Dimensions*. Oxford: Oxford University Press.
Butler, Judith. 1990. *Gender Trouble: Tenth Anniversary Edition*. London: Routledge.

Butler, Judith. 1993. *Bodies That Matter: On the Discursive Limits of "Sex."* London: Routledge.

Connell, Raewyn. 2008. "Masculinity Construction and Sports in Boys' Education: a Framework for Thinking About the Issue." *Sport, Education, and Society.* 13(2). 131–45.

Corona, Victor P. 2011. "Memory, Monsters, and Lady Gaga." *The Journal of Popular Culture.* doi: 10.1111/j.1540–5931.2011.00809.x. Accessed May 11, 2012.

Fouz-Hernández, Santiago and Freya Jarman-Ivens, eds. 2004. *Madonna's Drowned Worlds: New Approaches to her Cultural Transformations, 1983–2003.* Ashgate.

Gray, Richard J., ed. 2012. *The Performance Identities of Lady Gaga: Critical Essays.* Jefferson, NC: McFarland & Company, Inc.

Grimes, Ronald L. 1990. *Ritual Criticism: Case Studies in Its Practice, Essays on Its Theory.* Columbia: University of South Carolina Press.

Trothen, Tracy. 2009. "Holy Acceptable Violence? Violence in Hockey and Christian Atonement Theories." *Journal of Religion and Popular Culture.* Special Edition: Religion and Popular Culture in Canada. 21.

Video

Madonna. 1990. *The Immaculate Collection.* VHS. Warner Music (includes official videos for "Like a Virgin" and "Like a Prayer")

Madonna. 2006. *The Confessions Tour.* DVD. Warner Music

Online

Born This Way Foundation. http://bornthiswayfoundation.org/

Lady Gaga's website: http://ladygaga.com

Madonna's website: http://madonna.com

Madonna. 1990. "Like a Virgin (Blond Ambition Tour)." www.youtube.com/watch?v=2EUpeMSiQ8s

Madonna. 1990. "Like a Prayer (Blond Ambition Tour)." www.youtube.com/watch?v=zZ_RBZCo7Yw

Lady Gaga. 2011. "Born This Way." www.youtube.com/watch?v=wV1FrqwZyKw.

5

Feminist Theories

OBJECTIVES

This chapter will help you develop an understanding of

- the variety of feminist theories developed from the eighteenth to twenty-first centuries
- the way the sacred feminine is analyzed by differing feminist approaches to Dan Brown's *The Da Vinci Code*
- the "girl power" controversy in such icons as Wonder Woman and Xena, Warrior Princess

When I was starting my doctoral studies, a friend made up a mixed music cassette tape for my hour-long commute to the university (yes, this was a long time ago when people still used cassette tapes). The first song was the theme music to the 1970s TV show version of Wonder Woman. This song inspired me to keep on trekking through the grueling fight that pursuing a PhD can be. I have been known to use a picture of the comic version of Wonder Woman as my Facebook picture. I have a printout of the same picture pinned to my office bulletin board to inspire me through the equally grueling fight that being a university professor can be. Like for many before me, Wonder Woman has been a sign of female power, albeit a campy version. My question, though, has always been, why can't she wear more clothes?

The discussions around female and feminine representations in popular culture can certainly take the form of performativity theories, such as we've just seen with Judith Butler and our discussion of Madonna and Lady Gaga in Chapter 4. There are many other approaches to feminist theory, however. Taking a look at some of these feminist theories will make clear that what is one person's inspiration for female power is someone else's image of subjugation and continued sexist oppression. Where one feminist theorist valorizes a specific image as something new to be applauded, another cuts it down as reinforcing old gendered stereotypes. None of this is to say that feminist theory is so divided as to be irrelevant. Rather, it is to say that there are many different ways to think through gender and sex and it is important to consider them in their diversity rather than thinking there is only one feminism. This chapter demonstrates this by outlining some of the developments within feminism and the varieties of theories that have grown out of that development. It is impossible to speak to all feminist theories, as that in itself would take a whole book (or series of books), but this chapter will give a sense of the diversity and some of the important disagreements when it comes to the study of popular culture. To apply these theories more specifically, we look to the examples of how the sacred feminine has been represented in Dan Brown's novel *The Da Vinci Code* and its subsequent feminist analysis. We also look to how a couple of classic images of "girl power" such as Wonder Woman and Xena, Warrior Princess are understood to inspire change and/or collude with patriarchal systems.

Feminisms

First Wave

Though some people think of feminism as one kind of theory or perspective, there are in fact multiple kinds of feminisms. To understand how feminisms have been used to analyze religion and popular culture, it is necessary to look at the development of the feminist movement and its various approaches to gender, sexuality, and representation. Scholars often divide feminism into waves. This section outlines the first and second waves of feminisms and then explores the more controversial and disputed third wave.

MARY WOLLSTONECRAFT AND LIBERAL FEMINISM

First wave feminism began in the 1700s in Europe. Key to this movement was the influential text *Vindication of the Rights of Women* (1792) by the British Mary Wollstonecraft (1759–1797). One of the primary arguments in this text was that women should receive the same education as men. Wollstonecraft wrote,

> Contending for the rights of woman, my main argument is built on this simple principle, that if she be not prepared by education to become the companion of man, she will stop the progress of knowledge and virtue; for truth must be common to all, or it will be inefficacious with respect to its influence on general practice (1993, 70).

This text was written at a time when the theory of **liberalism** was developing, with its concurrent claims of the need for a liberal education for men of all classes.

Wollstonecraft supported this liberal ideal, but wanted it expanded to women as well. Thus **liberal feminism** was born. The concept of liberalism depends on three main themes: rationality, equality, and utilitarianism. Liberal thinkers of this era believed all men are rational but need to develop their rational skills, their reason, through education and freedom. Wollstonecraft pushed for the understanding of women as rational beings as well. Originally the equality of liberalism was based on class; all men regardless of their class are rational and thus we should start educating everyone. It is not clear that Wollstonecraft was arguing for actual equality between men and women, at least not in any sense that men and women were the same. However, she did advocate an equal education based on an equal ability to develop reason and virtue. The utilitarianism of liberalism required all members of society to be used for the good of society. This utilitarianism motivated the need for an educated citizenry. Though at the time that Wollstonecraft was writing, women were not typically thought of as citizens and certainly did not have access to voting rights in Europe or North America, her call for equal education soon led to the movement that would change this situation: the suffrage movement.

Suffrage is a term that means the right to vote in political election. The suffrage movement was a political activist movement starting mid-nineteenth century that rallied those in favour of Wollstonecraft's ideas to persuade their respective governments to grant women the right to vote, thus making them citizens. The arguments for this change came directly from the liberal ideology that was increasingly popular in nineteenth-century western democratic countries. Women had the capability to be rational, particularly if educated, thus the society should not neglect half the thinking population in the governmental system. Many women and men who were involved in this feminist movement were also involved in the abolition movement, that is, the movement to end slavery. Again, this was motivated by liberal values. Slavery was abolished in the British Empire, including Canada, thanks largely to the abolitionist movement, in 1833. It was not until 1865 after a civil war that slavery ended in the United States. It took a bit longer to get the vote for women. In Canada, white women achieved the vote in 1918, with the exception of the province of Quebec, where suffrage was not achieved until 1940, and Aboriginals, who got the vote in 1960. The United States followed quickly after Canada in 1920. In the United Kingdom, it took until 1928 until all women over 21 had the right to vote.

Second Wave

SIMONE DE BEAUVOIR AND SOCIAL CONSTRUCTION

Since this first wave of feminism was primarily about equal rights to citizenship and the vote, many felt that their goals had been achieved and a feminist movement was no longer needed. Activism died down and few considered women's lives as in need of improvement, with the exception of a few philosophers who continued to think through the issues first raised by first wave feminism, but outside the context of a particular goal such as suffrage. One of these was Simone de Beauvoir (1908–1986). De Beauvoir wrote the ground-breaking text *The Second Sex* (1949) in which she argues that "one is not born, but rather becomes, a woman" (1973, 301). This "becoming" is tied to the way men see themselves as human selves and see women as "Other." The expectations of how this "Other" is, in contradiction to how men should be, become socialized realities for female humans; as they adopt these socialized expectations, they become women. Much of second wave feminism has been influenced by this philosophical move to **social constructionism**.

The 1960s brought on what is called the second wave of feminism. It is in this second wave that we begin to see a diffusion of both motives and goals leading to the development of multiple feminist perspectives and actions. To begin, there were the liberal feminists who were interested in carrying on the fight for equal rights, as had the first wave feminists with the vote. Second wave liberal feminists expanded their fight to the work place, the education system, the law, and even religious organizations. Even though women may have the vote, they still were not equally represented in higher education, in professions, in the government, in religious leadership, or anywhere else that held public power. Liberal feminists in the 1960s believed that if the legal system provided for equal opportunities in jobs, salaries, public office, etc., then any sexist oppression of women would cease. Thus they fought for changes in laws to bring equality to all. This does not mean that liberal feminists, then or today, believed men and women to be the same. However, in all aspects of public life, they believed that women and men should be equal. To do this required some different treatment, such as the need for women to be allowed to take maternity leave from work without losing their jobs. Essentially, liberal feminism tries to work within the system to make changes.

LIBERAL VERSUS RADICAL FEMINISM

Liberal feminism is concerned with issues of equality. Not all feminists in the mid-twentieth century believed that to be a sufficient focus. Groups of women began arguing for liberation rather than equality. Liberation required a changing, even complete upheaval of the systems that liberal feminists were willing to work within. These feminists concerned with liberation became known as **radical feminists**. Radical feminists tended to get noticed in a way that liberal feminists did not. They tended to be more militaristic in their approaches to change and tended also to denigrate men and masculinity as the problem that needed eradication. Whereas liberal feminists believed **patriarchy** to be something women and men could overcome together by creating equal opportunities, radical feminists often saw patriarchy as essential to masculinity. Some radical feminists went so far as to advocate for reproductive technologies that would allow women to live completely without men. Needless to say, these feminists were given much press-time and became icons of feminism to many who were unfamiliar with the concerns of all the various feminist approaches.

CULTURAL FEMINISM

An off-shoot of radical feminism is **cultural feminism**. Cultural feminism is not necessarily a cultural studies approach to feminism (though it may be possible to do both). Cultural feminists argue for the importance of women's cultural space separate from men's. Like radical feminists they believe women need to disrupt the institutions that are in place and develop their own cultural institutions. This includes everything from music to art to religion. For cultural feminists, women and men are essentially different. Some believe this difference to be based completely on biology. Some believe it to be socially constructed but so ingrained that it cannot be changed in a single generation. In either case, what women need culturally is different from what men need, and the general culture of Western society has been male-centred, leading women to feel alienated. Important to our discussion of religion and popular culture is the development of cultural feminist religious and spiritual beliefs and practices. For cultural feminists, traditional institutional religions cannot meet the needs of women. Women need to look to a divine feminine which cultural feminists often argue is completely lacking in all Western religions, but can be found in other places, including pre-Christian European religions.

SOCIALIST FEMINISM

Another strain of second wave feminism that is concerned with the alienation of women within Western culture is **socialist feminism**. However, rather than seeing the alienation as being about any essentialized difference between women and men, socialist feminists draw on Marxism and the concerns of the economy and capitalism (see Chapter 2). Socialist feminists look to women's role in the capitalist system as both workers (proletariat) and as unpaid workers that make the system run smoothly. It is because women typically do all the housework and child-rearing that men can go out to work in the capitalist market. As women gained access to jobs in that market as well, their unpaid work at home did not necessarily lessen. Socialist feminists talk of the double work day for women, which leaves women with considerably less leisure time than men. The exception is upper-middle-class women who can afford to hire someone to do their domestic work. This situation then creates a class, and often racial, divide between women, as Black, Latina, or overseas women are hired to take on middle-class white women's domestic labour, sometimes to the detriment of their own domestic responsibilities. Socialist feminists have argued for a government funding of domestic work and/or a sharing of domestic work between men and women. Socialist feminists tend to be critical of the move toward middle-class, usually white women, drawing on the domestic work of working class, usually women of colour, to ease their burden of the double work day.

Third Wave

ANTI-RACIST FEMINISM

The second wave of feminism was largely made up of middle-class white women. They were not unaware of race and class issues, but these issues tended not to be front and centre to the movement. In the 1990s, women of colour began to speak out about their needs and the differences between various women's experiences of patriarchy and sexism. What was important in this movement was the insight that gender, race, and class intersect. This means that a woman's experience of sexism would be shaped by her race and class, just as her experience of racism would be shaped by her gender and class. For many scholars, this move to an **anti-racist feminism** that challenged the focus on gender and sexism, was the beginning of a third wave of feminism. Anti-racist feminists, beginning with Black feminists in the USA, wanted not only to consider race as part of the feminist equation, but also to challenge the collusion, recognizing that some women can be in fact be part of the oppressive systems, depending on their position in the equation. White women needed to recognize their role in racism; but Black women also needed to recognize that sometimes in supporting Black men's fight against white society, they were colluding with the sexism within their own communities. Anti-racist feminists refused to pick only one battle and argued that Black women must fight against both racism and sexism together (see the discussion of bell hooks in Chapter 6). Other anti-racist feminists argued for increased collaboration between various groups of previously alienated women from across the globe. **Transnational feminism** developed from the notion that women from various places could recognize their own local specificities while supporting women in other places to fight for their needs in their local context, without arguing that all women are the same and thus have the same needs. This is not to say that there are not common issues for women to address globally, such as rape, poverty, male control, etc., but the ways women address these issues while maintaining their cultural and religious contexts are different.

MULTIPLICITY OF EXPERIENCE AND PLURALISTIC THINKING

Other scholars see the third wave of feminists as beginning, also in the 1990s, with the development of a new do-it-yourself (DIY) kind of feminism in young women. These women were the ones who grew up with the advances made by their mothers: they could easily attend university; they could pick a career of their choice; they were not coerced into early marriage; they lived in a culture which was more accepting of lesbianism or bisexuality; they had choice. As Jennifer Baumgardner and

Amy Richards write in *Manifesta: Young Women, Feminism, and the Future*, "For our generation, feminism is like fluoride. We scarcely notice that we have it—it's simply in the water" (2000, 17). These feminists are concerned with the multiplicity of experiences and pluralistic thinking. They are embedded in a technological world that many second wave feminists were not. In fact, as that technological world developed some second wave feminists moved into asking similar questions and thus the line between second and third wave feminism is not so clear. Some second wave feminists, however, see this third wave as superficial; this third wave is more interested in doing their own thing than joining together as a movement to protest. However, third wave feminists counter that they are pushing the issues further into popular culture through their use of music, clothing, comics, and the Internet.[1]

POST-FEMINISM

Others have begun to articulate what they call "post-feminism" or "popular feminism." This post-feminism requires equality between men and women, but also embraces certain kinds of more "traditional" femininities and "girly" culture. It is here that we get the notion of "girl power" as something of a mixture between physical and emotional strength tied to a full embrace of sexuality, sexiness, and, what may be considered by some, appeals to conventional signs of beauty (make-up; high-heels; etc.). Post-feminism also tends to display a negative image of second wave feminists as old-fashioned, prudish, authoritarian, and ugly. As Angela McRobbie writes,

> Drawing on a vocabulary that includes words like 'empowerment' and 'choice', these [feminist] elements are then converted into a much more individualistic discourse, and they are deployed in this new guise, particularly in media and popular culture, but also by agencies of the state, as a kind of substitute for feminism (2009, 1).

This has led to "new issues such as the trend for pole-dancing being promoted as yet another form of women's empowerment" (McRobbie 2009, 3).

Representation

Feminists have always looked at popular culture as a site of analysis. For many feminists, representation of women is a key issue. Whether it be a liberal feminist concern that the media represent women in more professional positions or the

---

1. See Chris Klassen, ed. *Feminist Spirituality: The Next Generation* (Lanham: Lexington Books) for a more detailed discussion of the interactions between third wave feminists and spirituality.

radical feminist concern that the media too often represent women in pornographic ways or the social feminist concern that the media represent women in more diversity or the third wave concern that women from various locations need to do their own representing, representation has been at the top of the discussion of feminist theories on popular culture. Utilizing any of these various feminist standpoints, one can engage in feminist cultural analysis.

WHOSE GAZE?

An early example of feminist cultural analysis comes from the work of Laura Mulvey whose important essay "Visual Pleasure and Narrative Cinema" (1975) introduced the concept of the male gaze. In her theory, visual pleasure in Hollywood is based on a presumed male spectator looking at an objectified woman. Thus viewers are always encouraged to identify with the male spectator or male protagonist of a film. The woman protagonist, or supporting character, is only there to be looked at. Drawing on Mulvey, many feminists turned to alternative forms of art and culture assuming the mainstream was ultimately tied to the male gaze. However, other feminist theorists contested this perspective and followed from the culturalism approach to see popular culture as a site of negotiation of power. In 1988, Lorraine Gamman and Margaret Marshment edited a collection of essays entitled *The Female Gaze: Women as Viewers of Popular Culture*. In their introduction, they ask "So how do women look at women? Are female looks [that is, the gaze women direct] at other women always about identification or (by analogy with male looking) objectification?" (4). They suggest that there is more than just the male gaze; women, and particularly feminists, do have the agency to look in different ways.

ONE "REAL" IMAGE?

There have been shifts, therefore, in how feminists have looked at popular culture, particularly the image of women. In her 1995 book *Material Girls: Making Sense of Feminist Cultural Theory*, Suzanna Danuta Walters shows a progression from looking at images of women to the focus on woman as an image. In the 1970s, the feminist focus was on presentation of sex-roles and stereotypes in the media. Popular culture was believed to reflect dominant social values as well as being a socializing agent. Thus the feminist argument was for more positive images to counter the negative images found, so as to reflect the changing role of women and work to socialize in a different way. However, this perspective, according to Walters, was criticized because it assumed that there was one "real" image of women to be reflected, either truthfully or falsely. Walters asks, who gets to say what this "real" image of women is? Is there one "real" image? How do we locate it? The idea that popular culture socializes us into sex-roles also assumes that any given image has one meaning. Furthermore, this perspective seems to follow from the Frankfurt

School assumption that viewers do not participate in the constructing of meaning. The idea that popular culture socializes us through representations of stereotypes of sex-roles does not fully take into account viewer agency, or ability to negotiate meaning for themselves, in making sense of the images seen.

"WOMAN" AS A CONSTRUCTED IMAGE?

Walters suggests an alternative method for analyzing images of women is to switch to a focus on woman as image. This method follows from the question, Who gets to say what is the "real" image of women? Rather than trying to sift through the negative imagery found in popular culture, Walters suggests an understanding of the category of woman itself as always constructed. This means that there is no "real" image of women; the category of "woman" is, as de Beauvoir already has suggested, not natural but always shaped by our culture and society. What may seem like the "real" woman in middle-class white America is not the same as what is understood to be the "real" woman in African-American, or Asian, or working-class, or migrant worker contexts. The implication of thinking of women as always constructed—of thinking of "woman as image"—is that the focus turns to the signifying practice (the production of the image) rather than solely the sign. So how the images are produced (the signifying practice) is more important than what images are produced (the sign). And yet, some third wave feminists still contend that what images are produced cannot always be dismissed. Sometimes the images that are produced, regardless of how or for what intension, have been co-opted to become useful images.

Applying Feminist Theory: From the Sacred Feminine to Girl Power

Mary Magdalene and the Sacred Feminine: *The Da Vinci Code*

When Dan Brown's book *The Da Vinci Code* was published in 2003 it quickly gained a popularity the author's previous novels never reached. The story he told was not new; others had suggested it. So why were people so taken up with it at this point in time? In many ways the answer to that question lies in a popularization in the late twentieth to early twenty-first century interest in the sacred feminine and the increased interest in Goddess religions.

The Da Vinci Code tells two stories. The first, and most immediate, is a murder mystery in which main characters Robert Langdon and Sophie Neveu run around France and England trying to find clues as to who has killed Sophie's grandfather, while the French police chase them thinking Langdon is the culprit. Meanwhile, a fanatical monk associated with the Catholic Church chases after them, trying to keep Langdon and Neveu from revealing the secrets they discover. The secrets they find play into the second story of the novel. This story is presented as a historical account about Mary Magdalene, her relationship with Jesus, and the truth about the Holy Grail. In this story Mary Magdalene and Jesus were married. When Jesus was killed, Mary fled to France where she gave birth to a child, Sarah. The Holy Grail is not a drinking vessel as most think, but rather the vessel of the Holy Blood, which is Mary's womb. It turns out that Sophie's grandfather was the head of a secret society, the Priory of Sion, whose job it was to protect not only the secret of Mary's true role, but the continued blood line of Jesus. As Langdon and Neveu reveal secret after secret they eventually learn both the location of the protected tomb of Mary Magdalene and who the last remaining descendant of Mary and Jesus is: Sophie herself.

FEMINIST RESPONSES

The response to this book, and the later film released in 2006 with Tom Hanks as Robert Langdon, was varied. Its association with feminism was declared by fans and critics alike. It has been given "kudos for tackling women's lib issues" (Tubbs 2004) and accused of being "a radical feminist tirade" (Young 2003). The insistence on a valuing of a sacred feminine, Mary Magdalene as wife of Jesus, has been inspiring for many. Jennie S. Knight (2005) argues that this is one of the reasons *The Da Vinci Code* gained such popularity. Enough feminist thought (particularly cultural feminist) about the divine feminine or goddesses had become part of popular culture that society was ripe for a story introducing those themes within a specific Christian context. This allowed many Christian women to engage in consideration of the divine or sacred feminine without needing to leave Christianity.

However, many feminist cultural critics were less convinced about the inherent feminist nature of this text. Nancy Calvert-Koyzis (2006) argues that naming Mary Magdalene as Jesus' wife simply puts emphasis on her sexuality and reproductive capacities. How is that any different from other patriarchal assumptions of the role of women in society? Calvert-Koyzis is concerned with the way Brown interprets the traditions of the Gnostic Gospels, including the *Gospel of Mary*. These texts, as well as the canonical gospels (the gospels that made it into the New Testament), point to Mary Magdalene as an apostle, having spiritual insight, and perhaps even being the successor to Jesus' ministry. In the *Gospel of Mary* we get a situation where Mary tells the disciples a teaching that Jesus had told her. Some of the disciples do not want to listen. Peter is recorded as saying,

> Did he really speak with a woman without our knowledge (and) not openly? Are we to turn about and listen to her? Did he prefer her to us?" [. . .] Levi answered and said to Peter, [. . .]"Surely the Savior

knows her very well. That is why he loved her more than us. Rather, let us be ashamed and put on the perfect man and acquire him for ourselves as he commanded us, and preach the Gospel, not laying down any other rule or other law beyond what the Savior said (*The Gospel of Mary*, 9–18, quoted in Parrot 1990, 526)

This is a far cry from her importance being the vessel carrying the child of Jesus. Even in the canonical texts, Mary Magdalene is known for travelling with Jesus as a disciple and being the first witness to his resurrection when she is given the task to share the news (preach the gospel) to the other disciples. As Calvert-Koyzis argues, "Mary Magdalene is shown to have a close relationship with Jesus that is based upon her superior spiritual insight and maturity, not upon a sexual relationship with Jesus or her reproductive capacity" (2006). In contrast to these texts, how Brown portrays Mary is not so different from what the early Church did when they named her a prostitute which is not based on any biblical texts. Though now she is considered sacred rather than profane, she is still identified by her sexuality, not her spiritual authority.

While Calvert-Koyzis argues that *The Da Vinci Code* is anything but feminist, Kristy Maddux (2008) argues that the issue is not that Dan Brown's book is not actually feminist: it's what kind of feminism is represented. She suggests that what Brown's book (and later movie) presents is a celebration of the feminine as found in cultural feminism. Maddux's criticism of Brown's book, then, is both a criticism of Brown and a criticism of cultural feminism. She argues that "this very strand of feminist thought necessarily undermines the novel's liberatory potential in two ways: it limits [*The Da Vinci Code*'s] celebrations of womanhood to the private sphere, and it reinscribes binary notions of gender" (2008, 228); that is, there are two and only two genders because two genders are tied to two sexes that are necessary for reproduction. This binary also reinforces the need for compulsory heterosexuality. This is a similar idea to that of Judith Butler described in Chapter 4.

The story of the search for the murderer of Sophie's grandfather turns into the search for Sophie's own identity. As she becomes linked with the sacred feminine character of Mary Magdalene, the significance of that sacred feminine becomes privatized in Sophie's own experience. While many feminist theories advocate taking seriously individual women's experiences, Maddux believes *The Da Vinci Code* leaves the power in the private without actually expanding it into any public realm. The secret of Mary Magdalene remains a secret at the end of the book and film (or at least it does in the plot line, if not in the fact that millions of readers and viewers know it). The truth that has been revealed is about Sophie; it is not about all women. Additionally the importance of male/female binary in a heterosexual context is further reinforced. Mary is important as a mother and wife of Jesus. Again, this is a private relationship rather than the more public role of apostle. But it is also a

The Gnostic Gospels

When we talk about the Gnostic Gospels we are talking about a set of writings that are attributed to members of a tradition of "Gnosticism" from the time of the early Christian church. Many of these gospels are clearly Christian in theme and content. They mention specific teachings of Jesus and interactions between the disciples known to have travelled with Jesus. Others do not specifically seem Christian but seem to highlight more Jewish mysticism. Others seem to dwell on Indian worldviews of enlightenment and illusion. Some blend all these together. In any case, the writings of the Gnostics were considered **heretical** by the early orthodox Christian church and when those orthodox Christians gained the political support of the Roman Empire, Gnosticism was weeded out and the texts mostly destroyed. However, some of the texts, or copies of the texts, survived and were discovered in the late nineteenth and early twentieth centuries.

Gnosticism is a term that means knowledge or insight. The Gnostics differed from the orthodox Christians in a number of ways. First, the Gnostics believed that self-knowledge leads to knowledge about God, because the self and God were one and the same. Orthodox Christians believed God to be wholly other. Second, the sayings of Jesus in the Gnostic Gospels point less to concerns of sin and repentance, which were key to orthodox Christianity, and more to enlightenment: when one gained self-knowledge and spiritual understanding, one became like Jesus. This leads into the third difference: whereas the orthodox Christians believed Jesus to be the Son of God in a unique way, the Gnostics claimed that Jesus was more of a guide to help lead people to become just like him.

heterosexualized relationship that emphasizes the needed polarity of gender: masculinity and femininity. This polarity is key in cultural feminism where women are essentially feminine and men are essentially masculine. Because of these two trends, Maddux ultimately claims that *The Da Vinci Code* is anti-feminist. She sees this anti-feminism, however, as stemming from cultural feminism with its focus on women's essential femininity and biology. Cultural feminism itself, by its nature, can be too easily co-opted into conservative storytelling. It can too easily be used in novels, such as Dan Brown's, to reinforce an essentialized idea of femininity and masculinity that does little to change the prevailing patriarchal assumptions of what women are capable of and that gender itself may be more complicated than a simple binary.

Mythology, Girl Power, and Wonder Woman

Ancient mythologies are full of god-like heroes fighting cosmic evils. As such they can be sites of ripe imagery for modern-day popular culture, and have been, particularly in the realm of comic books and later film versions of superheroes. Specifically

The majority of the Gnostic Gospels to which we now have access were discovered in 1945 in the town of Nag Hammadi in Upper Egypt. They were discovered by a peasant digging for fertilizing soil who found an earthenware jar filled with papyrus books. The story about how they became known by authorities and then accessible to scholars is long and complicated (see Pagels 1979). It was not until the 1970s that we began to see significant amounts of scholarship being published on these texts and vernacular translations (the discovered texts are in Coptic, copies of early Greek texts). Included in this find were the *Gospel of Thomas*, the *Gospel of Philip*, the *Apocryphon of John*, the *Secret Book of James*, and the *Gospel of Truth*, among others. The *Gospel of Mary* was not included in this collection (a historical error Dan Brown makes in his book), but rather had been found earlier in 1896 along with a few other texts. Overall, the Gnostic Gospels, whether the ones found at Nag Hammadi, or other bits and pieces found over the past couple of hundred years, clarify some of the statements made by orthodox church leaders in early texts (140–200 CE) about the problem of heresy and the need to be harsh and wipe it out. Now that scholars have access to these texts we know more about what that heresy was and why it was considered so problematic by those who became the official orthodox and **catholic** church. We also know now that the early Christian church was much less unified than previously thought. And we know that those we now call the Gnostic Christians had a belief in deity that was both God the Father and God the Mother; the sacred feminine was as significant as the sacred masculine.

the mythologies of the ancient European world have found their way into modern American popular culture with the character of Thor (drawn from Norse mythology), Hercules (drawn from Greco-Roman mythology), and, of course, Wonder Woman (also from Greco-Roman mythology).

WONDER WOMAN

Wonder Woman was the first female superhero to gain a popular audience on her own, rather than as a side-kick for a more famous male superhero. She first appeared in the DC comic *All Star Comics* #8 in December 1941. Though most comic book heroes of the day were created by young men barely out of high school, Wonder Woman was created by psychologist William Moulton Marston. Marston's goal was very deliberate: he wanted to change gender perceptions to invert the hierarchy of men ruling women, thinking women would be better rulers. Marston himself said, "Wonder Woman is psychological propaganda for the new type of woman who should, I believe, rule the world" (quoted in Daniels 2000, 22). So, what was Marston's view of this "new woman"?

Wonder Woman is an Amazon. It is prudent then to take a look at the mythology surrounding the Amazons and how Marston reshapes their image to get a better sense of Marston's gender ideology. The Amazons were thought to be warrior women who lived completely outside of patriarchal culture. The Greco-Roman stories about the Amazons type them as fierce and worthy foes. Though they were said to be daughters of Ares, the god of war, they worshipped Artemis, the virgin goddess of the hunt, and Cybele, the earth mother. Elizabeth Danna, in her analysis of Wonder Woman and the Amazon myth from which she comes, argues that both Artemis and Cybele were goddesses who were imported into Greek religions from the Near East "hence, foreign gods" (2008, 72). Because of this, and because they were women warriors, "It is evident that the Greeks considered the Amazons to be different from themselves [. . .] and their country was considered an edgy part of the world where the 'natural' or patriarchal order of things ran in reverse" (72). As such, most of the stories about the Amazons involved their defeat by strong Greek heroes, such as Herakles (Hercules), in order to bring patriarchal order back to the world.

Marston's Amazons had escaped the wars with the Greeks and made themselves a secret home on a paradise island. As such they had been isolated from the world for thousands of years. However they were also given technological advancements that allowed them to observe what they deemed the patriarchal world. At the beginning of the Wonder Woman story, the Amazons realize that World War II is not only a battle between fascism and democracy, but also a battle between the continued patriarchal practices of the Nazis and the fight for women's rights, found, interestingly, in America. So they decide to intervene by sending their best warrior, Diana, the daughter of Queen Hippolyte (created out of clay, rather than with the assistance of a man), to help out in the American war effort.

The changes Marston makes to the Amazons in Wonder Woman are interesting and reflect his view of women. No longer do they worship Artemis, the goddess of the hunt, who refused all romantic advances, but now they worship Aphrodite, the goddess of love and beauty. No longer are the Amazons defined as fierce warriors only, but they now prefer the power of persuasion over violence: hence Wonder Woman's magic lasso which causes anyone caught in it to tell the truth.[2] It is used, not to imprison, but to have a truthful discussion. The Amazons in Marston's vision are a peaceful, woman-centred society, not unlike the kind of pre-historical society cultural feminists declare existed prior to the patriarchal systems that overtook them.[3]

---

2.   It is not incidental that Marston was also the inventor of the lie detector.
3.   For more information on the theories of pre-patriarchal Goddess societies see Klassen, *Storied Selves* (2008).

Not only did Marston want the peaceful, persuasive nature of women to gain power in American culture, he also thought it in the best interest of society for men to learn to submit to women. Ben Saunders, in his discussion of Wonder Woman in *Do the Gods Wear Capes? Spirituality, Fantasy, and Superheroes* (2011), outlines Marston's own relationship with women and views on submission and domination. Marston lived in a **polyamorous** relationship with two women and he seemed to have an interest in sexual bondage. His psychological work suggests that women are superior to men because they have interest in and find pleasure in both submission and dominance, with either men or women: it seems they are more sexually flexible. However, men have a problem with women having dominance over them. Thus they need to learn to be submissive. Hence, he created Wonder Woman, the strong, dominant woman. Her sexual allure is, thus, deliberate: her appearance is designed to induce men to submit to women and women's values through sexual appeal. Women's values here refer to the notion of peace and attempting to persuade rather than starting off with violent conflict. As Marc DiPaulo articulates it, "It is during these eras of global conflict [such as WWII] that she speaks as a priestess praying for a time when soldiers will finally lay down their weapons and men and women from all cultures will finally live in peace" (2011, 70).

Even though Wonder Woman was created by a man, and most of the stories were written and illustrated by men until the late twentieth century, Wonder Woman became somewhat of a feminist icon. She was often associated with the image of Rosie the Riveter, the strong woman designed to encourage women to take on factory work during the war period while the men were overseas. The posters of Rosie declared "We Can Do It!" Wonder Woman was Marston's declaration that women could do it not just in the factories but in the larger arena of the war effort. Some second wave feminists who grew up in this era drew on the image of Wonder Woman as exactly what Marston intended: an inspiration that they too could have power and be strong. In fact, well-known second wave feminist Gloria Steinem put the image of Wonder Woman on the very first cover of the *Ms.* magazine (December 1971), the premier magazine for second wave feminists, calling for Wonder Woman for president. For its fortieth anniversary, *Ms.* magazine once again put Wonder Woman on its cover (Fall 2012) with the slogan "Stop the War on Women."

Wonder Woman, though continually in the comics from the 1940s until today, has changed shape and message numerous times. At times she has become a master of martial arts without the Amazon background. In other times she has seemingly been denigrated to eye candy with little plot power. She is one of the few well-known superheroes not to be remade into a blockbuster Hollywood film in the twenty-first century (yet). However, she still persists as perhaps the only classic female superhero that most North Americans could name.

XENA, WARRIOR PRINCESS

A different kind of Amazon became popular in the 1990s and contributed to a whole movement of "girl power." Xena, Warrior Princess, also based on Greco-Roman mythology, began as a visiting character on the television show *Hercules: The Legendary Journeys*. She was so popular with fans that she was given her own show. Instead of the innocent and peace-loving Wonder Woman, Xena had a history of evil and violent actions. Her goal was, in part, to redeem herself, but she still had no compunction about using violence to do so. Like Wonder Woman, Xena is a character created by men. Also like Wonder Woman, women have found her inspiring, in fact, more so than with Wonder Woman whose audience always remained mainly a male audience. Xena came after the effects of second wave feminism and she became a kind of icon for some third wave feminists who were interested in seeing a powerful, yet sexually confident, woman unapologetically taking control of situations. As Suzanne Sheldon writes in her 1997 essay "Xena: Feminist Icon,"

> While channel surfing I happened upon the scene of a leather and armor-clad woman beating up a giant in order to save a blonde woman held in a cage. [. . .]I observed a warrior woman who defeated the odds and rescued her friend while making everything look easy. On top of that I was laughing hysterically. Here was the kind of woman that I wanted to see more of on television! Strong, intelligent, and independent, Xena was and is a character that I could look up to as a role model.

Not all feminist theorists agree with this perspective. Mary Magoulick, writing in the *Journal of Popular Culture* argues that Xena is a problematic character because she was shaped and formed by men. Not only were her creators men (as in the show creators Rob Tapert and Sam Raimi) but Xena herself as a warrior for justice was shaped by Hercules who "romances and reforms Xena before sending her off to do good deeds as a champion in her own right—thus making her" (2006, 730). Furthermore, Magoulick argues that throughout the series we see a joining together of sex and violence. Often Xena is forced in some way to fight against former lovers, or she takes on lovers who were former opponents. This is even the case with her companion and possible lesbian lover, Gabrielle. In either case the association of violence and aggression with sex and romance should, says Magoulick, put feminists on edge. Magoulick remarks, "One message is that women should expect such intense, violent, physical, and emotional combat on a regular basis if they seek independence or 'strength'" (2006, 749). We can see in Xena the continued debate about third wave feminism and/or post-feminism. For some Xena is negotiated into a sign of "girl power": we can do it, be strong and aggressive, and look hot at the same time. For others that simply plays into patriarchal desires to keep women as sexual objects and individualize their sense of power.

ANNABETH CHASE AND THE OLYMPIANS

If we move into the twenty-first century we can find another example of a female Greco-Roman inspired hero in the figure of Annabeth Chase, demi-god daughter of Athena, in the *Percy Jackson and the Olympians* series of books written by Rick Riordan. This set of books written for a youth audience tells the story of a group of teenage demi-gods in modern America who have to save the world from the return of Kronos, the Titan father of the Greek gods Zeus, Hades, and Poseidon (Percy Jackson's father). Annabeth Chase, like Xena, has the power of a warrior and the strategic intelligence one might expect from the daughter of the goddess of wisdom and just warfare. Also like Xena, and Wonder Woman before her, Annabeth is created by a man. Additionally she is linked romantically with Percy Jackson, giving up the opportunity to join the followers of Artemis (the modern equivalent of the Amazons) because of her love for a boy. She is once again a symbol of "girl power": strong, aggressive, attractive, and able to get a boyfriend even while she can kick his butt (sometimes).

So, what does religion have to do with these Greco-Roman inspired female superheroes? Few Westerners actually follow the Greco-Roman religions anymore, and while some contemporary Pagans may be returning to the worship of Aphrodite or Ares, generally it is not due to the influence of Wonder Woman or Xena. Ben Saunders suggests a more Christian value, at least to the Wonder Woman stories, and the seemingly strange combination of sexual and sacred submission. Saunders argues that Marston equated the necessary sexual submission that men needed to learn to a submission to a loving superior, even a god or goddess figure. Wonder Woman's mother Queen Hippolyta's closing line of the last Wonder Woman story Marston ever wrote was "The only real happiness for anybody is to be found in the obedience to loving authority" (quoted in Saunders 2011, 65). Saunders sees this idea as fitting nicely within some current Christian theology, including some feminist Christian theology. He draws on the work of Sarah Coakley who suggests in her *Powers and Submissions* (2002) that in current society submission is not typically thought of as a desirable position, particularly in light of current demands for personal autonomy or personal agency. Yet Christianity calls for a submission to God. A number of male theologians have been trying to get Christians to focus on Jesus' vulnerability and submission to God. Another feminist Christian theologian, Daphne Hampson, argues that while this focus might be good for Christian men, "for women, the theme of self-emptying and self-abnegation is far from helpful as a paradigm" (quoted in Coakley 2002, 3). This sounds similar to Marston's idea that men need to learn the value of submission to a loving authority, whereas women need to become that loving authority. For Saunders, the association of submission to God is legitimately tied to sexual submission because he argues that sexuality is sacred. Coakley does not herself make this connection.

As for Xena, her representation of aggressive and even dangerous femininity, has been drawn on by some Jewish Renewal members. In the Jewish Renewal Movement the aspect of God called the Shekhinah has been increasingly drawn upon. However there are gender politics involved in this usage. For some, the

Jewish Renewal Movement

The Jewish Renewal Movement is a modern movement that incorporates Jewish practitioners from a variety of Jewish denominations who are interested in emphasizing spirituality over law and doctrine. Jewish Renewal draws on the Jewish **mysticism** of Hasidism, an Orthodox Jewish version of mysticism that draws on Kabbalah. Jewish Renewalists also draw on other spiritual practices such as Buddhist meditation and Yoga. Chava Weissler has been studying the group *Aleph: the Alliance for Jewish Renewal* since 1999. She ties the movement to both a 1960s counter culture and a desire to embrace traditional Judaism. This happened through a move to the mystical. However, not only is this movement concerned with experiential spirituality and mysticism, but

> Renewal Jews are committed to *tikkun ha'olam* ("mending the world"), especially by means of ecological, peace, and social justice activism, and what they call *tikkun halev* ('mending the heart'), which encompasses the values of American psychotherapeutic culture. Finally, Aleph is explicitly feminist and explicitly welcoming to lesbian, gay, bisexual, and transgendered Jews (Weissler 2006, 57).

An important element of the Jewish Renewal Movement is the Kabbalistic understanding of God. In classical Kabbalah, God is unknowable. However, this unknowable God, called *Ein Sof*, manifests itself in 10 attributes, or *sefirot*. Two of the *sefirot* are specifically feminine, including the tenth, Shekhinah, who is the divine presence in the world. In traditional Kabbalah, Shekhinah is passive and receptive; she does not have any light of her own but reflects the light of the other *sefirot*. She can be a comforting mother, but also a "stern and punitive disciplinarian" (Weissler 2006, 62).

Renewal Jews tend to focus on Shekhinah as the feminine aspect of God and the inspiration for Jewish women to be present and powerful within Judaism. Interestingly, within Jewish Renewal, Shekhinah does not take on any of the punitive roles that traditional Kabbalah gives her. Thus she is motherly and nurturing only. Not all Renewal Jews appreciate this essentialist femininity, as was pointed out by the comment about Xena below.

Shekhinah is simply the feminine, in a traditional ideal of the nurturing and mothering aspects of God. Others display distaste for this stereotypical gendering of the feminine aspect of God. As Chava Weissler writes of her discussion with various feminist Jewish Renewal members, one of her participants "objected to the stereotypical warm, nurturing qualities associated with Shekhinah among Renewal Jews. 'For me,' she said, 'the "feminine" is Xena the warrior princess'" (Weissler 2006, 74). Here the image of a female warrior fighting for the justice of the weak can be seen as an image of the female face of the Jewish God.

Summary

There is much diversity within feminist theories. How these theories are then used to analyze religion and popular culture often leads to debate and controversy. Is the idea of Mary Magdalene as spouse of Jesus feminist or simply a reinforcement of a patriarchal assumption that women are only useful as bearers of children? Presumably one could be both a spouse and an apostle with community leadership, though this combination is rarely suggested by any scholars. Can a fictional character created by a man, for the purpose of shaping a dominant female with sexual appeal who can teach men to be submissive, be a feminist icon? This question assumes, of course, that there is one kind of feminism. For some feminists Wonder Woman *has* been inspirational as a feminist icon, for others not so much. This ties in to the question, Can a sexy superhero be a feminist? This question is complicated by the current heteronormative society (as discussed in Chapter 4). If we no longer think in terms of gendered and sexed binaries, perhaps sexiness takes on a whole different connotation. Can feminism itself be sexy without losing its transformative edge, if heteronormativity is disrupted? Disrupting heternormativity does not mean disallowing heterosexuality: it means opening up the options, which would include the option for a sexy feminist superhero to desire men and want to attract them, presumably. These debates continue within the feminist study of religion and popular culture. Understanding that there are such diverse feminist perspectives helps to deter any superficial dismissal of feminism as one political ideology that is no longer relevant.

Review Questions

1. What is the significance of Mary Wollstonecrafts's *The Vindication of the Rights of Women*?
2. What is the significance of Simone de Beauvoir's *The Second Sex*?
3. What is the difference between liberal and radical feminisms?
4. What is the difference between second wave feminisms and anti-racist feminisms?
5. What is the controversy around third wave feminism and post-feminism?

6. What kind of sacred feminine does Dan Brown's book *The Da Vinci Code* promote?
7. Why did early orthodox Christians deem the Gnostic Christians heretics?
8. For whom are Wonder Woman and Xena feminist icons?
9. Why do some feminist theorists dislike Wonder Woman and Xena?
10. How might Annabeth Chase fit into the legacy of Wonder Woman and Xena?
11. What is the Jewish Renewal Movement?

Useful Resources

Print

Brown, Dan. 2003. *The Da Vinci Code*. Doubleday Group.

Calvert-Koyzis. Nancy. 2006. "Re-sexualizing the Magdalene: Dan Brown's Misuses of Early Christine Documents in The Da Vinci Code." Journal of Religion and Popular Culture. Vol. 12. <http://utpjournals.metapress.com/content/c76j022214t55k88/fulltext.pdf. Date accessed June 3>, 2013.

McRobbie, Angela. 2009. *The Aftermath of Feminism: Gender, Culture and Social Change*. London: Sage Publications.

Oropeza, B. J., ed. 2005. *The Gospel According to Superheroes: Religion and Popular Culture*. New York: Peter Lang.

Riordan, Rick. 2005. *Percy Jackson and the Olympians: The Lightning Thief*. Miramax.

Riordan, Rick. 2007. *Percy Jackson and the Olympians: The Sea of Monsters*. Miramax.

Riordan, Rick. 2008. *Percy Jackson and the Olympians: The Titan's Curse*. Disney-Hyperion.

Riordan, Rick. 2009. *Percy Jackson and the Olympians: The Battle of the Labyrinth*. Disney-Hyperion.

Riordan, Rick. 2011. *Percy Jackson and the Olympians: The Last Olympian*. Disney-Hyperion.

Saunders, Ben. 2011. *Do the Gods Wear Capes? Spirituality, Fantasy, and Superheroes*. New York: Continuum.

Walters, Suzanna Danuta. 1995. *Material Girls: Making Sense of Feminist Cultural Theory*. Berkeley: University of California Press.

Video

Columbus, Chris. 2010. *Percy Jackson and the Olympians: The Lightning Thief*. 20th Century Fox.

Howard, Ron. 2006. *The Da Vinci Code*. Columbia Pictures.

Online

Ms. Blog: "*Ms*. Turns 40—and Wonder Woman is back on our cover": http://msmagazine.com/blog/blog/2012/10/01/ms-turns-40-and-wonder-womans-back-on-our-cover/

Tubbs, Sharon. 2004. "The Gospel According to Dan Brown." *St. Petersburg Times*. www.sptimes.com/2004/01/25/Floridian/The_gospel_according_.shtml. Date accessed January 8, 2013.

6

Racism and Anti-racism

OBJECTIVES

This chapter will help you develop an understanding of

- the anti-racism theories of Paul Gilroy and bell hooks
- the history and continuing legacy of the trans-Atlantic slave trade
- the religio-musical development of African-American music, particularly rap music

When thinking about the relationship between rap music and religion it is easy to think of it as a relationship of conflict. Religious folk often don't like rap music. However, a closer look may give surprise. Religious themes and language show up in all sorts of ways in rap music, from Talib Kweli's critique of organized religion to Tupac Shakur's appeal to a Black Jesus, to Erykah Badu and Busta Rhymes' celebration of the family values of the Muslim Five Percenters. Aside from religious themes, rap music follows in a trajectory of African and African diasporic musical traditions integrally tied to West African religious practices. However, the perception of these practices has been shaped by a history of racism and colonial exploitation.

This chapter explores the anti-racist critical theory of bell hooks and Paul Gilroy who both explore cultural representation within and in conversation with African diasporic communities: hooks in the US and Gilroy in the UK. Drawing on Gilroy's work on the Black Atlantic and hooks' critique of white supremacist patriarchy, this chapter explores specifically musical cultural formations with a focus on rap and hip hop as responses to racism from a religio-cultural positioning.

Race

"Race," as we understand it today, is a fundamentally modern concept. The term "race" first entered the English language in the sixteenth century as a term indicating family, lineage, and breed. By the eighteenth century, with the scientific turn of the Enlightenment, a more systematic understanding of "race" was sought. "Race" became a classification category, to interrogate whether humans were all one species. This classificatory system divided humans by skin colour and location (i.e., black Africans; white Europeans; etc.). As European white scientists were convinced of their own superior civilization, the ranking of these racial classifications became the norm, justified in the name of "science."

Racial Classification and the Slave Trade

The development of racial classification parallels the development of the trans-Atlantic slave trade that brought people from Africa to be slaves in the American colonies for the cultivation, extraction, and export of resources to Europe. The European association of blackness with ugliness—tied to their association of beauty with morality—led Europeans to view Africans and other "dark" people as both socially and morally inferior, thus justifying the European exploitation of African peoples as slaves. The continued development of slavery further legitimated the assumption that people who had dark skin were inferior. A conceptual circle was established: the racial classifications allowed Europeans to engage in race-based slavery, and the slavery reinforced their understanding of the racial classifications (Rattansi 2007).

The end of the slave trade (in 1807 for the British Empire and the United States of America) and emancipation of slaves (in 1833 for the British Empire and 1865 for the United States of America, following the American Civil War) did not resolve racial concepts. Though slavery was deemed immoral (by most), the assumptions of a ranked racial system were maintained through discriminatory laws and customs motivated by a science of race. This science of race insisted on the biological differences between racial groups, often called racial essentialism, that justified European/white control of all other racial groups due to theorized superior intellect and moral reasoning. By the end of the twentieth century, however, most scientists had moved away from this biological-based conception of race to insist on the existence of only one human race with multiple **phenotypes** (physical characteristics such as skin and eye colour, eye shape, etc.).

Franz Boas, Theodosius Dobzhansky, and M.F. Ashley-Montague

This shift began in the early twentieth century with the anthropological work of Franz Boas (1858–1942) and his students. This anthropological work challenged racial essentialism by focusing on culture through historical particularism; that is, that differences in groups had to do with their histories and the cultures that developed in specific times and places, rather than on any biological elements (see Boas 1925). Later in 1947 Theodosius Dobzhansky (1900–1975) and M.F. Ashley-Montague (1905–1999) furthered this position by publishing an article in *Science* that argued for a dual evolution: biological and cultural. In this essay they argued that all humans are the same species and thus have the same abilities. Any differences between groups of people were due to differences in environment, technologies, and ideologies: that is, culture. (see Cravens 2010). "Race" as a biological reality is no longer popularly accepted. This dismissal of a scientific understanding of "race," however, has not eliminated the ideas or practices of racism.

Paul Gilroy

Nationalism, Fascism and Racism

Paul Gilroy is a British theorist who engages in the interrogation of "race" and racism. His concerns about racism are largely integrated with concerns about **nationalism**. In *Between Camps* (2000) Gilroy tells some of his own story of growing up in post-World War II England in the shadow of the victory over the Nazis and the development of British fascist organizations. **Fascism** is an ideology based on ultra-nationalism where the nation must be protected at all costs from outside forces. Nationalism in this context involves cultural, ethnic, and racial unity. The German Nazis were fascist; they defined German nationalism as comprising the pure Aryan race and determined to cleanse Germany of any "impurities" such as Jews, Roma, homosexuals, disabled peoples, and anyone who disagreed with their nationalist agenda. As a boy, Gilroy was confused with the development of British fascism as the British constructed the Nazis as both evil and completely foreign (un-British). How could British people engage in fascism and still be completely against Hitler and the Nazis?

While the majority of Britain was not promoting the ultra-nationalism of fascist groups, the questions of British nationalism were, and still are, largely tied to concerns of "race." Gilroy sees racism and nationalism as closely tied. However, the current racism is less articulated by biological constructions of "race" and more articulated by cultural concerns. As increasing numbers of "black" people settled in Britain, the question of what it means to be British become more complex. Beginning in the 1980s, Gilroy pointed out the complications of being Black and British, particularly in the context of a cultural studies atmosphere that seemed highly invested in the articulation, and even construction, of British nationalism. With the increase of Black British population, largely due to immigration from the Caribbean and some African countries, as well as South Asia, following

World War II, the question of how these immigrants fit within a concept of British nationalism became paramount. In the face of a perceived national identity crisis, the construction of Black criminality stood as a way of marking Black settlers as "un-English." This construction brought attention to the criminal behaviours of, particularly, young blacks, as behaviour tied directly to race, rather than any other circumstance while the criminal behaviours of young whites were never thought of in terms of a racial group identity.

Anti-racism and Black Liberation

The concern about nationalism and Blackness is not solely a British concern. Gilroy is known for introducing the concept of the Black Atlantic to cultural studies (see Gilroy 1993). This concept, which looks at the history of Black migration, voluntary or forced, across the Atlantic Ocean and among the Atlantic territories, has become an important tool for thinking about the relationships between racism and nationalism, as well as anti-racism and Black liberation, throughout European, American, and Caribbean contexts. Gilroy draws on W.E.B. Du Bois' (1869–1963) notion of "double consciousness" to think about the constructions of race, racism and anti-racism for members of the African **diaspora** (see Du Bois 1989). Diaspora refers to the movement of people from their homeland to other lands. For Du Bois this double consciousness involved being both American and Black, though Gilroy extends that double consciousness to all African diasporic peoples with identities both in their current locations and in Africa, or at least in a conception of Blackness that often contradicted the popular nationalist identity of their home country. The concept of the Black Atlantic, rather than the narrower concept of Black Britain (or Black America for Du Bois), allows for a shift from a concern with a nationalism to a transnationalist perspective, which recognizes the multiple alliances with geographic regions. Thus African-Americans, for example, are Americans but also have familial, cultural, or nostalgic ties to Africa, and possibly to the islands in the Caribbean as well. This takes Gilroy into a form of anti-racism that does not rely on any nationalism.

To propose a transnationalist form of anti-racism requires Gilroy to engage with Black nationalist responses to racism. Gilroy insists that anti-racism and Black liberation are two distinct ideologies and practices. Black liberation movements have often been characterized by a "return" to Africentric cultural identities—a form of African or Black nationalism. This movement focuses on the regaining of roots in African cultures. Gilroy sees this move as problematic as it ignores the history of interactions between peoples through the processes of the slave trade and migration. Gilroy writes, "The history of the black Atlantic yields a course of lessons as to the instability and mutability of identities which are always unfinished, always being remade" (1993, xi). He is more interested in the history of routes of movement. Thus he focuses on the various movements of the Black Atlantic: from Africa to the Americas and Europe and back again; from the Caribbean to America or Europe and back again; from America to Europe and back again. Though Gilroy understands the motivation of the Black nationalist movements, he ultimately sees them as reinforcing racial categories. Anti-racism, for Gilroy, requires a move away from "race" to embrace concepts of **hybridity** and movement. For Gilroy a cultural studies exploration of "black music" allows for a particularly poignant example of this transnationalist, hybrid identity.

bell hooks

White Supremacist Capitalist Patriarchy

American cultural critic bell hooks[1] also utilizes popular culture to think about and through "race," racism, and anti-racism. In a video interview, hooks, however, asks us to move away from the more generic term "racism" to the more specific articulation of **"white supremacist capitalist patriarchy"** (Jhally 1997). This term, says hooks, incorporates the intersecting oppressions of racism, classism, and sexism, showing how they function simultaneously. White supremacy, for hooks, includes not only racialized categories, but the history and legacy of capitalist colonialism and the internalized racism of Black people. hooks is interested in interrogating, and deconstructing, both the way white supremacist capitalist patriarchy has been used against Black people, as well as the way Black people have **colluded** with the structures of racism to internalize their own sense of inferiority or white supremacy.

Representation and Identity Construction

In much of her work hooks emphasizes the importance of understanding how representations of race, class, and gender affect the choices we make on how to live our lives. While not seeing representation as absolute, it is important and significant in identity constructions. In *bell hooks: Cultural Criticism and Transformation* (Jhally 1997), hooks compellingly argues that mass media has been actively used as a backlash to feminism, to get women to identify with the more conservative and/or sexually complicit roles that maintain patriarchy. In *Black Looks: Race and*

1.　bell hooks, born Gloria Watkins, has chosen to take on her grandmother's name in honour of her grandmother's spirit. She uses the lowercase to reduce the importance of the author and put the significance onto what she has written.

Representation (1992) she makes similar arguments about race. In both texts, hooks uses the example of Black women in music videos. Typically these women, whether the artist herself or a background dancer for someone else, capitalize on their sex appeal and maintain an image of Black women as hypersexual. She writes,

> There is a direct and abiding connection between the maintenance of white supremacist patriarchy in this society and the institutional-ization via mass media of specific images, representations of race, of blackness that support and maintain the oppression, exploitation, and overall domination of all black people (1992, 2).

For hooks, Black people need to engage in **decolonization** processes. This includes not only political decolonization, but even more significantly, a decoloni-zation of the mind. To decolonize the mind requires Black people to learn to love Blackness rather than try to "become" white (or assimilate into white culture). This loving of Blackness can be as simple as seeing the colour of one's skin as beautiful and as complex as appreciating and acknowledging the histories of resistance and transformation of, particularly, African-Americans. hooks is concerned about the increasing drive for Black people (particularly Black youth) to "make it" in the cultural industries controlled largely by white elite Americans by perpetuating ste-reotypes of Blackness that continue the ideologies of white supremacist capitalist patriarchy. However, she is equally concerned with mainstream white society's insis-tence in the perpetuation of those stereotypical images. It is white audiences that crave and demand images of violent, **misogynistic**, Black men in gansta rap and then white critics that blame Black cultures for these images. It is the sexism and misogyny that often limits people's willingness to see any potential in rap and hip hop. However, Anthony Pinn points out,

> The sexism expressed by Saint Paul and other biblical figures, the homophobia that marks both testaments has not resulted in a huge theological backlash requiring the destruction of the Bible as a via-ble "sacred" text. Why not exercise the same hermeneutic of multiple meanings to rap lyrics and their creators? (2007, 293).

Pinn agrees with hooks that the sexism is a problem (in both rap and the Bible) but accusing one set of texts as being problematic while the other can be redeemed is hypocritical.

Both hooks and Gilroy see popular culture as an important site of inquiry to understand how "race" is continually constructed and as a potential site for anti-racism. While for both writers popular representations can continue the ideologies of colonialist, nationalist, white supremacist capitalist patriarchy, these representations, and our critical responses to them, are also places where, as hooks says, we can be "enlightened witnesses" (Jhally 1997). While hooks' work is more focused on film and literature, she also joins Gilroy in addressing the construction and consumption of rap music and hip hop culture, to which this chapter will now turn.

Applying Anti-Racist Cultural Theory: Rap and Hip Hop

Background

To understand the influence of African traditions on American popular music in general, and rap music specifically, we must look to West African possession religions, the trans-Atlantic slave trade, and the multiple ways African peoples coped with their experiences of slavery and oppression. While there are a number of African traditions that were transported to the Americas through the trans-Atlantic slave trade, there are some commonalities in worldview amongst these traditions. For the most part, these African worldviews saw the human condition as imperfect. That is, we live in an imperfect world which brings us suffering and pain. Suffering and pain is alleviated through ritual. The focus of ritual, then, is on this life, not a future afterlife. It is, they argue, important to repair social ruptures, maintain moral values, and build community. Thus ritual is focused on these goals. To reach these goals, the community must maintain harmonious relationships with the deities and/ or ancestors. These powerful beings can help to alleviate pain caused by social ruptures and physical illness; alternatively they can cause social ruptures and physical illness, if they are not adequately honoured.

The most prominent cultures of West Africa at the time of the trans-Atlantic slave trade, and thus the most common in the American settings, were the Fon and Yoruba (found in the modern-day regions of Benin, Togo, Nigeria, and Ghana). Each had a pantheon of deities: the *loa* for the Fon and the *orisha* for the Yoruba. Practitioners of these traditions used singing, drumming, and dancing to open themselves up to possession by *loa* or *orisha*. Once a person was possessed by a deity, indicated by a change in his or her movement, the deity could interact face-to-face with the rest of the community. In this ritual process, drumming is the key; music is a ritual tool linking the human community to the spiritual world. This ritual drumming involved two or more rhythms in tension with a single common beat; it is **polyrhythmic**. For example, you might have a four-beat rhythm laid over a three-beat rhythm. Often the dancers would supply additional rhythms, thus indicating the importance of community participation rather than simple observation.

Another element of this participation comes in the form of a call and response, either in the rhythm or in the singing. The priest or priestess calls out as the lead vocalist and the community of participants answers back as vocal accompaniment. The calling out involves improvisations as well, playing off the set rhythms to incorporate conversation with community and/or deity.

PLANTATION COLONIES

These religious and musical traditions were carried over into the Americas through the trans-Atlantic slave trade which began in the early sixteenth century. The trans-Atlantic slave trade involved the movement of Africans enslaved by Europeans largely to the so-called New World to work on agricultural plantations and gold mines. The most intense period of the slave trade was 1701–1810. In total, 12 to 15 million African people were transported across the Atlantic, though many did not make it, dying on the voyage. The majority of these African people were brought to the Caribbean and South America where a variety of European nations had set up **plantation colonies**. Plantation colonies were different from settlement colonies in that they were set up to exploit the resources to send them back to Europe. The plantation colonies had a small European population (typically Catholic) and a large non-European workforce, either enslaved Africans or, in some cases, indentured servants from Asia. In these contexts, Africans made up about 90 per cent of the population. Because of their numbers, they were able to preserve much of their African religious practices, though these were overlaid with Catholic images. So, while the possession rituals maintain with their musico-religious practices, the *loa* and *orisha* took on the form and name of Catholic saints. For example, in Santeria the *orisha* Chango, the god of fire, thunder, and lightning, is associated with Saint Barbara who is also associated with lightning and is the Catholic patron saint of artillerymen and gunsmiths. The introduction of additional deities/spirits from American indigenous traditions, as well as ancestors from the American contexts were also integrated in the West African traditions. Thus we have the development of religions such as Vodun in Haiti (see Chapter 3), Santeria in Cuba, and Candomble in Brazil.

SETTLEMENT COLONIES IN THE US AND BLACK CHRISTIAN CHURCH MUSIC

In the United States the situation was quite different. Only about 5 per cent of the Africans brought to the Americas through the trans-Atlantic slave trade were brought to the United States. The plantations were smaller and the colonies were largely **settlement colonies** rather than plantation colonies. This means that they were colonies designed to provide new homes for European immigrants rather than solely extraction of resources. Because of the higher number of Europeans and the lower number of Africans, there was more interaction between slaves and masters and less interaction amongst enslaved Africans. The US slave owners developed many restrictions on interactions between Africans and the maintenance of African cultures. Drums were forbidden as they were thought to lead to insurrection through group solidarity and African cultural identity. This resulted in a lack of opportunity for enslaved Africans to retain or establish strong African cultural identities. Additionally, the United States was largely Protestant rather than Catholic and thus there were no saint figures to lay over the West African deities; there was no obvious way to disguise West African *loa* or *orisha* as Christian. Because of this situation, West African religious forms went underground though there was certainly some continuity of practices. For example, enslaved Africans developed the musical practice of singing spirituals, songs drawn on Christian biblical ideas, particularly the stories of the Israelites escaping slavery in Egypt. In some contexts, the enslaved Africans were able to join together for what was called a ring shout: a gathering that involved the singing of these spirituals while rhythmically shuffling in a circle, replacing the drumming with foot stomping and clapping. This practice evolved into the musical styles of the Black Church. Hymn singing in the Black Church (the first of which were Baptist) continued the polyrhythmic patterns of West African traditions using clapping instead of drumming, but continuing the call and response, importance of improvisation, and participation by congregation. Even the possession by the spirits, though now articulated as the Holy Spirit of Christianity, became a mainstay of these churches.

Secular Music: Rap

In the secular realm an integration of African and European musical styles was also in play. Enslaved Africans were used to play European folk music for their masters, developing skills in stringed instruments such as fiddles, banjos, and guitars. As this music moved out of solely white contexts and with the end of slavery more and more West African styles began to permeate the European songs and instruments, creating a hybrid that once again incorporated polyrhythms through clapping and stringed instrument. Similarly the development of brass bands, again using European-style instruments, incorporated the polyrhythmic West African styles, call and response, and improvisation. These two styles—stringed and brass instrumentation—led into the development of blues and jazz.

Blues, in particular, emerged in the late 1800s, first in rural contexts, then shifting to the cities. The this-worldly concerns of the blues lyrics fit more closely with the West African theological and spiritual concerns than did at least surface readings of the Christian spirituals. The musical style also maintained the polyrhythms, improvisation, and call and response. In the late 1940s blues evolved into rhythm and blues which attracted a larger white teen audience, and became the first

Catholicism and Protestantism

Christianity has a number of different forms. The largest groupings are Eastern Orthodox, Catholic, and Protestant. In the development of the Americas and the practices of the trans-Atlantic slave trade, Catholics and Protestants are the most significant. Prior to the 1500s, the majority of Western Europe followed the Roman Catholic Church, under the leadership of the pope. In the 1500s, however, a number of religious leaders, most prominently Martin Luther, began to question the authority of the Catholic Church leaders. Though not necessarily intending to break away from the Catholic Church, Luther's arguments led to a split that we now call the **Protestant Reformation**. The Protestants believed that the Christian Bible should be the highest authority for Christians, and that individual Christians should be able to read it for themselves. Prior to this, the Bible was typically only read by priests in Latin and then interpreted for the people in their vernacular tongue. As printing developed, an increase in the translation and printing of Bibles in various vernaculars occurred. This allowed more people to read the Bible for themselves and determine what it meant. The Catholic Church maintained that the pope was the highest authority and that the priests, bishops, and cardinals were the only ones with the proper knowledge to interpret the sacred text.

Another critique the Protestants made of the Catholic Church was that it was too ritualistic. For example, the practices of lighting votive candles for blessings were perceived by Protestants as too magical. This was at the beginning of the scientific

expansive crossover of African American music into white culture. With the grooming of Elvis Presley to market rhythm and blues to a white audience, blues made its transition into rock and roll.

Rap music, and its attendant hip hop culture, first developed in the late 1970s in the South Bronx, New York. Like blues, rap developed first in predominantly Black communities. The centrality of rhythm, particularly the polyrhythmic patterns found in rap music, show the influence of West African musical traditions as permeated through African-American culture. The importance of dance, significantly the circular form of participants around a central breakdancer, shows a similar style to West African religious ritual. Rap music, however, has never been a solely African American musical form. The very base of rap music, the sampling of previously recorded music, develops from the introduction of the sound system culture from Jamaica into North America. The use of sound systems to broadcast music into the neighbourhood, what eventually becomes known as the ghettoblaster, was first found in Jamaican clubs or parties. This movement of musical technology from the Caribbean to New York to the rest of North America and beyond, highlights Paul Gilroy's articulation of the Black Atlantic as transnational and hybrid. In addition, revolution when ritual and magic was increasingly perceived as opposed to the more desirable world of reason. Other activities such as absolutions, where one confesses one's sins to a priest and receives a required action to absolve one of those sins, were perceived by Protestants to be contrary to Biblical teachings that they believed indicated salvation came through faith in Jesus, rather than any activity one could do. These ritual activities, for Protestants, were also tied to corruption whereby priests required monetary contributions for absolutions or absolved others of sins while living their own lives in gluttony and greed.

Because of these concerns, Protestants and Catholics have developed rather different practices. Protestants do not tend to honour or recognize saints in the way Catholics do. For Protestants there is no need for an intercessor with God and the asking for blessings is considered irrational. For Catholics, the saints are a sign of the grace of God and thus are closer to God than regular Christians, hence they can be asked to help out in both worldly and otherworldly concerns. Protestants hold the Bible to be the sole authority and Catholics hold the pope to be the final authority (though he is held to the teachings of the Bible as well). This difference means that the Roman Catholic Church has a singular structure and liturgy (though some Catholics deviate from this). However, there are multiple Protestant churches because if one can interpret the Bible for oneself, this leads to multiple interpretations of the Christian message and even conflicts among Protestant Christians on what the text says or means.

Hispanic communities of New York also quickly joined in the development of rap music adding their cultural spin to create a further hybrid of music of the ghettos.

MARTIN LUTHER KING, JR AND MALCOLM X

Embedded in the messages of early rap music, and continuing today in what many call "conscious rap," was a strong message of Black empowerment, sometimes taking the form of Black nationalism. In this trend, rap music took inspiration from the earlier soul music that developed alongside the civil rights movement of the 1960s, which often carried themes of Black pride. In the 1960s civil rights movement, there were two main strands of activism. The freedom movement of Martin Luther King, Jr took a predominantly non-violent position calling on moral values to motivate change in racial relationships and laws in the USA. Alongside this non-violent movement was the increasingly violent Black Power movement, identified with the Black Panthers among others, who advocated defensive violence and met with repressive response by government agencies. Malcolm X, a powerfully articulate member of the Nation of Islam (NOI), became a spokesperson for the Black Power movement, even though in his later years he began to advocate a more coalitional perspective.

NATION OF ISLAM

In the 1970s, after the heyday of both the Freedom movement and the Black Power movement, when both Martin Luther King, Jr and Malcolm X had been brutally murdered, the children of these movements living in the ghettos of major American cities responded to erosions of Black living standards through music drawing on the earlier messages of King and Malcolm X. Because of the importance of these two figures, their religious identifications also became significant in hip hop culture and the development of rap music. A significant number of early rappers considered themselves members of the Nation of Islam, or its offshoot, the Five Percenters. The rap music developed during this time drew on Islam, and particularly the image and message of Malcolm X, to articulate an "authentic" Blackness. Juan M. Floyd-Thomas (2003) names this appeal to Islam within rap music as engaging in a "jihad of words" much like Malcolm X did. With the mainstreaming of rap music, the messages of the Nation of Islam began to lose power in rap music. Rap musicians increasingly created more superficial music focusing on money and sex rather than resistance. Additionally, Floyd-Thomas argues that the commercial popularization of Malcolm X through the publicity campaign for Spike Lee's film adaptation of *The Autobiography of Malcolm,* turned the perception of the NOI message for many rappers into something passé. Most other rappers were born and bred in the Protestant Black Church and followed the teachings of the Reverend Dr. Martin Luther King, Jr. Joseph Sorett (2009) argues that the religious outlook of rap music and hip hop culture, while always multi-religious, has shifted focus from the early 1980s Islamic message to the twenty-first–century preoccupation with Christianity, particularly a prosperity gospel. With a proliferation of African-American–Christian **televangelism** and megachurch movements, Sorett observes that Christianity is overtaking Islam as the religious perspective of rap artists. However, this Christianity is not the revolutionary Christianity of Martin Luther King, Jr, but largely a prosperity gospel where God awards faithfulness with wealth and power. Sorett suggests that this shift to Christian prosperity gospel allows rap artists to "avail oneself of rhetorical, cultural and financial capital" (2009, 16).

Anthony Pinn (2003a) insists that rap music engages in responding to questions about what is ultimately important in life, thus, it is inherently engaged in religious issues, though these are not always explicit. Monica R. Miller agrees saying, "Cultural productions such as rap music ostensibly disrupt our neat, tidy, comfortable and coherent systems of religion and theology by re-signifying traditional language and concepts, while often displaying a level of comfort with religious and theological uncertainty" (2009, 40–41). An examination of a few examples within rap music will help us make sense of Pinn's and Miller's arguments and further allow us to explore the theories of Gilroy and hooks.

TALIB KWELI

Miller uses Talib Kweli as one of her foundational examples in showing the religious re-signifying found in rap music. Kweli began his rap career as a member of the Five Percenters, but has since moved away from association with any organized religion. While Kweli seems to maintain an articulate belief in God, he continually critiques organized religion. In his 2002 album *Quality*, he names religion as one more tool, like selling crack, to help disenfranchised Black people to get by. In his song "Get By," he rhymes: "Saturday sinners Sunday morning at the feet of the Father/ They need somethin to rely on, we get high on all types of drug." He further states that spirituality is more authentic than organized religion. In the 2007 album *Eardrum*, Kweli provides even stronger indictments of organized religion. The song "Give Em Hell" explores the existence and location of hell. In this song, Kweli refers to the various religions that have influenced him from Rastafarianism to the Five Percenters to Christianity. The first two are clearly given more positive representation as teachings that make sense to the inner city Black youth. Ultimately, however, he claims that "religion create the vision make the Muslim hate the Christian/make the Christian hate the Jew" and "More blood is spilled over religion than anything in world history." Hell, says Kweli, is here on earth, in the ghettos.

Kweli is certainly engaged in a critique of white supremacist capitalist patriarchy, though his concerns are not solely about white people. Following hooks' articulation, white supremacy is not a problem of white people but the problem of loving whiteness over and above anything else. Black people can be equally engaged in white supremacy when they collude with this system through their own self-hatred or dismissal of other Black people. Kweli calls for a decolonization of the ghettos, however, and like Gilroy, he does not seem interested in a specific black nationalism, though his early association with the Five Percenters may point in that direction. His movement away from the Nation of Gods and Earths, and his ultimate claim that all religions are promoting the same thing, seems to allow for a kind of transnational anti-racism that Gilroy advocates.

TUPAC SHAKUR

Pinn shows an interest in Tupac Shakur as an example of the concern with ultimate questions outside of the context of organized religion. For Pinn, Tupac represents an African-American humanism that both critiques American culture and religion and offers some, though limited, transformative vision. Tupac's thug life provides an embodied theology that disallows for a transcendent power. In Tupac's "Hail Mary" from the album *The Don Killuminati* (1996), this embodied theology reformulates the Christian story to put Tupac in the position of the sacrificed son of God: "Tell me I ain't God's son." This provides, says Pinn, a "radical humanizing of Christology" (2003b, 94).

The Nation of Islam and the Five Percenters

The Nation of Islam is a predominantly African-American branch of Islam. It began with the teaching of Wallace D. Fard in 1930 Detroit. Fard was a Muslim missionary to America, particularly the poor Black of Detroit. His message came at a time of increasing poverty and alienation for African-Americans in the Northern cities. During the Great Depression there was increased competition for jobs, housing, and food between European immigrants and Blacks who had earlier migrated up from the South. Unlike the European immigrants, Blacks were not given any opportunity to assimilate to mainstream white society. Thus with the increased poverty and little opportunity to escape that poverty, Black people of the ghettos were increasingly bitter about white society. Enter Fard and his attack on the white race, Christianity, and the Bible. Fard taught that Black people are the original human beings and Islam is their natural religion. White people are a mutation of Black people, a genetic experiment by a mad scientist called Yacub. When this experiment went bad, the white race overtook and enslaved the original Asiatic Black race, the tribe of Shabazz. Thus, all whites are devils and Black people are good and divine.

Fard called his new movement the Nation of Islam. He encouraged converts to rid themselves of their slave names by taking on Muslim names and eventually the practice of replacing one's last name with an "X" to represent their lost true name. Converts also adopted Muslim dress codes and worldview, yet they were set apart from other Muslims largely due to their racial-separatist position and the eventual belief that Fard, himself, was God. In 1934 Fard disappeared and Elijah Muhammad, his prime disciple, took over leadership of the movement.

Richard Brent Turner tells us that "The Nation of Islam in the 1960s saw a transition from the concept of signification as a personal search for religious identity to an institutional quest for a collective public identity" (1997, 176). This transition took the Nation of Islam from a localized movement largely in Detroit and Chicago, to the whole of America. At the forefront of this expansion was the skilled orator, Malcolm X. Malcolm X converted to Islam in 1948 while he was in prison. Turner argues that Malcolm X "became the most important twentieth-century public advocate for Islam in America, and arguably in the world" (1997, 185). However, in the 1960s Elijah Muhammad and Malcolm X developed significant disagreement about the goals of the movement. Muhammad was primarily a conservative Black nationalist. He advocated religious and racial separation and discouraged political alliances. Malcolm X, on the other hand, was increasingly a radical Black nationalist who saw the need for political alliances with other non-Muslim Blacks and non-Europeans and was willing to participate in more militant moves. By 1963, Malcolm's speeches began to emphasize politics more than religion, which eventually led to his suspension by Muhammad. In 1964 Malcolm X broke all ties with the Nation of Islam and shifted his perspective on racial-segregation radically. He established the Muslim Mosque Inc. based on orthodox Islam and established multiracial Islam as a valid option for Blacks. In doing this, he gave up the notion that whites were inherently demonic. Racism was a consequence of capitalism and whites could be allied with, if they were Muslim. On 21 February 1965, Malcolm X was killed by former NOI members while presenting a public speech.

In 1975 Elijah Muhammad died and his son, Wallace D. Muhammad, become the Supreme Minister of the Nation of Islam. W.D. Muhammad made sweeping changes to the movement. He moved away from the racial-separatist position and adopted a multi-racial orthodox Islam. With this move, he allowed whites to join the movement, rejected any notion of Black supremacy, and refuted the divinity of Fard. After a number of name changes, the Nation of Islam became the Muslim American Community and Muhammad changed his name to Warith Deen Mohammed. In 1978 Louis Farrakhan left W.D. Muhammad's group to reinstate the Nation of Islam. He returned to the belief in the divinity of Fard and discouraged integration with whites, claiming that they were literally devils.

In the 1960s, NOI member, Clarence 13X, began to question the organization's beliefs about the divinity of Fard. The problem, for Clarence, was that NOI taught that Asiatic Black man was divine, but Fard was very light skinned. Clarence began to teach that all Black men were God. In 1963 he was chastised by the NOI and left with a few other followers, changed his name to Allah, and began preaching to young folks on the streets of Harlem, beginning the movement of the Five Percenters, or the Nation of the Gods and Earths.

Father Allah taught that 85 per cent of the Black population was deluded and victimized by 10 per cent who manipulated them (which included the NOI). The remaining 5 per cent were Black men who have gained the knowledge of their divinity. The Five Percenters believe they will be able to save the 85 per cent from their victimhood as they show them the realities of their divinity. The teachings of the Five Percenters are called the "Lost-Found Muslim Lessons," the Supreme Mathematics and the Supreme Alphabet. The Supreme Alphabet involves breaking down words to learn their true esoteric meaning. For example, for the Five Percenters, Islam means "I Self Lord and Master."

According to Juan M. Floyd-Thomas, "Central to the mission of the Five Percent Nation has been an attempt to move beyond a critique of nihilism into a mode of empowerment for poor and working-class African Americans who are otherwise disenfranchised, disaffected, and desperate" (2003, 59). This makes the Five Percenters appealing to young Black men in the ghettos, as they can take control over their lives by becoming gods. Black women within this movement are the Earths. They are taught to submit to their men, respect themselves, and maintain a strong family and home.

Ultimately, Pinn sees the God in Tupac's music as rhetorical; the real answers to life are found in human activity. In contradiction, Michael Eric Dyson suggests that "Tupac was obsessed with God" (2001, 202), though clearly, Dyson agrees, Tupac's religious perspectives were complex and even contradictory. Like Talib Kweli, Tupac was influenced by a number of different religious traditions and he read voraciously a variety of spiritual teachings. Thus, the God Tupac references cannot be seen as solely a Christian God or a Muslim God. At times this God is likened to a cop beating Tupac down; at other times the sole support for those oppressed in the ghetto, as in the song "Black Jesus" from the album *Still I Rise* (1999).

As a representative of gangsta rap, with its typical misogynistic message and glorification of violence, hooks may suggest that Tupac Shakur could be seen as a cautionary tale about buying into white supremacist capitalist patriarchy. She writes, "The sexist, misogynist, patriarchal ways of thinking and behaving that are glorified in gangsta rap are a reflection of the prevailing values in our society, values created and sustained by white supremacist capitalist patriarchy" (1994, 135). She continues in a later passage, "The tragedy for young Black males is that they are so easily duped by a vision of manhood that can only lead to their destruction" (1994, 143). This seems clear with Tupac whose life was brutally ended with a bullet when he was only twenty-five years old. Ultimately, though, hooks critiques a mainstream society that sees the actions of rappers like Tupac as a symptom of Black maleness. Rather, hooks sees these actions as a symptom of the mainstream society that prefers these violent, yet desirable, images of Black youth to maintain the stereotypes of racial categories.

For Gilroy the problems with the kind of persona presented in gangsta rap lie in the questions of authenticity. Artists like Tupac, and his appeal to thug life, seem to present a certain image of authentic Black maleness from the ghetto. This appeal to authenticity is ultimately self-destructing though. It does not allow for a true anti-racist movement; it can only wallow in the oppression of poverty, violence, and hopelessness. To be fair to Tupac, however, he was a complicated character. He was well read in a whole range of topics and on many levels seemed to push against the white supremacist capitalist patriarchy. He could not, however, resist some of the rewards for furthering the stereotypical racial authenticity of the Black ghetto.

ERYKAH BADU AND BUSTA RHYMES

Erykah Badu is an artist whose work covers more than just rap; she also encompasses soul and rhythm and blues music, constructing a new hip hop blend called neo-soul. Badu incorporates religious perspectives in her music in quite obvious ways. For example, as explained by Anaya McMurry, in Badu's song "One" with Busta Rhymes, the perspective on family and theology of the Five Percenters is blazing. The importance of the family as a unity is significant in the Five Percenters, and so the theme and declaration of the song "One" reproduces this ideology, but like other rap musicians' engagement with religion, in somewhat unorthodox ways. Busta Rhymes states that "I self Lord am/so divine when me and my woman coincide with one mind." This statement aligns with the Five Percenter belief that the Black man who has learned his lessons (from the Five Percenters) is god. Women are earths, rather than gods and this idea is also represented in the song: "Yes yall my beautiful Mother Earth respect her to the max." Both Busta Rhymes and Erykah Badu reinforce the importance of unity between male and female in the family with men as gods and women as earths. Interestingly though, they add in some untraditional articulation of that unity. Badu sings about how the man can show his strength by coming home to watch the babies and let her make the money. Thus the unorthodoxy of their articulation of Five Percenter beliefs.

bell hooks is highly critical of a move toward increased patriarchal family values as a way to strengthen Black communities. However, the unorthodox version represented by Erykah Badu and Busta Rhymes does show some play with the role of male and female in heterosexual unions. The doctrines of the Five Percenters, though, do continue to maintain strict distinctions between men and women, and while Erykah Badu can sing about going out to work and Busta Rhymes can rap about staying home with the babies, she is still an earth while he is a god. As hooks sees racism, sexism, and classism as integrally tied together, a system that maintains one cannot adequately fight against the other. There is an insufficient decolonization happening here. Though Gilroy speaks less about sexism and gender, the position of the Five Percenters on racial-superiority cannot fit well within his transnational, hybrid anti-racism.

Holy Hip Hop

While many rappers and hip hop artists reference religious themes in their rhymes and contribute to complicated conversations about what is ultimately important in life, some rappers approach their craft with a specifically evangelistic goal. The development of holy hip hop or what others call gospel hip hop has lead to some controversy for established churches and their leaders, who often view hip hop as essentially problematic because of its association with drugs, sex, and crime. Regardless, holy hip hop artists take their message to the streets, to share their own stories of living in the drugs, sex, and crime world and coming out to see the redeeming grace of God. Christina Zanfagna conducted a study with some of these holy hip hop artists in Los Angeles and explains that "Sometimes considered musical mavericks in the church, corny Bible-thumpers in the streets or in hip hop clubs, and criminal youth by law enforcement in the so-called ghettos of Los Angeles, gospel rappers are often strained by accusations that their ways of being and expressing are blasphemous and/or inauthentic" (2011, 146). They persevere in their goals even in the face of these misunderstandings. These rappers do not want to be in the churches because they are concerned with those the churches have dismissed, which consists of many of the youth who have embraced hip hop culture. One of these gospel rappers is Nuwine who says in an interview "That's what ministry is about. Reachin' out to those who don't know God. [. . .] Jesus did it. He spent very little time in the synagogue" (quoted in Pinn 2007, 292). In his song "Mission Possible," from the 2002 album *Mission: Possible* he rhymes: "I love the Lord, not these material thangs/Just letting you know, living the life for Him is what it brangs."

Cassandra Thornton writes of the experience of attending a CD release party for a gospel rapper. She was so moved by the experience of seeing teenagers (herself in her early twenties) being visible moved by the rhymes. She concluded that "Most of the teens and young adults at the concert, as well as in churches, are part of the hip hop culture. The language of that culture is rap. Therefore, if you communicate the Gospel through rap, these people will understand and relate to it better than your traditional pastors teaching it to them from a pulpit" (2012, 115). This is a different position from Nuwine who takes his message to the streets. Thornton takes hers, as she developed her own artistic ministry as a mobile DJ, to various locations including churches that may welcome her. She calls the churches to welcome holy hip hop and challenges their dismissal of hip hop in general. Ralph Basui Watkins, a Christian theologian at Columbia Theological Seminary agrees with Thornton. While he admits that there is much in rap and hip hop that is problematic, from a Christian perspective, there are artists who use the genre to truthfully speak to and about God.

Summary

That rap musicians have a complex, and at times contradictory, relationship with organized religions should not come as a surprise to those familiar with Paul Gilroy's concept of the Black Atlantic. Embedded in this concept are the ideas of hybridity and intercultural interactions. Just as we can see movements of West African religious traditions moving and adapting to varying contexts in the Americas, creating new hybrid religious identities, so too we can see those new hybrid identities continuing to move and develop and adapt. As Gilroy writes, "the unashamedly hybrid character of these Black Atlantic cultures continually confounds any simplistic (essentialist or anti-essentialist) understanding of the relationship between racial identity and racial non-identity, between folk cultural authenticity and pop cultural betrayal" (1993, 99). These rap artists, like many others, are questioning authenticity from the perspectives of their hybrid identities, which includes religious hybridities. As this form of musical culture expands across the globe, even more elements, religious and otherwise, will be added to the call and response. This music, for Gilroy, if understood as transnational and hybrid in character, provides for a fertile soil of anti-racism. But it has also become a source of a reification of Black authenticity and

Black nationalism. For Gilroy this search for authenticity cannot be a core component of anti-racism which must move beyond race.

hooks understands rap and hip hop to have developed in specific response to white supremacist capitalist patriarchy. At its most revolutionary, rap is an example of loving Blackness, which hooks sees as so important for fighting white supremacy. Loving Blackness, though, is not the same thing as advocating Black nationalism. It is not just a task for Blacks to master. White supremacy will not be overcome until Blackness, in the whole of society, is seen as beautiful, good, and worthy of respect. Rap music, in many cases, demands this love. Unfortunately, rap music meets the same fate as others who love Blackness. hooks writes:

> black folk who "love blackness," that is, who have decolonized our minds and broken with the kind of white supremacist thinking that suggests we are inferior, inadequate, marked by victimization, etc., often find that we are punished by society for daring to break with the *status quo*. On our jobs, when we express ourselves from a decolonized standpoint, we risk being seen as unfriendly or dangerous" (1992, 17).

Rap music has been declared by the white supremacist society as dangerous and of little value. Many rap stars, themselves, have embraced this image and maintained the colonized, white supremacist vision of Black youth. hooks does not see it as coincidental that the most popular rap music is misogynistic gansta rap: popularized by white audiences reinforcing their assumptions of the dangerous, brutish nature of Black men. hooks argues that it is problematic to see this gangsta rap as endemic of Black culture; it is, rather, endemic of wider prevailing values in mainstream culture that are maintained by white supremacist capitalist patriarchy. As hooks argues: "It is much easier to attack gangsta rap than to confront the culture that produces that need" (1994, 143).

Review Questions

1. What is fascism and why is Paul Gilroy concerned with it?
2. What is the significance of the Black Atlantic?
3. Why does bell hooks use the term "white supremacist capitalist patriarchy" rather than "racism"?
4. According to hooks, how should black people engage in decolonization?
5. What are the differences between plantation and settlement colonies and how did those differences affect the Africans enslaved on them?
6. How does rap music reflect West African religious ritual?
7. What is the significance of Malcolm X's split from the Nation of Islam?

8. Why are the Five Percenters significant to a study of rap music?
9. How do Talib Kweli, Tupac Shakur, and Erykah Badu and Busta Rhymes "disrupt our neat, tidy, comfortable and coherent systems of religion and theology" (Miller 2009, 40–1)?
10. What is holy hip hop?

Useful Resources

Print

Dyson, Michael Eric. 2001. *Holler if You Hear Me: Searching for Tupac Shakur*. New York: Basic Civitas Books.

Gilroy, Paul. 1993. *The Black Atlantic: Modernity and Double Consciousness*. Cambridge: Harvard University Press

Miller, Monica R. 2009. "'The Promiscuous Gospel': The Religious *Complexity* and Theological *Multiplicity* of Rap Music." *Culture and Religion*. 10(1). 39–61.

Pinn, Anthony B., ed. 2003. *Noise and Spirit: The Religious and Spiritual Sensibilities of Rap Music*. New York: New York University Press.

Rattansi, Ali. 2007. *Racism: A Very Short Introduction*. Oxford University Press.

Sylvan, Robin. 2002. *Traces of the Spirit: The Religious Dimensions of Popular Music*. New York: New York University Press.

Watkins, Ralph Basui. 2011. *Hip-Hop Redemption: Finding God in the Rhythm and the Rhyme*. Grand Rapids: Baker Academic.

Video

Clift, Robert. 2009: *Blacking Up: Hip Hop's Remix of Race and Identity*. California News Reel. DVD.

Education Video Centre. 1999. *Hip Hop: A Culture of Influence*. VHS

Hurt, Byron. 2006. *Hip Hop: Beyond Beats and Rhymes*. Kinetic Video. DVD.

Jhally, Sut. 1995. *Material Witness: Race, Identity and the Politics of Gangsta-Rap*. Kinetic Video. VHS

Jhally, Sut. 1997. *bell hooks: Cultural Criticism and Transformation*. Media Education Foundation. VHS

Taylor, Jennifer Maytorena. 2009. *New Muslim Cool*. Seventh Art Releasing. DVD.

Audio

Busta Rhymes. 1997. *When Disaster Strikes*. Flipmode Records/Elektra Records

Nuwine. 2002. *Mission: Possible*. Wine-O

Talib Kweli. 2002. *Quality*. Rawkus/UMVD

Talib Kweli. 2007. *Eardrum*. Blacksmith Music/Warner Bros. Records

Tupac Shakur. 1996. *The Don Killumaniati*. Uni/Interscope

Tupac Shakur and Outlawz. 1999. *Still I Rise*. Uni/Interscope.

7

Orientalism

OBJECTIVES

This chapter will help you develop an understanding of

- the development of Orientalism as a lens for Western viewing of the East
- the relationship between Orientalism and Islamophobia
- the problems of stereotyping, even when seemingly positive
- Hollywood representations of Arab Muslims, Oriental spirituality, and Native Americans

What do *Aladdin* (1992), *Pocahontas* (1995), and *Kung Fu Panda* (2008) all have in common? If your answer is that they are animated children's movies, you would not be wrong. But, for the context of our current chapter, you would only be seeing the surface. Each of these films represents a particular people in an essentialized, stereotypical way. To analyze this representation, and the implications for our study of religion and popular culture, we need to explore Edward Said's concept of **Orientalism**.

Edward Said (1935–2003) argued that European (and later North American) cultural media typically viewed Middle Eastern peoples through the lens of Orientalism, thus limiting the "Orientals" to a primitive, exotic other. The reliance on an essentialized, singular representation of, particularly, Arab and Muslim cultures functioned to justify colonization and military action. This chapter uses Said's theory to analyze the way Hollywood films draw on such a singular representation to continuously present Arabs and Muslims as terrorists. In doing so, this chapter explores how current **Islamophobia** is similar to, but also different from, what Said saw in colonial European art and literature. We also look to how other scholars have used Said's argument to address Hollywood representations of other "Oriental" or "Othered" cultures. Jane Naomi Iwamura uses Orientalism as a way to analyze the seemingly positive image of the Oriental Monk, pointing out the problems of even positive stereotyping. We also explore the way Native Americans have been por-trayed in very similar ways to "Orientals" in Hollywood.

Edward Said

Edward Said's book *Orientalism*, originally published in 1978, offers a way to under-stand Western representations of the East and the very construction of that West/East distinction. Focusing on European literature of the eighteenth to twentieth cen-turies, Said shows how Europeans, and later Americans, came to view the "Orient," particularly the Middle East, Arabs, and Muslims, through a particular lens that limited the ability to see any complexity of identity. This lens, said Said, has more to do with the European observer than it has to do with actual people living in the areas designated as the Orient. As such, Orientalism, as a European practice, con-structed a particular image of the Middle East as the opposite of the European, so as to validate the European self-identity.

The Orientalist Image and an Essentialist Identity

A core element within Orientalism is that the Arab and Muslim is represented as a singular, **essentialist** identity. All Arabs are the same; all Muslims are the same. These vast generalizations disallow any recognition of the variety of cultures and Muslim identities to be found in the Middle East and other parts of the world. Not only is this representation essentialist—that is, based on an assumption of one identity for all Arabs or Muslims—but also constructed as static. This static nature removes the "Oriental" from history: Orientals are primitive and have been the same throughout all time. They do not progress. Thus the European Orientalists took this essentialist, static image and used it to show the complex, dynamic identities of Europeans. Europeans were civilized and continually developing. Modernization in European countries was a sign of this historical progress. Because the "Oriental" was not modern, they became the "Other" to the European.

POLITICAL INFLUENCE AND COLONIALISM

This Orientalist image was not just used by scholars or writers, however. The disci-pline of Orientalism that had developed in the nineteenth century—by the mid 1800s all major European universities had Oriental Studies as part of their curriculum—was used to influence political and economic decisions of European states. Said partic-ularly explores the relationship of the British and the French with Middle Eastern and North African countries. The eighteenth to twentieth centuries were times of European colonial conquest of many of these nations. The French occupied Egypt, eventually ceding it to the British. The French also occupied Algeria and Morroco, in North Africa, and Syria, in the Middle East. The British occupied Palestine and Iraq in the Middle East, as well as India. Much of this colonialism was justified and facilitated through the image constructed by Orientalist scholars. Imperialism, then, was not seen as conquering equally valid cultures, but about saving others from their primitiveness. The colonizing nations saw themselves as bringing the "Orient" into history, to bring Western values to these backward cultures, in order to uplift them. However, this uplift was only perceived as possible through the guidance and rule of the European nations who were more suited to civilization.

SCIENTIFIC EXPLORATION AND HISTORICAL PERSPECTIVE

Said outlines the development of Orientalism in Europe, particularly the shift from a specifically Christian opposition to Islam, to a more secular concern with liberal ideologies in the eighteenth century. This shift was composed of a number of elements largely associated with the move to "scientific" exploration and explanation of the world. With this move to science, the biblical framework of European understandings of the world expanded. Europeans became interested in the ancient histories of Egypt, India, and China, for example, allowing these histories and mythologies to be granted similar place to those of Jewish and Christian biblical history. This means that the stories of the beginnings of all these religious worldviews, including Christianity, were increasingly seen in historical terms rather than theological. This allowed for a new understanding of Islam and Mohammed as a historical figure rather than a "diabolical miscreant" (Said 2003, 120), a theologically defined associate of Satan. As European scholars increasingly engaged in "scientific" study of other cultures and regions, they also increasingly began to identify positively with some of these cultures and regions (or aspects of them). In this sense Orientalism was not necessarily always about a negative view of the Orient; at times European scholars showed a great love of Oriental cultures, even while they continued to see European civilization as more advanced or more complex than other civilizations (which were often not represented as civilizations at all). Much of what European scholars appreciated in these cultures was historical, thus allowing a love of, for example, Egyptian mythology and history, at the same time as a disdain of modern day Egyptian society. This eighteenth-century shift is exemplified, for Said, in the Napoleonic expedition of Egypt (1798–1801) when the French conquered Egypt not only with the military, but also through the "scientific" study of Egyptian culture.

What the Napoleonic expedition did was reinforce the role of the European scholar to be able to understand and record Oriental culture *better than* Orientals could themselves. As Said notes, the Orientalism this expedition represents constructed

> the picture of a learned Westerner surveying as if from a peculiarly suited vantage point the passive, seminal, feminine, even silent and

supine East, then going on to *articulate* the East, making the Orient deliver up its secrets under the learned authority of a philologist whose power derives from the ability to unlock secret, esoteric languages (2003, 138).

Philology was the study of languages and cultural groupings based on language forms. The European philologists would make vast cultural generalizations formed as scientific statements. Their comparisons between language and cultural groups, however, were typically evaluative rather than just descriptive. Thus Indo-European languages, and the cultures associated with those languages, were understood as more sophisticated than, in particular, Semitic languages (such as Hebrew and Arabic) and the cultures associated with those languages. In this construction of cultural generalizations, the European philologists, and other Orientalists, created the Orient as a discursive identity: that is, they created a **discourse** (see Chapter 1) about the Orient that allowed them, and Western governments, to act in a certain way in and toward the Orient. As such, Orientalism becomes "a political doctrine" (Said 2003, 204).

The Orientalism of the eighteenth to twentieth centuries, as discussed by Said, has not disappeared; it has become the basis for current Western understandings of Arabs and Muslims, both in political contexts as well as popular culture. As the United States became a significant global power in the twentieth century, the American role in maintaining Orientalism became stronger, particularly through the productions of Hollywood. This current Orientalism, however, is highly influenced by a number of political conflicts within the Middle East in the twentieth century, which push the Orientalism of the twentieth to twenty-first century into the arena of Islamophobia.

Islamophobia

Islamophobia is a term that has become salient in academic and political discourse since the 1990s. Though its origins and coinage are in dispute—some seeing it originating in the nineteenth-century others in the late twentieth century—the first firm definition of the term came in 1997 in a British report from the Runnymede Trust: Commission on British Muslims and Islamophobia called *Islamophobia: A Challenge For Us All*. In this report, Islamophobia is defined as "a shorthand way of referring to dread or hatred of Islam—and, therefore, to fear or dislike of all or most Muslims" (1997, 1). Islamophobia, while built upon Orientalism, involves a more direct mistrust and even hatred of Islam, typically focusing on "fundamentalist" Islam as normative. In this focus, Islam is represented as a monolithic hostile force out to destroy Western values. So, not only are Islam and Islamic cultures less advanced than Western cultures, as in Orientalism, but all Muslims are trying to take over the world and destroy the advances in liberal society the West has achieved.

Scholars who examine and critique Islamophobia point out three major political events that are tied to the shift to Islamophobia. The first is the creation of the State of Israel after World War II. In 1947 Britain decided to pull out of their colonial administration of Palestine. In 1948 the United Nations decided to create two states within Palestine: one Jewish and one Arab. The State of Israel declared its establishment on May 14, 1948. However, conflict between Israeli and Arab Palestinians (and other Arab nations) has continued to dominate the area. This complex situation is highly influenced by the American support of the State of Israel over the Palestinian people. Since 1948, American representation of Palestinians specifically, and other Arabs, has been coloured by the Israeli–Palestinian conflict. As Jack Shaheen points out in his book *Reel Bad Arabs: How Hollywood Vilifies a People* (2001), and the Media Education Foundation film of the same name (Jhally 2006), Hollywood has presented the conflict as one between a peaceful Western nation (Israel) and a lawless, primitive gang (Palestinians). All Palestinians are represented as terrorists beginning in the 1960s film *Exodus* continuing into blockbusters, such as the 1994 film *True Lies*. As Shaheen remarks, we (in the West) never see Palestinians in refugee camps or living under Israeli occupation. We never see them as human, only as monster. Thus the American support of the State of Israel has furthered the normalized image of the threatening, violent Arab.

The second conflict that contributed to the changed image of the Arab from simple, backward, exotic other to more specifically dangerous terrorist was the Arab oil embargo of 1967 (and again in 1973). This is when the Arab oil-producing nations stopped exporting oil to Western countries that were in support of Israel as a means of protesting that support in light of the continuing conflicts between the State of Israel and its neighbouring Arab nations. This embargo resulted in a huge increase in the price of oil in America, thus threatening the car-based culture that had become central to the American way of life. The image of the Arab trying to destroy American values became salient after these embargos.

The third event of the mid-twentieth century that contributed to American Islamophobia was the Iranian–Islamic revolution of 1979. Iran had been supported by the West and in turn was supportive of Western, particularly American, actions in the Middle East. Many Iranians felt that their leader, the Shah, was more concerned with supporting America than providing for his people. The growing disparity between rich and poor contributed to this perspective. In 1979, under the leadership of the Ayatollah Khomeini, a Shi'i Muslim cleric, Iranians ousted the Western-supported Shah and instituted an Islamic state that was not supportive of Western control in the Middle East. When the Shah was admitted into the United States rather than handed over to the Iranian people to stand trial for his presumed

Islamism

Islamism is, at its very basic, the integration of the religion of Islam with the politics of any given Muslim-majority state. Islamism developed in the response to colonial occupation by looking to Islam as a more just and valid system of government, economics, and social organization than the Western secularism represented in the colonial powers or the independent nation states drawing from Western systems. Islam has a system of law, called shari'a. While shari'a is interpreted differently by different Muslim groups, in Islamist perspectives it is seen as both sufficient and superior to other international law systems. Thus Islamists argue for an instigation of shari'a as their national law.

Islamism began as local groups responded to local situations. For example, the Iranian Revolution was an Islamist revolution that was concerned primarily with the local situation in Iran, including the perception that the Shah was overly influenced by Western governments and a return to shari'a would benefit the people of Iran not only religiously but economically and socially. By the end of the twentieth century, some Islamist groups took their struggle, or jihad (which should not be translated as "holy war" but as "struggle"), against the West more global, particularly in direct response to the actions of the State of Israel and the United States of America. Some of these groups have condoned the use of violence, specifically the use of suicide bombing, in their fight against the West. In particular, the group Al-Qaeda advocates the use of terror, as was evident in the events of September 11, 2001. Al-Qaeda also advocates

misdeads, a group of young **Islamists** invaded the American embassy in Tehran and kept its staff hostage for over one year. This action solidified the American image of the Muslim as terrorist and the assumption, as Chris Allen writes, "as a menacing power Islam irrefutably focused on bringing down and subsequently overthrowing the West and everything that it stood for" (2010, 40).

By the 1980s the image of the Arab Muslim as terrorist was well established. Later events of the twenty-first century, particularly the events of September 11, 2001, reinforced an image that was already a part of the American psyche, such that when the attacks on the World Trade Center and the Pentagon happened, we (the West) did not associate these acts of terrorism with a deviant fringe, but as representative of all Muslims. Until very recently—up until the 2012 change in the status of Palestine as a non-voting member in the United Nations—Palestinians in the news media or Hollywood were always terrorists, never working for peace; Islamic governments have been portrayed as backward and oppressive. "Arabs" are shown without differentiation and as vehemently anti-American while there are a great variety of peoples living in the Middle East, as well as millions of Americans and Canadians of Middle Eastern descent. Despite how they are portrayed in the a non-traditional use of the Qur'an. Whereas in many Muslim traditions, the Qur'an must be interpreted by trained scholars, Al-Qaeda follows the teachings of Ayman Al-Zawahri who argued for the right of any individual Muslim to interpret the Qur'an on his own. Zawahri also sanctioned the practice of suicide bombing as a religiously and politically valid action.

Not all Islamist groups are violent, however. Many groups advocate a non-violent approach to *jihad* that focuses on preaching Islam. For example, Wahhabism, an ultraconservative branch of Islam that began in the eighteenth century with the teachings of Muhammad ibn Abd al-Wahhab, in Saudi Arabia, is certainly anti-Western and pro *shari'a*, but it is also specifically anti-suicide bombing. They are more interested in forming Islamist states than directly fighting against the USA. An increasingly well-known Wahhabist group is the Muslim Brotherhood which originated in Egypt in 1928. The majority of Islamists fall under this category of non-violent struggle toward Islamist states, rather than violent struggle against the West. As Maha Azzan (2006) writes,

> The minority activists committed to violence are increasingly being seen as a threat by some of the most ardent and extremist Islamists who, while critical of the West and their own regimes, are committed to non-violent change. We are seeing the gradual formulation of a counterattack against the violent wing of the Islamist movement, emphasizing *daw'a* (preaching) rather than jihad (1131).

media and in film, only about 20 per cent of Muslims in the world are even Arab, 20 million Arabs in the Middle East are Christian, and there are many different kinds of Islam, just as there are many different kinds of Christianity or Judaism. Islamophobic imagery, like the Orientalist imagery before it, presents Islam as one singular identity, static in time, backward, primitive, and above all violent.

Applying Orientalism: The Hollywood Terrorist

The Orientalist image of Arabs and Muslims, including the assumption that all Arabs are Muslim and all Muslims are Arab, can be seen early in the Hollywood repertoire. A Hollywood mythology of what Jack Shaheen calls "Arabland" can be found in early silent films and carries on to today. For example, the 1921 silent film, *The Sheik*, brings to the silver screen the image of the aggressive, domineering seemingly Arab male, played by non-Arab Rudolph Valentino, abducting a high-class white British woman in the exotic context of the desert. Interestingly, in this film, once the woman, Lady Diana Mayo, realizes that the sheik is actually *not* Arab, but a European living as an Arab, she falls in love with him (even though he has violently assaulted her). This film both emphasizes the aggressive threat of Arabness, particularly to white women, and accepts aggressiveness as natural and attractive when in the form of European/white men over white women. Beginning in the early films and continuing throughout Hollywood's existence, the stock Arab characters, whether played by Arabs or non-Arabs, are caricatured as dangerous or inept figures.

Aladdin and the Arab Ineptitude

The ineptitude of Arabs is portrayed against American/European heroes either in comedic examples or as the losers in violent conflicts. An example of the comedic ineptitude of Arabs can be found in the Disney animated film *Aladdin* (1992). Beginning with the opening song, the image of the backward, aggressive Arab is mocked, with original lyrics, "Where they cut off your ear if they don't like your face, It's barbaric, but hey, it's home." Add to this images of a large Arab man trying to carry out the punishment of chopping off Princess Jasmine's hand for the crime of theft, and Aladdin's ability to ridicule the official, including cutting his pants to reveal polka-dotted boxer shorts. Though Aladdin and Jasmine are sympathetic Arab characters, this sympathy lies in their presumed defiance of "traditional" Arab roles.

True Lies and the Dangerous Arab

The Arab ineptitude, tied to the dangerous caricature, can be found in most action films that represent Arabs as terrorists, a role that became increasingly common after World War II with the American support of the State of Israel. In these films, the Arab/Muslim terrorist inevitably loses due to their inability to either think logically or be heroic enough. The film *True Lies* (1994) presents this image with the American/European character of Harry Tasker, played by Arnold Schwartzenegger, out-smarting and out-fighting groups of Arab Muslim terrorists. As Edward Said points out in the documentary film *Edward Said on Orientalism* (Jhally 1998), Hollywood movies contain a huge amount of dead Arabs and Muslims, reinforcing the idea that they need to be stamped out, they only understand the language of force, and they ultimately cannot stand up to the military strength of the United States or the clever prowess of Western heroes.

The demonization of Islam and Arabs in popular culture creates a mythology in which Islam becomes synonymous with terrorism. This is not solely for fictional, entertainment contexts. It became particularly obvious in the real life aftermath of the Oklahoma City bombing in 1995. After the bomb destroyed the Alfred P. Murrah Federal Building, killing 168 people, including 19 children under the age of six who were attending the daycare in the building, and injuring many more people, the news media alerted Americas to the "probability" that this was a Middle Eastern, Muslim terrorist act. Journalists informed us that "this has Middle Eastern terrorism written all over it" and that Oklahoma City was the centre of Muslim terrorist groups in America (Jhally 1998 and Jhally 2006). When it turned out that the bomb was planted by white American Timothy McVeigh, who was motivated by anger at the American government, somehow McVeigh's actions did not get reflected in the media as representative of all white American men, as terrorist acts committed by Arabs have been associated with all Arabs.

The Siege

The ongoing power of the Orientalist and Islamophobic imagery within Hollywood, resulting in the representation of Arabs and/or Muslims as inevitably terrorists, can be seen in the responses to the 1998 film *The Siege*. Karin Wilkins and John Downing (2002) conducted a study of this film to show the film as a site of struggle over the interpretation of Arabness. They provide a textual analysis of the film, an analysis of the protests that preceded and followed the release of the film, and an analysis of viewer responses to the film. What makes *The Siege* so significant for our discussion is that it "ostensibly was designed to present a diversified and civil-liberties-oriented portrayal of Arabs and Muslims" (Wilkins and Downing 2002, 419–20). As such it can be used to think through how Hollywood has tried to reform the Orientalist image of the Muslim terrorist, and evaluate the successfulness of that endeavour.

The story of *The Siege* revolves around the response of American agencies to terrorist acts in New York City committed by Muslim Arabs. While the FBI, personified in the characters of Special Agent Anthony Hubbard (played by Denzel Washington), and his assistant, the Arab American Frank Haddad (played by Tony Shalhoub), and CIA, represented by Elise Kraft/Sharon Bridger[1] (played by Annette Bening), attempt to locate the terrorists, the bombings become increasingly devastating. When a truck bomb is detonated at the New York City FBI headquarters, the US Army under Major General William Devereaux (played by Bruce Willis), takes over and seals off Brooklyn in an attempt to find the terrorist cell. All Arab Americans, including Haddad's son, in Brooklyn are rounded up and detained. Eventually we discover that the terrorist cell is led by an Arab lecturer, Samir Nazhde

---

1. The spelling of names in Wilkins and Downing does not always match that of the script. Where Wilkins and Downing use the names "Sharon Breccia" and "Samir Najdi" the script uses the names "Sharon Bridger" and "Samir Nazhde" (http://www.imsdb.com/scripts/Siege,-The.html).

(played by Sami Bouajila), who had been presented at the beginning of the film as anti-terrorist and supportive of the CIA agent's attempts to find the terrorists.

Wilkins and Downing, in their textual analysis of the film, conclude that *The Siege* maintains the hegemonic discourses of Orientalism, though it does include some internal contradictions. One of the most significant signs of Orientalism comes in the character of Elise Kraft, the CIA agent who is represented as the expert in the Middle East. Even though we are given a positive Arab-American character in the FBI agent, Haddad, he is not allowed to be an expert on Arabness or the Middle East. As in all Orientalist representations, the Westerner is the one who can hold authority over the understanding of Arab and Muslim culture. Kraft, then, is the Western expert who interprets the Oriental. However, she committed the error of "going native" and engaging in too intimate a relationship with Nazhde. Because of her sexual relationship with Nazhde she is unable to see his true nature as a Muslim extremist and terrorist. Of course, Nazhde's duplicity in his relationship with Kraft and his representation of himself as anti-terrorist reinforces the image of Arabs as deceitful.

While the Arab-American figure of FBI agent Haddad provides a more positive image of Arabness, Wilkins and Downing point out that this is an Arabness that is specifically contrasted to that of Nazhde who is an immigrant. Haddad clearly balances his Arabness and his Americanness with a heavier emphasis on the American side. Though he is critical of the Army move to detaining Arab Americans in Brooklyn, he is still fundamentally pro-American. Nazhde, however, is a Palestinian, and thus falls into the Orientalist and Islamophobic stereotype of Arabness. So while we get some sympathy for Arab Americans—if they are fully and committed Americans—non-American Arabs are still Muslim terrorists. This focus on Americans is carried through to the focus on the domestic arena, rather than tying American events to the context of the Middle East. Thus we, as viewers, are given minimal understanding of all sides of a conflict that could lead to Arab actions in America. As Wilkins and Downing point out, "*The Siege* pushes violence into American awareness, though only as a threat *to* Americans, never as a threat emanating from the USA and its foreign government allies" (2002, 427).

Wilkins and Downing do not only supply us with a textual analysis of the film (looking at performance, narrative, and genre), but they also provide analysis of some viewer responses, including Arab-American organizations that protested the film, journalists and reviewers, and a group of university students. The analysis of these viewer responses show that *The Siege* can be seen as a site of struggle in determining meaning.

The two groups most involved in protesting the portrayal of Arabs and Muslims in *The Siege* were the American-Arab Anti-Discrimination Committee (ADC) and the Council on American-Islamic Relations (CAIR). These groups saw the film as perpetuating the stereotype of the Arab Muslim as terrorist, even if there is a sympathetic Arab character in Haddad. Members of these organizations protested at the release of the film and handed out flyers with information on what Islam actually is to film viewers. Interestingly, Wilkins and Downing's analysis of newspaper articles shows a significant shift in representing this protest over time. Prior to the full release of the film, about half the newspaper articles were unsympathetic to the concerns of the ADC and CAIR (who had been given a pre-release viewing). After the premiere well over half the newspaper articles shifted to a sympathetic portrayal of the protests. The movie reviewers were split down the middle: about half had similar concerns to the ADC and CAIR about continued stereotypes; the other half, while admitting that there were stereotypes represented in *The Siege* saw the stereotypes as realistic and thus justified.

Wilkins and Downing also asked their own university students for responses to the film. They had them watch the film in small groups and provide written feedback. They found that almost half of their students specifically associated terrorism with Islam and only about 10 per cent seemed to notice that there was a more sympathetic Arab portrayal in this film (at least only 10 per cent felt it important enough to remark upon).

Overall, Wilkins and Downing's study shows that this film is a complex text: while the filmmakers claim to try to provide a more balanced view on Arabs and Muslims, that balanced view is not necessarily decoded by the majority of viewers in the way intended. The Orientalist and Islamophobic image of the Arab Muslim is so ingrained in Western minds that it seems natural to many viewers, even when alternatives are provided. These images continue into the twenty-first century in such TV series as *24* (2001–2010) and *Sleeper Cell* (2005–2006).

Applying Orientalism: The Oriental Monk

Though in his discussion of Orientalism Edward Said focused on the Middle East and Islam, he did acknowledge the same process in Western concepts of further East in India, China, Japan, and other South East Asian contexts. Drawing on Said's conception of Orientalism, Jane Naomi Iwamura (2011) pulls out newsmedia, film, and television images of what she calls the Oriental Monk as a way to think through some of the Orientalist imagery of India and the Far East. Unlike the Muslim Arab terrorist image, though, the Oriental Monk is one that on the surface is positive and beneficial. Iwamura argues that the positive elements of the Oriental Monk image may be preferable to the negative elements of the Muslim Arab terrorist, but neither image recognizes the complex varieties in the people supposedly represented. The Oriental Monk sets up a specific image as acceptable based on largely American understandings and expectations of Asian spirituality. Any actual living

Asian people who do not fit the stereotype are, thus, not taken seriously or even seen as suspicious and inauthentic in the American viewers' eyes.

Kung Fu

The Oriental Monk can be Japanese, Chinese, Indian, Tibetan, or any other Asian background. However, the distinctions between these cultures and the religious traditions tied to them are rarely highlighted. What is most significant about the Oriental Monk is not the specifics of his beliefs or teachings, but, as Iwamura suggests, "his spiritual commitment, his calm demeanor, his Asian face, his manner of dress, and—most obviously—his peculiar gendered character" (2011, 6). This gendered character is both masculine—as in the Oriental Monk is always male—and feminine—as in the Oriental Monk is always gentle, calm, and not aggressive in a Western masculine fashion, thus, non-threatening to American men. The narrative of the Oriental Monk in both representations of actual Asian spiritual teachers in America and in fictional stories such as the iconic television series, *Kung Fu* (1972–1975), is as such:

> A lone monk figure [. . .] takes under his wing a fatherless, often parentless, child (usually a boy). This child embodies a tension—although he signifies the dominant culture in racial terms, he has an ambivalent relationship with that culture. This allows him to make a break with the Western tradition that is radical enough to allow him to embrace his marginalized self. The Oriental Monk figure discerns this yearning for difference, develops it, and nurtures it. As a result of this relationship, a transmission takes place: Oriental wisdom and spiritual insight is passed [on]. (Iwamura 2011, 20).

Iwamura focuses much of her study on the development of this figure in *Kung Fu*, though she also gives significant space to thinking about the implications for real life Asian spiritual teachers in America, such as the Japanese Zen philosopher, D.T. Suzuki, and the Indian Hindu guru, Maharishi Mahesh Yogi. In these two characters, as represented by the Western media, Iwamura sees Suzuki as more successful because he could be slotted into the Oriental Monk figure. Even though he typically wore American style clothing, in newsmedia he was photographed in Japanese-style robes showing his exotic, and feminized (in the American eye), persona. He was known for transmitting his Zen Buddhism to American disciples, both those of the Beat subculture, such as Jack Kerouac, and more conventional Americans such as Alan Watts. In both contexts, it is in America that Zen will further develop, having been dismissed in its homeland of Japan, having been replaced with modern industrialism (according to the American news reports; see Iwamura 2011).

Zen

Zen Buddhism is a type of Mahayana Buddhism. Mahayana Buddhism, also known as the Great Vehicle, is the most prominent type of Buddhism in East Asia. It is most commonly contrasted with Theravada Buddhism, which is common in South Asia and Tibet. An important teaching with Mahayana Buddhism is the idea of compassion as leading some people who have reached enlightenment to postpone nirvana, or their final enlightenment, and remain in the earthly realm to teach others. These people are considered bodhisattvas. Zen developed in China in the sixth century as Ch'an Buddhism and then was introduced to Japan in the eleventh century where it took on the name Zen. The formation of Zen is tied to stories about a disciple of the Buddha in India named Mahakasyapa. The story goes that the Buddha was going to give a sermon. Instead of speaking he simply held out a flower. Mahakasyapa smiled. This was an indication that he understood what the Buddha meant while others did not. This story led to the idea of a mind-to-mind transmission of teaching found within Zen. The focus is not on scholarship and text, but on meditation and breaking attachment. Zen teaches that all people have inherent Buddha-nature—that is, the potential to be enlightened. Two schools of Zen Buddhism developed. One school, called Rinzai in Japan, taught that people could suddenly reach enlightenment through a shift in their consciousness. Sometimes this sudden shift comes via the meditation on a *koan*, a seemingly illogical dialogue between student and master that forces the student to think in different ways. The other school, Soto, teaches that students can gradually come to enlightenment through the long practice of meditation.

Zen Buddhists practice *zazen*, sitting meditation. However, this meditation practice is not about thinking through the *koan* or meditation on the Buddha. In *zazen* one is simply sitting in awareness, not thinking at all. Rather than meditating *to* reach enlightenment, this practice is about *demonstrating* one's enlightenment. As Mavis L. Fenn writes (2013), *zazen* is about meditating "as an expression of one's Buddha nature" (188).

The Maharishi Mahesh Yogi, and his teaching of Transcendental Meditation, was less successfully adopted by Americans. Though highly popular for a time with celebrities such as the Beatles and Mia Farrow, this Indian spiritual leader was often criticized in American media for his adoption of modern technologies and methods of marketing to get his spiritual message across. The American people were already expecting a certain kind of Asian spiritual leader who would emphasize the differences between East and West and eschew Western progress. Mahesh was suspect because of his willingness to cross over the divide. His popularity, and that of Transcendental Meditation, did not last much beyond the 1960s.

As Iwamura remarks, "While 'real' Oriental Monks like the Maharishi Mahesh would disappoint, ones spun directly from imagination could not, as the television and film characters such as Kwai Chang Caine would prove" (2011, 111). Kwai Chang Caine, the protagonist of the 1970s television movie and series *Kung Fu*, was a biracial (Chinese and American) Shaolin monk trained in China and exiled to America where he wanders the Wild West encountering various people requiring his help. Though he always counselled a pacifistic approach to conflict, he invariably needed to resolve situations using his martial arts skills. While the show presented Chinese philosophy and people in more positive ways than previously found in Hollywood, and provided opportunities for more positive representations of other minority figures and women, the way these minorities were encouraged to address their situations of oppression was largely based on individualistic approaches. This was during the period of great upheaval in American society following the civil rights movement. Many minority groups were forming more militaristic organizations, such as the Black Panthers encountered in Chapter 6. The approach to minority concerns in *Kung Fu* "assumed that *changing the hearts of individuals will automatically lead to changing society*. To a post-1960s liberal audience who obviously felt sympathy toward the plight of racial minorities but who nevertheless were wary of certain measures taken by these groups toward self-determination and weary from extended conflict, this simple adage proved seductive" (Iwamura 2011, 135, italics original). Kwai Chang Caine, and his Chinese teachers, as Oriental Monks, provided a more passive, gentle approach (until Caine needed to assert his American aggression with his fighting) based on Buddhist (but read more generally as "Oriental") wisdom.

Kung Fu Panda and *Broken Blossoms or the Yellow Man and the Girl*

Iwamura maintains that the various Oriental Monks she discusses, including the ones mentioned above, as well as figures as early as the yellow man in D.W. Griffith's *Broken Blossoms or the Yellow Man and the Girl* (1919) or as late as Master Oogway and Master Shifu in DreamWork's *Kung Fu Panda* (2008), are essentially interchangeable for American viewers. As long as they are passing on ancient, rather than modern, spiritual wisdom of an Eastern variety, they are recognizable as the Oriental Monk. However, the distinctions of location are usually significant as they are tied to specific geopolitical relationships. When relations between Japan and the United States are good, for example, we are more likely to see Japanese Oriental Monks. However, when Japan was a major economic competitor with the United States, the Japanese Monk was less in the forefront (though not necessarily absent). The most evident Oriental Monk in the early twenty-first century is the Tibetan one, emphasized by the figure of the Dalai Lama, who represents what many Americans see as a noble cause for the support of a disempowered people, who are, incidentally, no political or economic threat to the United States.

Applying Orientalism: Reel Injuns?

In 2009 Cree filmmaker Neil Diamond directed a documentary, *Reel Injun*, that explored the image of North American native peoples in Hollywood. Much of what he found fits very close with the Orientalist lens as described by Said. Many scholars have used the theories around Orientalism to think through the Western relationship with other colonized peoples, including myself in a study of *Avatar* (see the Conclusion and Klassen 2013). While the history of relationships between Western nations and the various peoples and places they colonized are different, the way Westerners viewed these colonized peoples are similar. The twentieth-century (and beyond) representations of those colonized peoples are largely dominated by Hollywood imagery. Thus in *Reel Injun* we again see the use of stereotypes that present essentialist notions of a static, ahistorical people that reflect very little of the actual diversity and experience of indigenous peoples. Diamond points out a number of these stereotypes, and like the Oriental Monk, some of them are seemingly positive. While we do have particularly early images of the Fearless Warrior who can be very dangerous and destructive for the white people, there is also the Noble Savage who, like the Oriental Monk, has a spiritual wisdom that "we" (white/Western folk) can draw on. This spirituality is typically tied to the land and an appreciation of the earth, such as found in Disney's *Pocahontas* (1995). The important observation Diamond makes is that in Hollywood all Indians are the same. They typically wear the feather headdress and buckskin, even though that is a specific costume of the Plains Indians, not all native peoples. There is little recognition of the variety of nations, and differing worldviews they may hold. This is very similar to the way Arabs and Muslims, or other "Orientals," are portrayed.

Avatar

While in the late twentieth century we do begin to see an increased diversity of images of native American peoples, and particularly an increase in Native-made films, the Hollywood representations still draw on Orientalist ideas, even if focusing on the more positive spiritually mystical, close-to-the-land versions. For example, in James Cameron's *Avatar* (2009), while representing a fictional people, the Na'vi are similarly represented as Native Americans that are living in harmony with the land and offering some kind of spiritual message that the colonizers/Western societies need. They also are necessarily saved by a representative of that very same colonizing society who has been taught their wisdom and can thus be their saviour (much like the narrative of the Oriental Monk).

Challenging Orientalism: Multiculturalism

One of the critiques of Said's discourse of Orientalism is the lack of any serious consideration of how this Orientalism has been challenged by Arabs, Muslims, Asians, and Indigenous peoples. Whether this challenge has been overwhelmingly successful is less important than the fact that by not addressing it Said himself represents the "Oriental" as passive. So as not to make the same mistake, we will end this chapter with a few examples of speaking back to the Orientalist constructions.

Little Mosque on the Prairie

In 2007 one response to Orientalist discourse began its run on the Canadian Broadcasting Corporation on Monday nights. This was the comedy *Little Mosque on the Prairie*, created by Canadian Muslim filmmaker Zarqa Nawaz, which aired until 2012. As a story about a small Muslim community in a small town in the Canadian prairies, this situation comedy attempted to be, as Sandra Cañas suggests, "A challenge to this orientalist orthodoxy cultivated and nurtured by hegemonic media discourse" that, interestingly for Cañas, "has emerged from within this very media space itself" (2008, 196). What *Little Mosque on the Prairie* does is interrupt the Orientalists' assumption of static and universal Muslim identity to show a range of Muslim identities and conflicting perspectives in one small community. The show has young Canadian-born Muslims as well as immigrants from Pakistan, Lebanon, and Nigeria. It includes a white convert. Some of the women veil; some of them do not. Some of the members are conservative; some of the members are liberal; at least one is a feminist. The members of this community challenge assumptions about Muslims in general and Muslims in the North American context. Their interactions with the largely white Christian population of their small town comedically highlight the assumptions held by this larger Canadian population using an Orientalist lens. This show also highlights some of the challenges of multiculturalism, a particularly salient concern in Canada where multiculturalism is so ingrained in Canadian identity. In this show, multiculturalism is challenged by the bigotry of some of the non-Muslim townsfolk as well as some of the Muslims themselves. Ultimately, Cañas argues that "this Canadian serial shows that the Islamic world is multifaceted and contradictory, calling into question static, monolithic ideas of this religion and its practitioners" (2008, 207). That said, *Little Mosque on the Prairie* does not address all the issues of diversity necessary to have a full understanding of the Muslim world. There are little to no discussions of sectarian differences, such as disagreements and conflicts between Sunnis and Shiites. The show also tends to romanticize Canadian multiculturalism. There always seems to be a solution to solving the problems of miscommunication and misunderstanding. As a sitcom this may be necessary but it does not reflect the complex realities of multiculturalism. That said, Aliaa Dakroury argues that *Little Mosque on the Prairie* "opened a public space" to begin talking about the place of Muslim Canadians in multiculturalism (2012, 162). But this opened space is not limited to Canada. *Little Mosque on the Prairie* has gone global with syndication in European countries, the United Arab Emirates, the United States, and even Israel. In all these contexts, whether the show is satisfactory in discussion of multiculturalism or the fullness of diverse Muslim identities, Dakroury insists that "the show further contributes to dialogical encounters inside and outside of the Muslim community" (2012, 176). This dialogue challenges the Orientalist lens.

Challenging Orientalism: Visual Sovereignty

Atanarjuat

An even more deliberate challenge of the "Orientalist" lens can be seen in the production of the Inuit film *Atanarjuat (The Fast Runner)*, (2001), a Cannes Film Festival award winner. This film tells an ancient Inuit legend. The story is set in the far past in the eastern arctic. It starts with a strange shaman coming to a village. The strange shaman and the local shaman engage in a spiritual duel, which is meant to be relatively friendly. However, the local shaman dies. This event brings evil into the community. A few decades later we get the story of Amaqjuaq and Atanarjuat, brothers who are nephews of the new local shaman. They have a particular rivalry with the shaman's son, Oki. Atanarjuat falls in love with Atuat who has been promised in marriage to Oki. He fights Oki for the right to marry Atuat, and wins the fight. After this much complication ensues with multiple marriages and deceptions. Atanarjuat becomes the "fast runner" who flees, naked and barefoot, across the ice. Eventually, through another shamanic challenge, peace is brought to the village.

Michelle Raheja argues that this film provides a "visual sovereignty" that draws on Western ethnographic approaches to indigenous peoples, while turning the gaze around. This film uses Inuit actors, is produced by an Inuit production company, is filmed completely in the Inuktitut language on location in Nunavut, Canada, and addresses multiple audiences: Inuit who are familiar with both the story and visual strategies of the filmmakers, non-Inuit aboriginal peoples who can translate some of the elements of the story to their own situations of colonial struggle, and non-indigenous peoples who may have little understanding of the context and narrative. Raheja calls this visual sovereignty in that it "offers up not only the possibility of engaging and deconstructing white-generated representations of indigenous people, but more broadly and importantly [. . .] it intervenes in larger discussions of Native American sovereignty by locating and advocating for indigenous cultural and political power both within and outside of Western legal jurisprudence" (2007, 1161). This visual sovereignty involves self-representation rather than reliance on the "Orientalist" lens of the anthropologists who constructed various ethnographic films and literature, casting themselves as the experts on indigenous cultures.

What *Atanarjuat* does is incorporate Inuit visual aesthetics within what on first sight appears to be an ethnographic film. The setting is in the past and thus we see the "traditional" dress and appearance of the Inuit, not unlike the famous *Nanook of the North* by Robert Flaherty (1922). But we are given this imagery without the colonialist explanation. In other words, we are not given this explanation. For those of us who do not share the Inuit culture, we are not told what is symbolic of what; what is significant to the culture and what is simply plot device. Without the ethnographic, authoritative scholarly voice, the film becomes a story, a representation of the filmmakers' vision, "as opposed to an 'authentic' visual record of a vanished past" (Raheja 2007, 1174). This play on the ethnographic whilst removing the authenticating voice is also evident at the end of the film when we are given images of the actors in modern dress while we see the credits. The film is a *story*; it is not meant to explain Inuit culture in total. The story, however, does hold meaning as a challenge to the simplistic "Orientalist" image of the "primitive Eskimo." Ultimately, Raheja argues, the film tells of the struggle to heal from destruction and make the community whole again. Though the context of the narrative is pre-European contact, the implications are that the stranger bringing destruction is a foreshadowing of the coming colonists. Through its use of visual sovereignty, though, the filmmakers do not represent the Inuit as victimized innocents, as savage primitives, or as noble savages. They are complicated individuals working through a complicated issue that is only partially understandable by the non-Inuit viewer.

Summary

Orientalism, as explained by Edward Said, is a lens through which European and American scholars, governments, and producers of entertainment have viewed the "East." This lens provides an image of a static, primitive people who are all the same, simplistic and never changing. For the image of the Middle East, this Orientalist lens has developed into one of Islamophobia, even though the majority of Muslims in the world are not Middle Eastern. Thus Muslims and Arabs (and typically the two categories are collapsed together) are generally represented as backward, anti-American terrorists who will ultimately be overcome due to their own ineptitude and American skillful heroics. Although the image of Indian or far Eastern spirituality is more positive than that of Islam, these images also present Orientalist tendencies. The Oriental Monk is also a static, ancient person who represents a more simplistic spirituality based on meditation rather than scholarly endeavour. While this image does not have quite the same damaging effect as the Muslim terrorist image, it is still limiting and essentializing, lacking any recognition of variety and, in fact, humanity of Asian spiritual leaders in particular, and Asian people in general. We also see that the Orientalist lens is also evident in the representations of Native Americans in Hollywood, again as static, primitive people.

While some representations within Hollywood have begun to attempt to dismantle these images, providing examples of films, such as *The Siege*, that can be seen as sites of struggle for meaning, ultimately the legacy of Orientalism is still with us. Examples of stronger challenges to Orientalism come not from Hollywood but from the so-called "Orientals" themselves. *Little Mosque on the Prairie*, written by Canadian Muslim filmmaker Zarqa Nawaz, and *Atanarjuat (The Fast Runner)* created by Inuit Zacharias Kunuk and his fully Inuit team, provide examples of complicated characters and diverse identities that challenge the static, monolithic images of Orientalism.

Review Questions

1. What are the core elements of Orientalism?
2. What is the relationship between Orientalism and colonialism/imperialism?
3. How was Napoleon's conquest of Egypt influential in the shaping of Orientalism?
4. What is Islamophobia and how is it related to Orientalism?
5. What are the goals of Islamist movements?
6. How does Hollywood represent Arab Muslims as inept?
7. How does the film *The Siege* both replicate and complicate Orientalist and Islamophobic imagery?
8. What are the characteristics of the Oriental Monk and how do these fit within the concept of Orientalism?
9. How might Hollywood representations of Native Americans fit within the concept of Orientalism?
10. How do *Little Mosque on the Prairie* and *Atanarjuat (The Fast Runner)* challenge the Orientalist lens?

Useful Resources

Print

Allen, Chris. 2010. *Islamophobia*. Ashgate.

Cañas, Sandra. 2008. "*The Little Mosque on the Prairie*: Examining (Multi) Cultural Spaces of Nation and Religion." *Cultural Dynamics*. 20(3). 195–211.

Iwamura, Jane Naomi. 2011. *Virtual Orientalism: Asian Religions and American Popular Culture*. Oxford University Press.

Said, Edward W. 2003 [1978]. *Orientalism*. Penguin Books.

Shaheen, Jack. 2001. *Reel Bad Arabs: How Hollywood Vilifies a People*. Interlink Publishing Group.

Video

Cameron, James. 1994. *True Lies*. Lightstorm Entertainment and 20th Century Fox.

Cameron, James. 2009. *Avatar*. Lightstorm Entertainment and 20th Century Fox.

Clements, Ron and John Musker. 1992. *Aladdin*. Walt Disney Pictures.

Diamond, Neil. 2009. *Reel Injun*. National Filmboard of Canada.

Goldberg, Eric and Mike Gabriel. 1995. *Pocahontas*. Walt Disney Pictures.

Griffith, D.W. 1919. *Broken Blossoms or the Yellow Man and the Girl*. Paramount Pictures. Available at http://video.google.com/videoplay?docid=5636171007327735796#

Jhally, Sut. 1998. *Edward Said on Orientalism*. Media Education Foundation. VHS.

Jhally, Sut. 2006. *Reel Bad Arabs: How Hollywood Vilifies a People*. Media Education Foundation. DVD.

Kunuk, Zacharias. 2001. *Atanarjuat (The Fast Runner)*. Igloolik Isuma Productions, Inc.

Melford, George. 1921. *The Sheik*. Famous Players-Lasky.

Nawaz, Zarqa. 2007–2012. *Little Mosque on the Priarie*. Canadian Broadcasting Corporation.

Osborn, Mark and John Wayne Stevenson. 2008. *Kung Fu Panda*. DreamWorks.

Thorpe, Jerry. 1972–1975. *Kung Fu*. Warner Bros. Television.

Zwick, Edward. 1998. *The Siege*. 20th Century Fox.

8

Subcultures and Post-subcultures

OBJECTIVES

This chapter will help you develop an understanding of

- subcultural theory
- the move into post-subcultural theory
- the parareligious elements of Goth
- the Burning Man festival as a "carnival of protest"

You see her walking into your classroom wearing a long black skirt and black tank-top. She sports a dog collar around her neck and thick leather bands on her wrists. Her hair is deep red, face powdered pale, and her eye and lip make-up are dark purple. From her ears hang silver pentacles and in her eyebrow and nose (and possibly elsewhere) are silver rings. She may not represent the mainstream culture of your university, but her style is recognizable. Likely she is interested in electronic trance music, vampire fiction (but not the *Twilight* series), and hanging out in graveyards. She is Goth.

A group of students come in behind the Goth. One is dressed fairly conservatively in jeans and a long-sleeved t-shirt. He has short blond hair and no piercings. The second is wearing cut off cargo pants and a t-shirt that says "unlearn." His hair is brown, long, and uncombed. He has earplugs in his earlobes and a tattoo on his arm in the form of a serpent. The third is a large woman wearing a batik sundress and sandals. She is not wearing makeup, but has a nose ring and a small tattoo on her foot in the shape of a turtle. What these three students have in common is their conversation about their participation the week before at Burning Man in the Nevada desert. They stayed in the same theme camp, partied all night at the dance parties, and let loose all inhibitions for a ritual burning of a wooden effigy. They may not look like they are part of the same group but they are all Burners.

Each of these students is participating in something beyond the mainstream popular culture. But how do we make sense of these participations? For some scholars, it has been useful to theorize about the creation and role of **subcultures** within larger cultures. For others, the concept of subcultures is limiting and does not allow for a full understanding of what these groups offer their participants and how they relate to larger mainstream culture(s). This chapter explores subcultural and **post-subcultural** theories. We then explore the examples above—Goth and Burning Man—to see how these theories work and how they can be useful for understanding the relationships between religion and subcultures/post-subcultures.

Dick Hebdige and the CCCS

The first significant studies of subcultures occurred in the United States at the University of Chicago. Beginning in the 1920s the newly developed sociology department was interested in the study of urbanization and deviancy. Chicago was a perfect location for this study as a fast growing city with its developing multiple sub-cultural groupings. Subcultures are smaller groups within society that challenge the dominant mainstream culture by showing the hegemonic ideals and values of the mainstream to be constructed rather than natural. The concerns for these scholars looking at these Chicago subcultures focused on a criminological interest, trying to determine what was at the root of deviant behaviour leading to crime. For example, in 1927 Frederic Thrasher (1892–1962) published a study of youth gangs in Chicago and in 1932 Paul Cressey published a study of taxi-dancers, women who danced with men for money in private clubs, often leading them into prostitution. The Chicago school used both quantitative (surveys, questionnaires, etc.) and qualitative (interviews, etc.) methods. What made their studies unique at the time was the premise that deviancy was based on social phenomena rather than psychological or biological elements. However, they did approach subcultures as a problem—particularly a problem of youth—which needed to be fixed, thus their emphasis on the criminological elements of subcultures.

Sites of Resistance

A cultural studies approach to subcultures did not develop until the 1970s, when the scholars of the Centre for Contemporary Cultural Studies (CCCS) in Birmingham, such as Stuart Hall (Chapter 3) and Dick Hebdige, began to study working-class youth in the UK. Rather than focusing on deviancy, the CCCS approach was neo-Marxist in that it focused on class and ideology, viewing subcultures as sites of resistance to hegemonic dominant culture. To explain this position further, we look specifically at Hebdige's influential text, *Subculture: the Meaning of Style* (1979).

Hebdige, like the other CCCS scholars, understood subcultures to be youth cultures developed in "a fundamental tension between those in power and those condemned to subordinate positions and second-class lives" (1979, 132). Thus subcultures came to be associated with class (and to some extent racial) divisions. However, not only were subcultures class-based, but also, in the post-World War II British world, they represented changes in perceptions of class and expectations of class mobility. The working-class youth of Britain were torn between the increasingly accessible middle-class consumer lifestyle and their working-class heritage. Their construction of subcultural styles brought this tension to the surface by integrating mundane objects with double meaning: both consumerist and anti-consumerist, hegemonic and counterhegemonic. The styles developed (Hebdige focuses on punk specifically) push the boundaries of the normalization of dominant society, offering alternative meanings to objects. This disrupted the cultural consensus that is so necessary for the maintenance of hegemonic power structures. For example, the use of the Union Jack (British flag) in the wardrobe of punks both represented British identity and a critique of British normative culture. As Hebdige writes, though, "the challenge to hegemony which subcultures represent is not issued directly by them. Rather it is expressed obliquely, in style. The objections are lodged, the contradictions displayed [. . .] at the profoundly superficial level of appearance: that is, at the level of signs" (1979, 17).

SIGNS, SIGNIFIERS, AND SIGNIFIED

Because Hebdige was focused on style and the interpretations of **signs**, his study was primarily a **semiotic** one. Semiotics involves the interpretation of language or signs. Signs can be words or symbols (or, as in Hebdige's study, style) which are made up of a **signifier** (the physical form) and a **signified** (the mental concept). So, for example, as you read this you are looking at words on a page in a book. Each of these signs (words, page, book) have signifiers—the physical thing itself, and the signified—the cultural and linguistic association (meaning) given to that thing. A word is simply a set of signifiers linked together (w-o-r-d). The things themselves have no meaning until they are interpreted to be associated with the signified. For Hebdige, the subcultural theorist is trying to interpret the signs of the style constructed by subcultural youth. Rather than assuming the signifiers are linked to dominant understandings of the signified, Hebdige looks to the larger class-based context of these subcultures, and the tensions with the middle-class dominant hegemonic mainstream, to decipher the signified. In this study, then, style is not simply superficial, but "pregnant with significance" (Hebdige 1979, 18).

Ultimately, for Hebdige:

> Subcultures represent "noise" (as opposed to sound): interference in
> the orderly sequence which leads from real events and phenomena to

their representation in the media. We should therefore not underes-
timate the signifying power of the spectacular subculture not only as
a metaphor for potential anarchy "out there" but as an actual mecha-
nism of semantic disorder: a kind of temporary blockage in the system
of representation (1979, 90).

For Hebdige, subcultures represent challenges to the hegemonic order. These challenges lie in the realm of style. However, that does not make them insignificant. They
mark the very arbitrariness of the hegemonic values they resist. Since hegemony
(see Chapter 2) relies on convincing subordinate groups that the dominant group's
values are *natural*, the act of marking these values as arbitrary (or constructed) is
inherently a challenge to that hegemony.

As sites of resistance to hegemony, Hebdige sees the commodification of subcultural styles as a process of recuperation by the hegemonic cultural forces. In
order to maintain the dominant hegemony, the mainstream needs to co-opt the
subcultural styles to make them less potent as resistance. This happens through
the mainstreaming of subculture away from the original class-based political statements. So, for example, the use of punk style in fashion magazines, advertising, and
other disseminations of mainstream style, reduces the power of punk as a resistance to hegemony. Punk becomes normalized. For Hebdige, this commodification
freezes the subcultural style thus rendering it impotent. This commodification then
leads to the construction of new subcultural styles that seek to disrupt the hegemonic mainstream. These new styles then go through a process of commodification
and the cycle of hegemony continues.

Post-Subcultural Theory

Sarah Thornton and the Subcultural Capital

The approach of the CCCS, exemplified by Hebdige, became something of an orthodoxy in the study of subcultures/youth cultures. Subcultures were understood largely
as class-based critiques of hegemonic values and cultural productions. However,
beginning in the 1990s the study of subcultures began to move away from a focus on
marginalized groups (working-class youth particularly) to conceive of subcultures
as non-normative groups that may not be associated with distinct classes, races,
genders, etc. A significant study that moved in this direction was Sarah Thornton's
Club Cultures: Music, Media and Subcultural Capital (1996). In this study, Thornton
moved away from a strictly semiotic approach to one that included ethnographic
study and allowed subculturalists a voice alongside the academic theorizations. Her

focus on musical and dance style in club and rave subcultures of Britain posits the importance of **subcultural capital** in understanding the way people interact within subcultures.

Thornton is drawing on the concept of cultural capital developed by Pierre Bourdieu (1984). Bourdieu (1930–2002) talks about various types of capital: economic capital, cultural capital, and social capital. Cultural capital has to do with what you know (education, manners, etc.) that gives a person social status. Often cultural capital is tied to economic capital, in that the more cultural capital one has the more likely one is to have economic capital and vice versa. A significant piece of cultural capital is the idea of **taste**. Those with cultural capital have a specific taste in clothing, music, art, etc., that is tied to a higher education. For example, knowing and appreciating the works of Shakespeare, wearing designer clothing, and watching alternative art films could all be signs of higher cultural capital in Western culture.

Thornton uses this idea of cultural capital to coin the term subcultural capital that places the same idea of the significance of taste within the subcultural context of club culture. Here subcultural capital still has to do with how one dresses, what music one listens to, how one dances, what films one watches, and so on. However, the subcultural capital is marked off from the mainstream notions of cultural capital in that the taste desired is specific to the subculture. Those who seem authentic within the subculture are those with the higher subcultural capital, perceived as "hip." Those who do not dress quite right, or are awkward in their adoption of musical and dance styles, are less authentic, even perceived as wannabes.

In Thornton's study, subcultural capital was rarely, if ever, associated with class, thus her study in many ways contradicts the theories of Hebdige that subcultures are about class divisions and the class-based resistance to hegemony. Thornton does, though, maintain the focus on style that Hebdige and the CCCS began. But style is not necessarily a sign of resistance for Thornton. It is more of a sign of youth and the process of finding identity in the liminal stage between childhood and adulthood. The concept of the liminal stage comes from Victor Turner's ritual theory. As we saw in Chapter 4, Turner saw ritual as social drama whereby the tensions of society could be worked out. Through ritual, participants enter a liminal stage in which they are no longer part of the social order but can in some ways defy that social order. At the end of the ritual, participants exit the liminal stage to rejoin the social order transformed. For Thornton, subcultural participation could be viewed as this liminal stage toward adulthood.

Scholars following from Thornton have begun to look at the multiplicity of styles within subcultures and the increasing disruption of the notion of one singular dominant culture in the context of **postmodernity**. Many of these scholars have adopted the term post-subcultural studies to indicate their difference from the

Postmodernism/Postmodernity

While postmodernism is difficult to define, it is possible to describe it as a system of thought that attempts to destabilize presumptions of coherent and stable truths. The term was introduced by Jean-François Lyotard (1924–1998) in his 1979 work *The Postmodern Condition*. He wrote about the postmodern condition as the rejection of **metanarratives** and the death of meaning. Instead of finding meaning in narrative processes (i.e., ideas of truth), postmodernists find meaning in the performative, and thus meaning is contextual and constantly changing. We construct our truths through our actions and interactions; truth is not out there simply waiting to be understood. Judith Butler's conception of gender as performative is a postmodern conception (see Chapter 4). Because meaning is contextual and performative, it is also always only partial, or fragmented. There is no one whole meaning that is true for everyone; there are only pieces of meaning that may overlap and/or contradict each other. Thus postmodernism can be disconcerting in its disavowal of unities and boundaries. However, if postmodernism is true to itself, its own fragmentation is also contextual and performative.

Postmodernism is primarily understood as a rejection of modernism, which involved the search for universal truths or metanarratives. However, David Muggleton (2006) argues that modernism was never the monolithic mindset that many assume it to have been. Muggleton argues that while there certainly has been a modernity of order, what he calls Enlightenment modernity, there has also been an Aesthetic modernity characterized by disorder. Aesthetic modernity involved expressivity and experience of social change. Muggleton writes, "My argument for invoking this distinction is that while the postmodern represents a break with many of the tendencies in enlightenment modernity, it expresses substantial continuities with aesthetic modernity, and could be regarded as an intensification of such features" (2006, 36). This continuity is important as it allows for a look at the commonalities in postmodernity, the time period in which postmodernism holds sway, and earlier times in modernity.

CCCS approach. Post-subcultures are also small groups within society, but they are characterized by more diversity and fluidity. In other words, one is not necessarily a member of one post-subculture as much as one may interact with a number of post-subcultures that fit one's sense of self. Furthermore, post-subcultural studies scholars tend to minimize the idea that there is one dominant hegemonic society to challenge or resist, suggesting instead that society is made up of multiple cultures and ideologies, some of which have more power then others, but there is no longer simply one hegemonic social or political system in place.

David Muggleton and the Rejection of Metanarratives

David Muggleton suggests that "perhaps the very concept of subculture is becoming less applicable in postmodernity, for the breakdown of mass society has ensured that there is no longer a coherent dominant culture against which a subculture can express its resistance" (2006, 48). Muggleton characterizes postmodernism as a collapse of Enlightenment modern boundaries leading to fragmented cultures. While Enlightenment modernity focused on scientific order, postmodernity disrupts that order by rejecting **metanarratives**, coherent truths, or totalizing stories, for a context-based understanding of reality and a notion of truth as in flux. For postmodern scholars, hegemony itself is a metanarrative that belies the unpredictability of cultural processes and the multiplicity of tastes, styles, and cultures. Without a coherent dominant culture to respond to, it becomes difficult to speak of subcultures. Instead, we have multiple cultural groupings based on style, some with a larger following than others. However, it is significant that the *idea* of a dominant mainstream culture is still held by many who would see themselves as subculturalists. Thus, though Muggleton disputes the idea that there is one dominant culture, in his research he found that participants in various subcultures did maintain the notion of an "Other" in the mainstream that they were defining themselves against. What they weren't doing, however, was associating solely with one type of subculture. Muggleton found significant crossover in subcultural boundaries, something the CCCS did not allow for in their semiotic study.

Michel Maffesoli and Neo-tribalism

A common term used by post-subcultural studies scholars for the groups/cultures they study is that of **neo-tribalism**. This term comes from the work of Michel Maffesoli (1995) who wrote about the urban "tribe" as a small-scale social grouping joined together by common consumption patterns rather than class, race, or religion. Maffesoli sees these tribes as moving away from the strict individualism of late modernity and consumerism to preference community. However, the community formed is also based on individual need: one joins or creates a tribe to fulfill one's individual needs. Should those needs no longer be fulfilled, one leaves the tribe to join or create something else. This tribalism, however, is not so bound that one is only part of one tribe. The Maffesolian neo-tribes are based on "passional logic" or "orgiasm," which Maffesoli describes as "contrary to a morality of 'ought to be' [. . .] refers to an *ethical immoralism* which consolidates the symbolic link of all society" (1993, 2). What this jargon means is that neo-tribes are sensual rather than moral. They are based on shared pleasures and doing what feels good. These passional logics reach their climax in the "festal," or festival type settings. Thus for Maffesoli, neo-tribes are based on pleasures rather than political activity, where people enjoy themselves and do not tell others what to do or think.

Graham St John and "Carnivals of Protest"

Graham St John is one post-subcultural studies scholar who takes on Maffesoli's notion of the tribe in his study of what he calls "technotribalism" and the post-rave cultures. However, St John argues that rather than seeing these neo-tribes as solely based on pleasure, he sees them integrating pleasure and politics in what he calls "carnivals of protest" (2003, 65). For St John, and the technotribes he studies, the party can also be political, particularly when, "in its temporary duration, [it] is beyond corporate media representation, commodification and state control" (2003, 74). The technoparties and raves St John is speaking of happen in non-commercial contexts, largely for no fee (or a minimal fee going toward activist fundraisers). Participants in these tribes also utilize their skills in technology for activist purposes, particularly around "risk-aware ecological sensibilities and non-colonialist attitudes" (St John 2003, 72). St John concludes his study saying that these technotribes "are orgiastic and ideological, their intention a combination of party and protest, their rendezvous carnivals of dissent—often a cross pollination of the *festival* and direct *action*" (2003, 78).

While the CCCS approach was based on neo-Marxist theory, thus seeing subcultures as political resistance, post-subcultural studies does not see these groups as necessarily politically motivated. That said, Muggleton agrees with St John that we need to be careful not to assume that they are never politically motivated. In fact, some of these groups are more directly political than the CCCS even allowed for. For the CCCS approach the politics were solely located in style, with little actual political or social action beyond how one looks or what music one listens to. For Muggleton, many post-subcultural groups mobilize for direct political action as well as engaging in purely hedonistic stylistic behaviours. Muggleton, along with Rupert Weinzierl, writes,

> The assumption that youth cultures are mainly hedonistic, individualistic and politically disengaged, or are concerned only to assert their authenticity via the accumulation of subcultural capital, has been significantly undermined by the political activism and media visibility of new post-subcultural protest formations (Weinzierl and Muggleton 2003, 14).

Though there are certainly youth cultures that are purely style focused and apolitical, some are creating "carnivals of protest."

(Post) Subcultures and Religion

When we talk about subcultures and religion, we can certainly look at religious sub-cultures, such as the Promise Keepers, a group of evangelical Christian men who get together to support each other in creating Christian patriarchal families. However, much of the work on religion and subcultural studies takes the form of looking at the religious elements of subcultures, or the ways subcultures and post-subcultures operate like religions. We were introduced in Chapter 1 to the four relationships between religion and popular culture as outlined in Forbes and Mahan's text *Religion and Popular Culture in America* (2000). The third of these relationships was "popular culture as religion." It is important to note that thinking of the religious functions of popular culture, particularly subcultures, does not mean the people involved in these subcultures see them as religious. It is also significant, though, that for many people subcultures do what Durkheim sees as the function of religion: to provide social cohesion and mark off the sacred and the profane. When thinking of religion and popular culture in this way, we are also confronted with questions of authenticity. Is this real? Is it really religious? Is it sufficiently religious? As David Chidester reminds us in his book *Authentic Fakes* (2005), invented religions, popular cultural practices that seem anti-religious, and religious deceptions, "can be doing a kind of symbolic, cultural, and religious work that is real" (9). However, many scholars of popular culture *as* religion articulate the relationship as one of popular culture operating *like* a religion, rather than specific subgroups of popular culture, such as fans or other subcultures or post-subcultures, actually *being* religious. This is possibly a mistake, according to Jennifer Porter.

Jennifer Porter, Edward Bailey, and Implicit Religion

Porter studies fandom and admits that she has fallen into this tendency to say fandom is *like* religion rather than actually *being* religion. However, by drawing on the theoretical concept of **implicit religion**, Porter asks "If something looks like, if someone acts like, if someone sees the world like, a religious person, does this not make the object, the action, and/or the perception 'religious,' regardless of what secular category might also be applied to the phenomenon?" (2009, 272). The concept of implicit religion is credited to the work of Edward Bailey who suggests that the strict distinction religious scholars like to make between the sacred and the profane does not reflect what is actually going on in people's lives. He suggests that implicit religion involves three elements. The first element is Commitments. This does not mean all the minor commitments made in one's life. It means "what people are determined *about*, as distinct from what they are determined *by*" (Bailey 2012, 196). What people are fully committed to, whether explicitly religious or not, is part of their religious life. Implicit religion recognizes that even if those commitments are not explicitly religious (i.e., commitment to Jesus or Allah) they are still important for religious studies scholars to take seriously. The second element is Integrating Foci. This means that studying implicit religion requires looking at "the Causes (with a capital C) *for* which [people] live, and sometimes die, as distinct from the causes (with a small c) *of* their living and dying" (2012, 196). The third element in Bailey's conception of implicit religion is Intensive Concerns with Extensive Effects. What this means is that the commitments and foci for any individual goes beyond the specific situation and affects their whole life. Implicit religion thus is holistic in the sense of incorporating all elements of the sacred and the profane. For Porter, then,

> Uncovering what a person stands for, what they feel they must or must not do, who they feel they are, who they belong with, and how they ultimately situate themselves in their own personal history, their community, the world, and the cosmos, is the essence of understanding implicit religion in pop culture fandom contexts (2009, 277).

This is the same for subcultures and post-subcultures. Implicit religion is tied to the concept of lived religion that we have already encountered (see Chapter 1). As Robert Orsi suggests, "Lived religion cannot be separated from other practices of everyday life, from the ways that humans do other necessary and important things, or from other cultural structures and discourses (legal, political, medical, and so on)" (2003, 172). While a lived religion approach can focus on explicit as well as implicit religion, a study of implicit religion cannot do without a lived religion approach. In the next two sections we will look more specifically at some examples to see how these theories of subcultures, post-subcultures, and implicit religion can be applied to some group activities. First we will use the subcultural theory of Hebdige to think about the style and religion, both explicit and implicit, of Goths. Then we will use post-subcultural theory to explore the "carnival of protest" that is the Burning Man festival in the Nevada desert.

Subcultural Theory Applied: Goth As Implicit Religion

Goth is a subculture that developed in the 1980s in the UK as a derivative of punk. It soon spread to other locations, particularly North America. The Goth subculture is largely defined by its dark and morose style with a focus on death and the macabre. Goths tend to wear black, dye their hair black or bright garish colours, paint their faces with pale makeup and striking eye and lip colour. They are fascinated with Gothic literature and imagery, a genre that Catherine Spooner says deals with "the legacies of the past and its burdens on the present; the radically provisional or divided nature of the self; the construction of peoples or individuals as monstrous or "other"; the preoccupation with bodies that are modified, grotesque or diseased" (2006, 8). Tales of vampires and sexual fantasy, particularly of a sadomasochistic variety, are common to this genre, and are common interests of Goths today as well.

Amy Wilkins and Style

As a subculture, Goths are noticeable, and in fact tend to be suspicious of those who are only part-time Goths (i.e., Goths at night but passing as "normal" in their day-time jobs). According to Amy Wilkins, Goth style "deliberately and vocally rejects the consumerism they associate with hip-hop" (2008, 5). Many of the Goths she spoke with rejected Goth-specialty stores as pandering to wannabes, and even did their own sewing to create their style. Tied to their concerns with consumerism, Goths are also critical of the cult of happiness they perceive as central to mainstream middle-class life. As such, says Wilkins, they cultivate personalities characterized by psychological or psychiatric disorders of angst and depression, even while claiming to find contentment in the Goth community (Wilkins 2008, 31). Wilkins is using a similar theoretical position to Hebdige here: Goth, as a subculture, resists the dominant mainstream as a way to show its falseness. This is not, however, a deliberately political statement, nor one that moves into the larger political scene. It is an oblique statement through style not activism.

However, it has become clear through mainstream responses to the Goth subculture, that Goths threaten the mainstream culture to some degree. Hebdige argues that subcultures are typically eventually co-opted into the mainstream through commodification. Before this happens, though, they are explained through concepts of deviancy and anti-social behaviour. In many cases members of subcultures are labelled "as 'folk devil', as Other, as Enemy" (Hebdige 1979, 94). This labelling helps to repair the fracture of the hegemonic order to which the subculture has contributed. This can certainly be applied to the situation of the mainstream response to Goths.

Goths are often associated with Satanic religion and violent behaviour. This association, tied to the Goth fascination with death, graveyards, and vampires, was made early on in the development of the Goth subculture; however, it was solidified with the tying of Goth style to the Columbine school shootings of 1999. While the shooters were not specifically Goth, their style was tied to Goth in the media because they wore black trench coats and were socially isolated. This public association created increased stigma for actual Goths and created a **moral panic** around Goth in many contexts, particularly that of conservative Christian United States.

Stan Cohen and Moral Panic

Subcultural theorist Stan Cohen, in his 1972 book *Folk Devils and Moral Panics*, defines moral panics as

> [a] condition, episode, person or group of persons emerges to become defined as a threat to societal values and interests; its nature is presented in a stylized and stereotypical fashion by the mass media; the moral barricades are manned by editors, bishops, politicians and other right-thinking people; socially accredited experts pronounce their diagnoses and solutions; ways of coping are evolved or (more often) resorted to; the condition then disappears, submerges or deteriorates and becomes more visible (28).

Moral panics, in this sense, create a fear around something that is illusory, building it to a frenzy based on perception rather than actual fact. The sensational association of Goth with Satanism and the Columbine shootings created a fear that all youth who dressed in black or had any interest in the occult were heading toward a violent rampage.

That Goths are often interested in the occult does seem to be true. In Wilkins' study, though she was not specifically looking at religious affiliation, she does make passing reference to a number of her participants as "pagans." This sense of an overlap between Goth and Paganism is also mentioned in Helen A. Berger and Douglas Ezzy's 2007 study of teenage Witches. While certainly not all Witches are Goths, nor are all Goth Witches, the common interest in the occult has led some Goths into Paganism. Berger and Ezzy note that these Goth Witches are "quick to note that Goth is distinct from the Witchcraft movement, but that there are some overlaps" (2007, 81).

Anna Powell and the Parareligious

A study that looks more specifically at religious or **parareligious** affiliation of Goths is that of Anna Powell. Powell asked Goths in the UK about their religious and spiritual affiliations. Though she is clear that the Goth subculture is largely secular, as in few members hold specific religious affiliation, Powell argues that Goth is also "parareligious." She defines parareligious as "the use of religious-style practices, paradigms, or symbols that are inherent in various aspects of Goth subculture" (2007, 359). In other words, for Powell, Goth operates in a similar way to religion for its members, even as it is not specifically *a* religion.

Julia Winden Fey and Cult/ure

Similarly, Julia Winden Fey's study of Generation X Goths in North America (2000) points to a religion-like element of the Goth subculture. Fey, in fact, calls Goth a "cult/ure" which she describes as "something existing somewhere between, or perhaps beyond, the traditional concepts of subculture and cult" (2000, 32). By using the term cult, Fey is drawing on the sociological meaning, rather than the popular negative meaning. For sociologists of religion, a cult is a group that has moved away from dominant religion and tends to focus on individual needs rather than group needs. While a cult may have a charismatic leader, the concerns of the cult tend toward self well-being. This is significantly different from the popular understanding of a cult as an isolated group requiring people to leave their families and follow a presumed crazed leader in strange rituals that often lead to suicide pacts. This popular notion is based on the experience of a small group of religious movements that have been labelled as cults in the media, but does not represent the sociological understanding of a cult. As such, most scholars of cults or cult-like groups have shifted to the term "new religious movements." As Lorne Dawson, a prominent scholar in cults and new religious movements writes, cults "offer their believers some more direct kind of ecstatic or transfiguring experience than traditional modes of religious life" (1998, 31). They tend to be loosely organized and short-lived. Drawing on this notion of the cult, Fey sees Gothic culture as providing a specific understanding of the world, particularly in terms of "the cosmos as consisting of complementary forces that must be kept in balance" (2000, 46). Since most of society is focused on attaining happiness, Goths focus on the negative to bring the balance back. Fey sees very clear ethical codes within Gothic "cult/ure," such as the acceptance of all sexes, genders, sexualities, and races. Ritual takes the form of dance and costuming. And the "cult/ure" provides community. Thus Fey concludes that "As a cult/ure, Gothic, like many other current movements, points to the increasing difficulties of separating religion from other aspects of contemporary and popular culture, and of defining exactly what is meant by the term *religion*" (2000, 51).

It would seem here that what both Powell and Fey are pointing to is that Goth could very well be an implicit religion, much like Porter's study of fandom. Goth provides ceremony and ritual, in the context of Goth nightclubs, as well as providing community. It utilizes multiple religious imagery to motivate spiritual effects (such as Christian crosses or Pagan pentacles). Many of these images and symbols are also associated with the occult, and a number of participants in both Powell's and Fey's studies did claim affiliation with occult religious traditions in a more explicit way than the "parareligious" "cult/ure" of Goth on its own.

Contemporary Paganism and Modern Satanism

Contemporary **Paganism** (sometimes called Neo-Paganism) is an umbrella term referring to a number of different religious groups who find their primary source of inspiration in ancient European (pre-Christian) religious and ritual practices. For some Pagans, there is a focus on recreating specific religious traditions, such as ancient Celtic, Greek, Norse, etc., for a modern context. So, for example, the Asatru (sometimes called Heathens) worship the Norse gods and try to follow the seasonal agricultural calendar in similar ways as the ancient Norse/Vikings did through festivals and rituals.

Other groups are more eclectic in their constructions, drawing from a number of different traditions and interpretations of ancient religions. In this category, groups such as Wicca developed through the combinations of Western magical traditions and predominantly British folk cultures. For Wiccans, ritual takes the form of a magical circle in which members draw on their own energies to combine their wills for the purpose of making some sort of change in the world. The ritual cycle is based on both the solar cycles, with solstices and equinoxes as high holidays, as well as the lunar cycle, with full and new moons as regular ritual days. Wiccans have an initiatory system, and thus can be seen as a secret society. Those who are initiated are given the secrets of the group and knowledge of how magic works. As one progresses in the magical practice, one achieves higher degrees (a system borrowed from Freemasonry)

As mentioned in Chapter 3, the occult is characterized by things hidden or concealed, often with an association of ancient and archaic traditions. Christopher Partridge argues that the occult is increasingly popular in Western cultures as evidenced by its manifestations in movements as diverse as contemporary Paganism, the New Age movement, alternative health movements, interest in vampires, witches and zombies in popular culture, and alien invasion or secret society conspiracy theories. Many Goths have a fascination with vampires and some go so far as to develop vampire spiritualities and rituals (see Chapter 3 for more on vampire religion today). Fey's study also shows an interest in Eastern spiritualities such as Buddhism and Taoism. Some in the study were drawn to aspects of Scientology. Contemporary Paganism seems to be a tradition many Goths find appealing, as was noted by Powell, Fey, and Berger and Ezzy. Though there are a number of very different kinds of Paganisms, Goths tend toward focusing on a revaluing of the dark elements of life: life, death, and rebirth as a natural system; as well as the magical rituals found particularly in **Wicca**. Other Goths would associate themselves with modern **Satanism**. However, this Satanism is something very different than the perception of Satanism represented in the mainstream or Christian media. Satanism until becoming a high priest or high priestess and then is eligible to break off from the original coven to start a new one. Covens (ritual meeting groups) are typically small, though multiple covens may come together for ritual at the high holidays. Wiccans are duotheistic; they believe in two deities, the Goddess and the God. These two represent the balance of the feminine and masculine necessary for fertility.

Some Pagans do not affiliate themselves with a particular group, such as Wiccans or Asatru, but rather simply find their spiritual fulfillment in nature. For them, nature is ultimate and may or may not be associated with deities from various world mythologies. Considerable variety exists amongst contemporary Pagans, though most would consider themselves more nature-based in their spirituality than other world religions.

Modern Satanism is not a form of Paganism. Nor is Paganism a form of Satanism. Pagans typically do not believe in Satan and see him as a god of evil within Christianity. Most modern Satanists also do not typically believe in Satan as Christians do. Rather they see Satan as a metaphor for breaking out of the bonds of rules and regulations placed upon one by a larger (religious) authority. The Church of Satan, founded by Anton LeVey (1930–1997), who wrote *The Satanic Bible* (1969), was specifically designed as an opposition to mainstream Christianity in America. Satan, in this organization, is not understood to be an actual person, but a metaphoric figure through which Satanists can realize their own self-desires; he represents the attributes Satanists want to achieve (indulgence, vengeance, animalism, etc.).

in this context does not involve the worship of a creature of evil named Satan. Rather it involves a glorification of the individual and a philosophy of radical self-determination. Each of these various traditions are elements of the occulture that Partridge sees as blossoming in current Western culture.

Drawing on subcultural theory, then, the Goth subculture can be seen as a resistance to the hegemonic values of middle-class Western culture, including consumerism and optimism. While Goth does not seem to be motivated by a primarily working-class group, its antipathy towards the middle-class does fall loosely within the same concerns as Hebdige promotes. Its movement away from dominant religious forms into both an implicit religious sensibility alongside individuals' involvement in various occulture traditions and practices also shows the desire to resist mainstream society. That Goth has been perceived as a threat by the mainstream shows the power of style, whether of clothing, music, or occult imagery, to denaturalize hegemonic values. One could also argue that the co-option of Goth style into mainstream interests with Gothic themes (such as vampires in such acclaimed TV shows as *True Blood* and books such as the *Twilight* series) involves the commodification of Goth in order to render its power to disrupt the status quo null.

Post-subcultural Theory Applied: Burning Man Festival

Burning Man is a festival that takes place during the September long weekend and the week leading up to it each year on the Black Rock playa in the Nevada desert. It began as a casual gathering on a San Francisco beach during the 1986 summer solstice when Larry Harvey and Jerry James decided to burn a wooden effigy. As the annual event grew, it eventually moved out to the desert. It now draws over 48,000 participants creating a temporary Black Rock City each year. The "Man" that is burned has also grown in size and the festivities surrounding the burn have increased to include multiple art installations (many of which are also burned), performative art, dance parties, and other participatory events. The central aspects of the festival are participation, creativity, and non-commercialism, celebrating an alternative life to what "Burners" call the default life. Buying and selling is prohibited in Black Rock City, though some forms of bartering do occur. All participants must bring in everything they need for the week (including immense amounts of water for the hot, dry environment) and remove everything they brought in. There is a clear culture of "No Spectators" at Burning Man. Art installations are largely participatory as are other events. The space becomes a hub of creativity, with people dressing in shiny, exotic costumes, and acting in ways freed from regular social inhibitions.

Lee Gilmore and Burning Man Spirituality

Burning Man is not a religious festival; at least, it is not affiliated with any religious organization and the majority of participants are not affiliated with religious organizations or understand the event to be religious. However, in Lee Gilmore's 2010 book, *Theater in a Crowded Fire: Ritual and Spirituality at Burning Man*, many participants, including organizers, indicated that there was something deeply *spiritual* about Burning Man. As we noted in Chapter 2, spirituality is often popularly associated with a more individual kind of spiritual development while religion is associated with organized and dogmatic traditions. Many of Gilmore's interviewees held this same view and considered themselves to be spiritual, but not religious. As such, Burning Man fits into a larger social movement "in which creative expressions of spirituality and alternative conceptualizations of religions are favored, thereby destabilizing and reinventing normative cultural assumptions about what constitutes 'religion'" (Gilmore 2010, 2). "Religion" for many Burners is perceived as negative and part of the default world from which they choose to escape. Escaping this default world, however, involves a cleansing of the spirit and a creation of spiritual community, which for some extends beyond the week-long festival.

Many Burners understand spirituality in a way that could be labelled as post-modern. Gilmore writes,

> Spirituality as performed in this context is fundamentally *experiential* (based on the primacy of personal experience and personal authority), *reflexive* (inspiring reflection on self, self/other, and self/culture), and *heterodoxic* (constituted by multiply layered, fluid, and noncentralized constructions of meanings) (2010, 57).

There is no one way to be spiritual at Burning Man. For some, their spiritual experience may be tied to specific artistic sites. For others, it may be the interaction with fellow Burners. There is no one truth of spiritual experience here. As such, this performance of spirituality points to Burning Man as being a post-subculture rather than a strictly defined subculture. There is considerable multiplicity of identities allowable within the festival and for the Burner: not only is spirituality itself experiential, reflexive, and heterodoxic, so is Burning Man. In fact, a number of Gilmore's interviewees denied there was any spirituality in Burning Man, while others (a minority) saw Burning Man as renewing their commitment to organized religion. A whole range of experiences are evident within Burning Man. As Gilmore concludes, "Burners desire transformative, direct, and visceral encounters that are inherently diverse and disputable as the event remains at core 'whatever you want it to be'" (154–5).

Steven T. Jones and Counterculture

In making Burning Man "whatever you want it to be," a variety of cultural styles have emerged as prominent in the festival. Fire arts are highlighted (from sculpture with fire elements to fire performances). Each year there is a Temple created for more soulful contemplation (as well as art temples/shrines with often parodic and blasphemous purposes). An increasingly popular element of Burning Man, since the late 90s, is the expansion of the dance parties, largely focused on techno-rave-style music. To study Burning Man, one clearly needs to move out of a strictly "sub-cultural" studies mode to embrace the postmodern approach of post-subcultural studies. Steven T. Jones, a participant in Burning Man and San Francisco journalist, has done this, in a non-academic way, in his book *The Tribes of Burning Man: How an Experimental City in the Desert is Shaping the New American Counterculture* (2011). As his title indicates, Jones, much like St John in his study of technotribes, sees Burning Man as a kind of carnival of protest, incorporating both the "orgiasm" (as discussed by Maffesoli) and the political activism. He also uses the term counterculture, presumably to draw parallels with the counterculture of the 1960s hippie and civil rights movements that made significant political and social changes to American society. In this sense, a counterculture could be seen to be a set of post-subcultures that have political and social success in promoting their particular ideologies and practices.

Burners Without Borders

To show the political side of Burning Man, Jones points to Burners' response to Hurricane Katrina. Hurricane Katrina struck Louisiana and Mississippi during the 2005 Burning Man festival. Not only did Burners collect money and supplies to send to the devastated area, a group of Burners went to help with the clean-up and stayed for over eight months. They eventually named themselves Burners without Borders (BwB) and have continued to this day to work on community projects where cultural and social systems have failed. In 2012, BwB were involved in community development in Kenya, supplying sleeping bags to homeless youth in Santa Fe, New Mexico, and an environmental awareness campaign through arts and culture in Beijing, China, to name a few projects. The point of BwB is to bring the ethos and cultural values of Burning Man (i.e., participation, creativity, non-commercialism) out into the default world to create alternatives. BwB also brings the party. In Louisianna and Mississippi, for example, BwB participants stayed together in a Burning Man-like camp. They worked hard in the day and danced hard at night. Integral to this non-profit movement is the incorporation of both pleasure and politics, leading some, such as Jones, to name Burning Man and its Burners as a counterculture with significantly more political power and motivation than subcultures such as Goth may hold.

Summary

Subcultures are challenges to the dominant mainstream culture. They are statements of dissatisfaction. In providing alternatives to the mainstream, they show the constructed nature of the mainstream, thus, by their very nature, resist hegemonic consensus. As such, subcultural theorists such as Dick Hebdige see subcultures as political, if only obliquely so. However, in an increasingly postmodern world, the distinctions between mainstream and subculture become blurry and individual identities become fragmented. No longer is there one dominant mainstream and discrete subcultures; rather, there are multiple cultural formations that both compete and interact. In this context, many scholars are moving to the language of post-subcultures with its embedded fluidity and diversity. Festivals such as Burning Man show the way multiple styles can come together in one context. That said, these multiple styles of post-subcultures are still positing a resistance to a perceived dominant culture. The Burners call it the default world. Whether the default world can actually be characterized as a universal culture or not, Burners define themselves in opposition to it. They also take a more specifically political stance against the values of the default world, integrating their pleasure and politics in a "carnival of protest" and transferring the experience of Burning Man into external contexts, such as the community service work of Burners without Borders. Post-subcultural theorists argue that these kinds of movements or groups go beyond a simple resistance of hegemonic consensus to creatively construct multiple styles and cultures. Sometimes these are deliberately political as in Burners without Borders. Others are more focused on the pleasure aspect. But all of them reject clear definitions of identity and group coherence. Interaction between post-subcultures is fluid and constantly in flux. In both these examples we see what could be called implicit religion: activity that looks like religion and provides spiritual nourishment for people, even though the activities seem secular and have nothing to do with organized, traditional religion.

Review Questions

1. What does it mean to call Hebdige's study of subcultures semiotic?
2. How, according to Hebdige, do subcultures challenge the hegemonic order?
3. What might subcultural capital look like to a Goth?
4. What is postmodernism?
5. What does the concept of neo-tribalism contribute to post-subcultural theory?
6. What is implicit religion?
7. How does implicit religion relate to the study of subcultures and post-subcultures?
8. What elements of mainstream middle-class culture do Goths resist?
9. How is Goth parareligious and an example of cult/ure?
10. How is spirituality understood by Burners?
11. What is the post-subcultural significance of Burners without Borders?

Useful Resources

Print

Bailey, Edward. 2012. "'Implicit Religion?': What Might That Be?" *Implicit Religion*. 15(2). 195–207.

Fey, Julia Winden. 2000. "Spirituality Bites: Xers and the Gothic Cult/ure." In *GenX Religion*. Eds., Richard W. Flory and Donald E. Miller. New York: Routledge. 31–53.

Gilmore, Lee. 2010. *Theater in a Crowded Fire: Ritual and Spirituality at Burning Man*. University of California Press. Includes DVD.

Hebdige, Dick. 1979. *Subculture: The Meaning of Style*. New York: Methuan & Co. Ltd.

Jones, Steven T. 2011. *The Tribes of Burning Man: How an Experimental City in the Desert is Shaping the New American Counterculture*. Consortium of Collective Consciousness.

Muggleton, David. 2006. *Inside Subculture: The Postmodern Meaning of Style*. Oxford: Berg.

Muggleton, David and Rupert Weinzierl, eds. 2003. *The Post-subcultures Reader*. Oxford: Berg.

Powell, Anna. 2007. "God's Own Medicine: Religion and Parareligion in U.K. Goth Culture." In *Goth: Undead Subculture*. Eds., Lauren M. E. Goodlad and Michael Bibby. Durahm NC: Duke University Press.

Williams, J. Patrick. 2011. *Subcultural Theory: Traditions and Concepts*. Cambridge: Polity.

Online

Burning Man, www.burningman.com/

Burners without Borders, www.burnerswithoutborders.org/

Church of Satan, www.churchofsatan.com/home.html

Goth.Net, www.goth.net/goth.html

9

Digital Media and Hyper-real Religion

OBJECTIVES

This chapter will help you develop an understanding of

- the shifts from print to electronic to digital media
- the postmodern development of the hyper-real
- practices of Christianity through digital media and in virtual reality
- the development of hyper-real religion in online role-playing games

Tarma walks through the doors of the House of Prayer Church on a quiet Wednesday morning. She turns right and enters the prayer room. It is almost empty; only one other person is there at this time. Soft Christian music is playing, drawing attention to the love of Jesus. Tarma heads for the prayer bench and kneels, hands together in prayer position. She stays that way for a few minutes and then stands up and goes on her way to the rest of her day. Tarma is an avatar in the online virtual world, *Second Life*.

Another Tarma is starting her day with a trek through the virtual world of Azeroth with a selection of allies. As they search for various magical items necessary for their quest, they are attacked by a horde of orcs. Tarma, the shaman in the group, uses her spiritual power to heal her companions so they can continue fighting, eventually overcoming the attacking group. This Tarma is an avatar in *World of Warcraft*.

Is either Tarma real? Does the *Second Life* Tarma actually pray? If so, to whom? Does the *World of Warcraft* Tarma actually have spiritual powers? If so, where do they come from? These two scenarios reflect some of the challenges of thinking about religion within the context of digital media. This chapter explores those challenges by looking to the field of media studies and the implications digital media have on communication and meaning-making in the twenty-first century. We will discuss the way digital media affects the practice of both traditional religions, such as Christianity, as well as hyper-real religions, such as that created for the role-playing game *World of Warcraft*.

Media Studies

Marshall McLuhan

Marshall McLuhan (1911–1980) is one of the most well-known and widely quoted **media studies** scholars. Media studies involves the study of communication technologies as well as the cultural uses of those technologies. Writing in the mid- to late-twentieth century, McLuhan coined the phrases "the medium is the message" and "the global village." For McLuhan the proper objective of media studies was not the content of media, but the technology itself and how it shapes human interactions. He wrote, in 1964, that "the 'message' of any medium or technology is the change of scale or pace or pattern that it introduces into human affairs" (8). Regardless of what, say, the television projects, the form and function of television alter how people understand their world and thus, how they receive or interpret the content projected. Some media require high participation; others require minimal participation. McLuhan labelled these hot (low participation) and cold (high participation) media. **Hot media** give us lots of data, so we can sit passively and receive it. **Cold media** give us minimal data, so we need to fill in the blanks and work harder to understand. Movies, for McLuhan, are hot media. Comics, on the other hand, with their low detail drawing, are cold media. The effect these media have on the audience is significantly different. If we have to participate in the meaning-making, as in cold media, we are less likely to passively absorb content.

Though he was writing prior to the development of the World Wide Web, McLuhan anticipated a computer-based media system which would bring the world together in a "global village." He saw this form of electronic media, which would be interactive and thus cold media, as shifting society away from the individualism of print media. Engagement with this kind of media would change the way we view the world, each other, and ourselves, regardless of the content passed through that media. For McLuhan, this was an interesting possibility that he posited with some optimism. Other media studies scholars have not been quite so positively oriented towards electronic and digital media.

Neil Postman

Neil Postman (1931–2003), writing a bit later in the 1980s, took McLuhan's formulation of the medium is the message and altered it slightly to posit the medium as the *metaphor*. Postman, unlike McLuhan, still saw a content-based message as significant for media studies, but recognized, like McLuhan, that the content possible would be shaped by the medium. He saw media as like languages, which "classify the world for us, sequence it, frame it, enlarge it, color it, argue a case for what the world is like" (1985, 10). Postman focused his study on television, suggesting that by the 1980s society took television for granted. We were only concerned with questions about the content of television without asking any questions about the medium itself and what kinds of content it allowed.

The technology of television, argued Postman, flows from the earlier technologies of communication developed in the late nineteenth century. Primary in these was the invention of telegraphy. The telegraph, though obsolete today, changed the way we think about information and thus changed the kind of information thought of as important. Prior to telegraphy, we were limited by time and space. We could learn of things in our own locale relatively quickly, but anything further away we only knew about after days or weeks of courier travel. With the telegraph, however, we could learn about things happening across the globe within the day. Postman argues that this "gave a form of legitimacy to the idea of context-free information" (1985, 65). We could know what was happening to people we had no connection to, and events that did not affect us in any way. What was considered important information was now based on novelty and curiosity rather than how much it affected personal or local situations. Additionally, the telegraph did not allow for prolonged conversation or in-depth analyses of events. As Postman writes, telegraphy's "language was the language of headlines—sensational, fragmented, impersonal" (1985, 70). The invention of the telegraph was the first step toward the limited attention span of Western audiences. What was a necessity of the technology became a way of thinking. Information must be concise, yet catch our attention amidst the plethora of options.

For Postman this move to the electronic media, beginning with telegraphy and culminating in television (in the 1980s), was a sign of intellectual decline from the era of print media. Unlike McLuhan, Postman was not optimistic about the future of electronic media to bring the world into closer communication to create a global village. He saw the development of television as a metaphor, a way of framing the world, which limited any public discourse to entertainment and sound-bites. In fact, the title of his influential book, *Amusing Ourselves to Death* (1985) speaks volumes about Postman's position.

Digital Media

Both McLuhan and Postman were writing during the heyday of television and observing the changes from primarily print-based media to electronic-based media. Electronic media, however, have not remained the same and in the late twentieth and early twenty-first centuries the move to digital media has resulted in significant changes to the way most people engage with their world. These changes do not necessarily make McLuhan's and Postman's analyses obsolete, but they do suggest further avenues of analysis.

Andrea L. Press and Bruce A. Williams: Digital Options and Interactions

Andrea L. Press and Bruce A. Williams argue in their book *The New Media Environment: An Introduction* (2010) that "a change is now occurring that is every bit as profound as the change from typography to television" (16). This change involves both the proliferation of options within digital media, and also the way people interact through digital media. In the mid-twentieth century when television was the epitome of entertainment and informational media, the media environment was largely controlled by a small number of corporations or networks. There were the big networks: ABC, NBC, and CBS. There were also local stations that were fairly amateurish in their production and reached a limited audience. In the twenty-first century, however, that is no longer the case. Specialty cable stations have sprung up to offer alternatives to the main networks who have typically tried to appeal to the masses. The masses, it seems, are no longer interested in one dominant form of entertainment or news media perspective. We want unique offerings. For those who love sports, there are sports networks. For those who love sci-fi, there are sci-fi networks. For those who love cooking, there are cooking networks. Our television options have increased immensely.

Not only do we have a proliferation of television offerings, but with the development and popularization of the Internet and other digital technologies like smart phones, we no longer need to rely on the television for either entertainment or information. We can login to news websites; we can sign up for informational tweets; we can download an app that tells us the weather; we can play interactive games with people across the globe. Our options are vast. With this increase in media options we are increasingly able to customize our interactions according to our own peculiar desires.

The way we engage with each other through these digital media has also shifted away from a separation between producer and consumer. In television, the shows are produced, offered to us for consumption, and we choose whether to consume or not consume. Interaction is limited to response to the production, but that response rarely actually affects the production. Digital media, particularly via the Internet, allows for much greater interaction in a way that, as Press and Williams write, "is eroding the distinction between producers and consumers of media and even between elites and the broader society" (2010, 20). Now, anyone can post their opinions in a blog. We can connect instantly via Facebook, Twitter, texting, and email. These methods of interaction have had profound influence on the ways ordinary people have been able to interact and make changes in their world. Furthermore, anyone can post a video of themselves (or other people/events) on YouTube, resulting in a de-commodification of entertainment and art forms, in some cases. We can participate in fan websites and contribute fan fiction to add to, or alter, fictional worlds. We can play games with thousands of other people, and meet, date, and get married in virtual spaces like *Second Life*.

Henry Jenkins: Convergence and Collective Intelligence

Media studies scholar Henry Jenkins calls this "participatory culture" and "convergence culture." He suggests that "Rather than talking about media producers and consumers as occupying separate roles, we might now see them as participants who interact with each other according to a new set of rules that none of us fully understands" (2006, 3). There is something exciting, according to Jenkins, to this new interaction. Even though we don't necessarily know the rules, we—as both "consumers" and "producers"—can work together to make new ways of both shaping media, and using media to shape our world. **Convergence**, for Jenkins, means that media functions converge in single technologies whereby a mobile device is a phone, camera, web-browser, instant messenger, etc. Convergence also means that we use multiple technologies for the same thing, such as listening to music on ipods, smart phones, computers, CD or MP3 players, etc. Additionally, convergence means we interact more fully with one another as consumers and producers, creating a collective intelligence. Jenkins writes,

> Each of us constructs our own personal mythology from bits and fragments of information extracted from the media flow and transformed into resources through which we make sense of our everyday lives. Because there is more information on any given topic than anyone can store in their head, there is an added incentive for us to talk among ourselves about the media we consume. [. . .] None of us can know everything; each of us knows something; and we can put the pieces together if we pool our resources and combine our skills (2006, 4).

This idea of convergence culture as creating collective intelligence seems to echo McLuhan's optimism for the future of a truly global village.

If the medium is the message, as McLuhan argues, or the medium is the metaphor, as Postman argues, how do the new digital media affect our public discourse, or change our social patterns? In many ways, McLuhan was correct in foreseeing a global village. The new digital media does allow for a closer interaction around the globe than we have ever had before. However, many have argued that the very nature of digital media—the profusion of options and the interactive qualities—increases the naturalization of individualism, meaning that we are more connected to each other, but only insofar as those connections personally benefit us. We have a decreased commitment to community (particularly local community) and an increased commitment to our own well-being. Rather than moving us away from the collective to an isolating individualism, Jenkins alternatively suggests a convergence: our uses of these new digital media allow for both an emphasis on the individual and the collective. This shift in social patterns, the way these digital media frame our interactions, has had some interesting consequences for religion.

Rachel Wagner and the Digitally Sacred?

Rachel Wagner argues that "rapid and incredible changes" are occurring in the way people practise their religion because of the new digital media. For her, "these experiences are raising profound questions about the nature of sacred space, about technology as a vehicle for sacred text, about who we are when we go online, about how religious ritual works, and about whether or not it is possible to gather for worship in online space" (2012, 1). One of the issues Wagner discusses in her book *Godwired: Religion, Ritual and Virtual Reality* is that of the way holy scripture is understood in the digital age. In the print age, the holy scriptures were physical books that were sacred and static. For example, as a young Mennonite girl, I was given a Bible. This Bible, while there were some differences based on translation practices, was static, as in I could not change it, I could only read it, think about it, and choose to believe or not believe in the importance of the words. It was sacred, as in I was expected to use it for religious purposes and keep it safe. I was not supposed to use it to prop up a wiggly table. However, with holy scriptures increasingly put in digital form, the way we can interact with them changes. To what extent is scripture still static when it is hyperlinked to other texts? As a girl I was not also given all the other ancient texts that were voted out of the Christian Bible. How does our interaction with the Bible (or other sacred texts) change when these other options are available online as easily as the sanctioned scriptures? If I download scripture onto my smart phone, does that make my phone sacred? Do I then need to keep it separate from my Marilyn Manson music?

Most importantly, the questions Wagner raises about this new digital access and interaction with sacred texts has to do with authority. We no longer need religious leaders to interpret texts for us; we can access multiple versions, interpretations, and critiques easily without ever needing to adopt, or in some cases even recognize, the orthodoxy of religious authorities. The increase of interactive media shapes our social patterns to privilege interactivity. We want to customize our religion for our own personal well-being as much as we want to customize our smart phones or game avatars. But we do that in conversations across the globe that create communities based on interaction rather than acceptance of authoritative stances.

Hyper-realism

Jean Baudrillard and Simulation

The move into the virtual worlds that digital media allow for brings us to questions about the nature of who we are on- and off-line, what is real, and what is the relationship between the real and the imaginary. Jean Baudrillard (1929–2007), in his 1981 text *Simulacra and Simulation*, argues that the late twentieth century, and presumably moving into the twenty-first century, is characterized by a fascination with **simulation** rather than reality. Baudrillard draws on the image of the **simulacra**, which in Plato's philosophy was a false copy of something else. Baudrillard however alters the meaning of the simulacra; for him, it is a copy of something that does not, or no longer, exists. Simulation, says Baudrillard, involves "feign[ing] to have what one doesn't have" (1994 [1981], 3). Simulation creates a model of something without an actual origin or reality. Baudriallard called these simulations, or simulacra, hyper-reality. So, for example, we see television shows as more real than our real lives and, in fact, try to copy the simulacra of sitcoms, dramas, and "reality" shows that are simulations without an actual referent. We become friends with digital characters—either in games or through chat rooms—with little or no tie to non-digital life. Actors not only play heroes, they become heroes, governors, or presidents.

Umberto Eco and the "Absolute Fake"

Umberto Eco similarly argues that Americans, in particular, are more interested in the **hyper-real**, what Eco calls the "Absolute Fake" (1983, 56), than the real. He is interested in the way Americans construct and consume museums, amusement parks, and zoos, where if something looks real it must be real regardless of whether if reflects something else. In other words, simulations, like Disney's Animal Kingdom, are perceived as real, even though they do not reflect any real physical nature outside of the Disney franchise. In discussing Disneyland, a model of this Absolute Fake, Eco argues, "Disneyland tells us that technology can give us more reality than nature can" (1983, 44). Baudrillard also discussed Disneyland, though he sees it less as the model of the Absolute Fake as much as the sign of the hyper-reality of the world around it. He writes,

> Disneyland is presented as imaginary in order to make us believe
> that the rest is real, whereas all of Los Angeles and the America that

surrounds it are no longer real, but belong to the hyperreal order and to the order of simulation. It is no longer a question of a false representation of reality (ideology) but of concealing the fact that the real is no longer real, and thus of saving the reality principle (1994 [1981], 12–13).

Disneyland, for Eco, is the hyper-real with no referent in reality. For Baudrillard, it is the sign that all of modern American life is hyper-real. We make up our world through simulation, but the simulation is not a reflection of something that actually exists. It is all make-believe. Our popular culture no longer reflects reality but shapes it. The simulation comes first, then our imitation of the simulation. There is no longer any reality prior to the simulacra.

Jediism

The origins of the new religious movement called Jediism comes from the *Star Wars* world created by George Lucas. The first of the films, *Star Wars: A New Hope*, episode IV, came out in 1977 and since then multiple films, books, comics, games, and merchandise have been created and consumed. The original trilogy in the *Star Wars* saga had definite religious themes around the notion of the Force and the Jedi who could use this Force. Immediately upon release of the film in 1977, discussion ensued in fan newsletters, general media, and even academic sources, about the religious mythology Lucas constructed. As technology developed, online *Star Wars* games developed, which allowed for an increased interaction between people worldwide in the role-playing of their favourite characters. As the Internet became more interactive, an increasing number of sites supplying teaching practices for becoming a Jedi developed. These involve largely, as Debbie McCormick writes, "a combination of moral and philosophical development through assigned readings [. . .], physical fitness through the practice of martial arts; and mental exercises designed to harness the power of *The Force*" (2012, 173). Beyond Internet activity, Jedi groups have encouraged off-line interaction as well. Ordination ceremonies have developed, as have birth, marriage, and death ceremonies. The *Temple of the Jedi Order* insists that Jediism is not solely a created religion from the *Star Wars* world. It claims that its philosophies are based on Eastern traditions such as Buddhism and Taoism. In 2005, the *Temple of the Jedi Order*, was the first Jedi church to be incorporated as a legal religious institution in Texas, USA. In 2009, Canada followed suit to legalize the Order of the Jedi as a recognized religious institution (McCormick 2012,178).

Adam Possamai and Postmodern Religion

While both Baudrillard and Eco are critical of the hyper-real, seeing it as a sign of social and cultural degeneration, others scholars suggest there is some legitimacy in the construction of the hyper-real that should be taken more seriously. For example, Adam Possamai suggests that this culture of hyper-reality has extended into the realm of religious ideas, practices, and associations to such an extent that scholars can no longer ignore these "hyper-real religions," as he calls them. In fact, most of the scholars Possamai gathers together in his *Handbook of Hyper-real Religions* (2012) not only take these religions seriously but see them as valid and interesting examples of postmodern religion. For Possami, "a hyper-real religion is a simulacrum of a religion created out of, or in symbiosis with, commodified popular culture which provides inspiration at a metaphorical level and/or is a source of beliefs for everyday life" (2012, 20). These are religions based on fictional worlds, such as Jediism, or ritual practices within spaces such as role-playing games, online or off. These hyper-real religions develop through the digital framework that decreases religious authority and increases personal interaction and creation of individualized worldviews. Thus, the digital media create different kinds of religions—religions that are based on interaction amongst various sources, including popular culture, developed in individualistic contexts to create what works best for one's personal well-being. They also are created in community. Drawing on Jenkins, we could also call these convergence religions.

The rest of this chapter explores two examples of this digital framing of religion. In the first case we look at the way digital media can mediate traditional religious ideas and practices by looking at the presence and practice of Christianity in virtual reality, especially the online site, *Second Life*. The second case explores more fully hyper-real religious practice through the role-playing game *World of Warcraft*.

Applying Media Studies: Virtual Christianity in Second Life

Phylis Johnson and Virtual Life

Both *Second Life* and *World of Warcraft* are Massive Multiplayer Online Role Playing Games (**MMORPGs**; see break-out box below). However, unlike *World of Warcraft*, many participants of *Second Life* do not view it as "just" a game. As Phylis Johnson points out in her study of *Second Life*, many view it as "a community of residents who work and play in this second space, which actually exists, but is accessed online through the computer" (2010, xii). *Second Life* is an online virtual space where paying members can build houses and businesses and interact with one another via their custom-designed **avatar** or visual representation of themselves. Non-paying members can also interact in *Second Life*, but cannot own property and build buildings. Unlike other MMORPGs, *Second Life* does not have a plot, or quest, or any goals one must achieve. It is a free-flowing environment where one can basically do whatever one might do off-line: work, play, buy, sell, walk in the park, visit museums, and, of course, worship, pray, meditate, and do other religious rituals. The difference from off-line life is that one can be whomever one wants to be (including animals) and one can fly. People from across the globe are interacting in *Second Life*. Johnson suggests that *Second Life* might, in fact, be "that idealistic global village [envisioned by McLuhan], if we are particularly discussing the notion of how mediated communication connects us throughout the world, initially as avatars, encouraging us to learn about one another in real spaces" (2010, 19).

Sher Salmson and a Virtual Church

Johnson explores a number of social aspects of *Second Life*, including the practice of religion. One of the "organizations" she explores is that of Hope Springs Eternal, an **evangelical** Christian place that hosts Christian dance parties and prayer meetings, developed by Sher Salmson, the avatar of a real-life Christian counsellor. Many Second Lifers come to her to talk about both real and in-world (that is, in the *Second Life* world) problems, from marriage to finances to spiritual questions. Salmson, and a group of helpers, try to respond with love and a lack of judgment, from a Christian perspective. Johnson sees Hope Springs Eternal as an open, welcoming space: "Biblically, it could be easily argued this fellowship is how communing through God was intended—through loving one another" (2010, 250). Salmson herself thought *Second Life* was just a game when she first encountered it. But she then realized that there were real people behind the avatars—real people with real needs. "What I found is there are a lot of people who had lost hope. Not just *Second Life*, but in real life. In fact, some people had lost hope in real life and had come to *Second Life* seeking. And again these people come seeking one thing, but many times God finds them right here in *Second Life*" (Salmson quoted in Johnson 2010, 251–252). Salmson then decided that God had called her to minister to these people in *Second Life*.

Evangelical Christians have a history of using electronic media to share their message with the larger world. They began with radio and progressed to television early in the lives of these technologies. They are well known for the creation of **televangelism** as a method of witnessing and sharing their worldview in a fully mediatized way. The move into digital media has been embraced by most evangelical Christians as well, with multiple websites, mega-churches with online ministries, and customized apps for religious education and practice (see Chapter 3 for more on evangelical Christians).

For Salmson, the virtual reality environment is a real environment where she interacts with real people. These real people need God, and thus she is called to share God with them, even online. She believes that the work she does in *Second Life* is as real a ministry as the work done off-line, even if she never physically encounters the people she is counselling and praying with. And the prayers in *Second Life* are true prayers, received by God.

It might not be so hard to understand how Christians like Salmson can create Christian communities and conduct prayer meetings online. But, in *Second Life*, some people go beyond their real-life commitments to experiment with other realities and relationships. Johnson also draws attention to a discussion in a Christian group in *Second Life* that questioned some of these practices, particularly the practice of getting married in *Second Life*. *Second Life* allows you to "partner" with someone, meaning living in the same place. For many in *Second Life* this is the equivalent of marriage. Others even go through wedding ceremonies to mark this. At times, these are ceremonies involving people who are already married in real life. However, that is not always the case. Some people meet, date, and marry completely through *Second Life*, never having met in the real world. Are these marriages real? For Christians, does the ritual of marriage hold? Is it sanctified if it is happening solely in the virtual world? For some Second Lifers it is; for others, this is taking the reality of *Second Life* too far. One participant in the conversation asked the question "Is it right to partner in SL [*Second Life*] when you are not married in RL [real life]?" While it seemed that most of the Christian participants were a bit hesitant to accept solely *Second Life* marriage, many did see *Second Life* as a valid place to meet and date, providing you actually then met in real life. Others were opposed to even dating online. Many argued that *Second Life* is not a game, and thus what you do in *Second Life* must follow "the Lord's will" (quoted in Johnson 2010, 259–61).

Johnson ultimately concludes that traditional religions, such as Christianity, exist in *Second Life* to mirror, or replicate, off-line services and beliefs. Christians involved in these groups, for the most part, are less interested in the role-playing potential of an environment like *Second Life*—as in being someone different than they are off-line—and more interested in the networking and community-building aspects. In this case, then, digital media become one more way of building the church without necessarily radically changing it.

That said, the question still remains, to what extent is the virtual world as real a place for religious practice and communion as the physical world? Wagner continually asks this question in *Godwired*. She is particularly interested in the idea of virtual prayer. If one is living in a virtual reality like *Second Life*, it seems that the prayer one might participate in would simply be another aspect of the virtual life. But what if one only prays virtually? Or, what might the relationship be between God and virtual reality? Wagner explores the development of prayer apps for smart phones with these questions in mind. Some prayer apps are wall spaces where one can publically display one's prayers. Are these prayers displayed simply to share prayer concerns with others? If that's the case, what about prayer apps that are not digital wall spaces? Wagner discusses the app "Pray." For this app, you simply type in your prayer and send it. It doesn't go to a public space or anywhere recorded at all. The point is to send a prayer. But send it where? Wagner writes,

> Such programming suggests that increasingly we *do* view digital space as identified in some ways with sacred heavenly space, and we see messages sent via virtual reality as having the ability to be delivered to God via that space. In fact, such prayers may arguably have *more* potency, having been sent through the most reliable message-delivery system available for most people today (2012, 25–26).

Sending prayers via virtual reality may suggest that a collective view of God, or the sacred, has shifted. If God is accessible via virtual reality and digital media, does that mean God is *in* virtual reality and digital media? Is God virtual? In Wagner's example it seems as if God is hyper-real. In this case, prayer itself could become a simulation of something that no longer exists in any reality beyond the virtual. Praying with or through or in digital media is more real than any other prayer. This suggests that digital media are not solely new locations for interaction, but ultimately change the way we understand that interaction. It is only real when hyper-real.

Applying Media Studies: Hyper-real Religion in World of Warcraft

World of Warcraft, like other MMORPGs, follows a model of role-playing games that are based on a fantasy world, complete with magical powers and created mythologies. As such it is a very good example of what Possamai calls "hyper-real religion." Participation in the game, then, allows gamers to choose to engage in ritual and mythology that is deliberately created. These creations may draw from pre-modern traditions, ancient mythologies, and bygone ritual practices, but they are "cut and pasted" into new conglomerations of worldviews and game goals.

MMORPGs

Massive Multiplayer Online Role-Playing Games (**MMORPG**) have become very popular in the twenty-first century. They developed from a tradition of role-playing games that originated in the 1970s with the creation of the *Dungeons and Dragons* games. *Dungeons and Dragons* was first released by Tactical Studies Rules in 1974 and is a pen-and-paper role-playing game based on the world created by Tolkien in *The Hobbit* and *The Lord of the Rings* trilogy. In *Dungeons and Dragons*, players select a race or species for their character. This determines strengths and weakness according to the set-out rules. Players also select a class, such as fighter or mage. Once characters are developed, players go through various quests and adventures to work through a specific storyline determined by either a Dungeon Master (one of the players) or by a set scenario created by the *Dungeons and Dragons* game makers. This system of creating a character based on race/species and class/skill has become central to most role-playing games including the MMORPGs.

In 1978 the first computer-based role-playing games developed. These were called Multi User Dungeons (MUDs) and were similar to *Dungeons and Dragons* but based in online communication. They were text-based, rather than the current graphic-based games. The first graphic-based computer role-playing games were single-player games. Many of these games moved to a real-time environment, rather than the turn-taking environment of the MUDs and *Dungeons and Dragons*. Soon these games were also offered as multiplayer, but in a local network context, so you could play with your friends.

The first generation of MMORPGs was developed in the 1990s. In 1996, 3DO release Meridian 59, considered the first MMORPG. This game, with its global server, allowed for thousands of players to play at once. It also offered a persistent world—a world that continued regardless of whether you were logged in or not—where players could play at any time and come and go as they pleased.

The second generation of MMORPGs was developed in the early twenty-first century characterized by improved graphics and interface. They tend to be more customizable and include the possibilities of player-crafted items. The most popular of these is *World of Warcraft*, which in 2010 exceeded 12 million players worldwide (Achterbosch et al 2008; Blizzard Entertainment 2010).

Stef Aupers and Hyper-real Religion

In an interview study of players of *World of Warcraft*, Stef Aupers discovered that the majority of players he talked with named themselves atheists and specifically rejected traditional religions. They were also, largely, disenchanted with modern life:

"the 'emptiness' of politics, the problem of unchecked modern capitalism, relentless consumption and the unforeseen consequences of science and technology" (2012, 236). Interestingly, though, these same self-proclaimed atheists held a fairly romantic view of pre-modern life, including pre-modern belief in magic. As Aupers writes, "gamers cannot believe in the supernatural but, argue, very much like FBI agent Fox Mulder in the popular television series the *X-Files* that they '*want to believe*'" (2012, 237). What does this mean for the practice of religion in *World of Warcraft*? Is it just a game or does it have any implication for real life?

Aupers wants to push us to think of the practice of magical religions in games like *World of Warcraft* as something more than just superficial play. He argues that in *experiencing* the magical world, these players are experiencing something real for them, not just entertainment. Role-playing, for him, is an important ritual process that may not lead to real-life conversion to a specific religious tradition, but does go beyond simple play. Make-believe here, like in other religions discussed in the *Handbook of Hyper-real Religion* (2012), can have powerful transformative powers. Aupers suggests that "in the process of role-playing, fiction becomes real, make-belief instigates belief and play is gradually experienced as serious magic" (2012, 239).

Aupers bases his conclusions on the accounts of players who indicate that they strongly identify with their avatars, even if their avatars are invented characters that do not resemble them off-line. Players typically indicate that the avatar becomes a part of them, tied to them, even a piece of their "soul." If this is the case, what the avatar experiences is also closely tied to the player's real life person and thus, Aupers concludes, the magical world the avatar is embedded in becomes a part of the overall worldview of the real-life players. *World of Warcraft* provides an immersion into a virtual magical world, but that immersion does not honour boundaries between virtual and real life. Role-playing transgresses these boundaries.

If we return to Christopher Partridge's theory about occulture in Western society from Chapter 3, we can see that games such as *World of Warcraft* make the occult—that is, the magical realms, mythologies of multiple deities from ancient periods, other-worldly creatures such as ghosts, fairies, vampires, etc., and divination rituals—increasingly popular and familiar. It is not that all of the millions of *World of Warcraft* players are going out to become Pagans or practise other occult traditions, but they are engaged, on some level, with occult religious worldviews that shapes the way they can understand these worldviews off-line. That the versions of occulture they encounter in *World of Warcraft* are constructs drawn from fantasy fiction and percolated through the minds of game developers does not decrease their validity as religious worldviews. These are hyper-real religions, with little to no referent in the non-virtual world, but they provide real experiences for gamers.

Lauren Bernauer and Christian Gaming

Interestingly this perspective is shared by some Christian gamers and opponents of gaming. Lauren Bernauer looks at Christian gaming and participation in mainstream gaming. She suggests that for many Christians, particularly evangelical Christians, playing games such as *World of Warcraft* does bring potential harm. She writes, "given the nature of hyper-reality within the gaming genre, playing games that have strong occultic overtones is considered dangerous because it is not truly a fantasy, non-real, world in which the player's actions are taking place. The players are engaging with 'evil' supernatural forces and in some games actually performing sorcery or devotion to Pagan deities" (2012, 350). Some Christians get around this by creating guilds within the group that are Christian focused, so as to help each other maintain a Christian playing model. Bernauer notes that some within these Christian guilds push for an evangelical presence in *World of Warcraft*. One particular member she discusses "demonstrates how the seemingly non-real world can impact faith. [. . .] By witnessing to other gamers in the virtual reality of their chosen game, they are doing their work as Christians, and getting the Word out to non-believers" (2012, 353).

Another option for Christians is to opt for specifically Christian games. However, though there have been Christian-themed games from the 1970s, they have not had the same kind of success as mainstream games, largely because the Christian companies do not have the same fund base as the mainstream companies. Christian games started as console games designed (without licence) for the Nintendo Entertainment System. As Nintendo continually changed its console system, it became less feasible for Christian games to be made for these systems. Christian games then moved to computer-based games. The point of these games was to provide biblically based stories and significantly less violence. Most of the Christian games created were based closely on mainstream games such as *The Legend of Zelda* and *Mario Brothers*. These have remained single-player computer games. Christians interested in MMORPGs have had little other option than playing the mainstream games.

Summary

Digital media, with its increased opportunities and more interactive relationships between users, can have some profound effects on the practice of religion. While not everyone engages in religion online or through digital media, many do, and in this engagement people are increasingly forming their own understandings of religion. For some, this new understanding has to do with the location and way of communicating with the divine. Virtual reality becomes a new way of thinking about the sacred, otherworldly home of God or the gods. For others, the digital interactions available allow for a mashing of various traditions—ancient, traditional, new, and completely fictional—to develop unique religious worlds to engage with. At times these religious worlds remain solely accessible and valid in virtual space, such as the religion and spirituality of *World of Warcraft* (for most players). At other times, this hyper-real religion can take on a life outside the digital, fictional world, such as the development of Jediism, the influence of the fantasy genre on the development of modern occult practices like contemporary Paganism, and the justifying of game playing by evangelical Christians as a real-life mission.

Thinking about how the media allow certain kinds of frameworks of ideas and information helps us to see how we both are shaped by and shape our cultural worlds, as well as the various ways we communicate with one another. If the medium is the message, we are in a time of both close interaction and fragmented identity. If the medium is the metaphor, we are able to take that fragmentation and reshape our own individual identities, in communication with others, to create new selves. In either case, the real is no longer presumed to be something other than the virtual. Or perhaps it is better phrased as the virtual is as real as anything else might be.

Review Questions

1. What are the differences between McLuhan's and Postman's approaches to media studies?
2. How have digital media caused a change in the relationship between producer and consumer?
3. What, according to Jenkins, is convergence culture?
4. What questions can be raised about digital media and the practice of religion?
5. What is hyper-real religion? Give some examples.
6. In what ways do some Christians use virtual reality, like *Second Life*, for real ministry?
7. What is the significance of the app "Pray" for Wagner's discussion of religion?
8. Are players of *World of Warcraft* engaging in actual religion? What would Aupers say?
9. What is the main roadblock to the creation of good Christian MMORPGs?

Useful Resources

Print

Aupers, Stef. 2012. "'An Infinity of Experiences.' Hyper-Real Paganism and Real Enchantment in *World of Warcraft*." In *Handbook of Hyper-real Religions*. Ed., Adam Possamai. Leiden: Brill. 225–45.

Baudrillard, Jean. 1994 [1981] *Simulacra and Simulation*. Trans. Sheila Faria Glaser. Ann Arbor: University of Michigan Press.

Bernauer, Lauren. 2012. "Playing for Christ: Christians and Computer Games." In *Handbook of Hyper-real Religions*. Ed., Adam Possamai. Leiden: Brill. 227–357.

Eco, Umberto. 1983. *Travels in Hyperreality*. Trans. William Weaver. New York: Harcourt Brace Jovanovich.

Jenkins, Henry. 2006. *Convergence Culture: Where Old and New Media Collide*. New York: New York University Press.

Johnson, Phylis, 2010. *Second Life, Media, and the Other Society*. New York: Peter Lang.

McCormick, Debbie. 2012. "The Sanctification of *Star Wars*: From Fans to Followers." In *Handbook of Hyper-real Religions*. Ed., Adam Possamai. Leiden: Brill. 165–84.

McLuhan, Marshall. 1964. *Understanding Media: The Extensions of Man*. New York: McGraw-Hill Book Company.

Possamai, Adam, ed. 2012. *Handbook of Hyper-real Religions*. Leiden: Brill.

Postman, Neil. 1985. *Amusing Ourselves to Death: Public Discourse in the Age of Show Business*. New York: Viking.

Wagner, Rachel. 2012. *Godwired: Religion, Ritual and Virtual Reality*. Routledge.

Online

Order of the Jedi: www.orderofthejedi.org/

Second Life website: http://secondlife.com/

Temple of the Jedi Order: www.templeofthejediorder.org/

World of Warcraft website: http://us.battle.net/wow/en/

Conclusion: Multiple Readings of *Avatar*

In the Introduction we looked briefly at the example of James Cameron's 2009 film *Avatar* as a film religious studies scholars might want to take seriously. Now that we have explored a number of differing cultural studies approaches to popular culture we are in a good position to explore Cameron's film in more detail. We will look at what each theory allows us to see in the film. Some of these various glimpses will bring us to contradictory conclusions, but that is the nature of academic study: the competition between varying theories and the attempt to show that one's own theory is correct. What I hope to show you here, though, is that each of these theories has something to offer that is thoughtful and useful in the discussion of religion and popular culture.

First a brief synopsis of the film: *Avatar* revolves around the experiences of a former marine, Jake Sully, who is now a paraplegic. He is brought into a project to pacify the indigenous population on a far away moon, Pandora, where humans have discovered a rare mineral that is necessary for further technology on a ravished Earth. Working with both the Company and its paramilitary support, Sully is able to transfer his mind into an avatar, made in the image of the indigenous people, the Na'vi. As he interacts with the Na'vi in his avatar form, he learns the ways of these people, falls in love with the chief's daughter, and eventually helps the Na'vi fight against the colonizing forces of the Company. After conquering the human colonists, Sully uses the spiritual power of the Na'vi, which is based on the connection of all life energy of the moon, to fully integrate into his avatar, forsaking his disabled body forever.

Marxist or Neo-Marxist Theories

Theorists like Adorno and Horkheimer would see a film like *Avatar* as part of the culture industry designed to keep us entertained but not particularly engaged politically. They may add to this the standardization of the story providing consumers with a sense of pseudo-individuality that re-enforces (and naturalizes) the hegemony of heterosexual, middle-class, capitalist values of the individual. What does this mean? Well, taking a culture industry approach one could argue that the story in *Avatar* is not particularly new. There are two opposing sides and one has more power (military, technology, etc.) than the other. There is also a romance between a boy from one side and a girl from the other. As the two interact, the one who is on the more powerful side begins to side with the marginalized people and fights against his own people to bring justice. The seemingly less powerful group finds their own psychological, spiritual, intuitive resources to stand up to the bully and they win the day. Have you heard a story like this already? A few films come to mind: *Dirty Dancing* (1987), *Pocahontas* (1995); *Gnomeo and Juliet* (2011). While these films do not seem to hold quite the popular power as *Avatar*, they are all, as the last listed implied, highly influenced by Shakespeare's *Romeo and Juliet*. Of course, all of these examples, including *Avatar*, allow for the hero and heroine to live in the end. This, in a culture industry perspective, is exactly what is needed to keep people satisfied. We have the same story as *Romeo and Juliet*, but with a happy ending. Thus, we can leave the theatre feeling uplifted and ready to continue to work and consume in our regular lives. The problem has been solved, no need for any action on our part. The spirituality that is so attractive, should we wish to engage in it further, can be purchased at the local New Age bookstore, or through meditative workshops. A film like *Avatar* is simply a reformulated version of a frequently told story that makes us feel good and commodifies a holistic spirituality that we can find, should we wish, in consumer contexts.

Culturalism

The culturalists, like Williams and Hall, would take a very different approach. Sure some people may just watch the film and be entertained and that's it. But others may, in fact, have very different responses. So how people consume *Avatar* is as important as how it might fit in a larger culture industry, if there even is such a thing. A good example of a culturalist perspective comes in the work of Britt Istoft (2010) who looks at viewer responses to this film. Istof looked at various online discussion groups based on fan responses to the film, particularly the religious aspects. Many fans were quite interested in the holistic spirituality constructed for this film—the notion that all living energy is integrated into a unity, called Eywa, a goddess-like figure. Some fans found this appealing and similar to their already Pagan perceptions of nature. Others took a more scientific interpretation saying this was not really "religion" as much as a bio-scientific aspect of the moon. For some fans the religious elements motivated them to take more of an interest in environmental issues, though Istoft was unable to actually verify real-life actions as the study focused on what people wrote online rather than what they actually did off-line. Matthew Holtmeier (2010) conducted a similar study with online groups. His study showed that while certainly many fans were Na'vi sympathizers, some fans of *Avatar* descended into what he called "Post-Pandoran Depression." These folks wanted to live on Pandora and were unable to bring any hope from the film into "real" life on earth. They simply kept watching the film losing more hope for their own reality. These studies show there are varying ways of interpreting the film from fan perspectives. What James Cameron may have encoded into his film is not necessarily decoded in the same way by all viewers.

Performativity

A scholar concerned with performativity, such as Judith Butler, may look at the ways normative notions of the body are performed in this film. This would include issues around gender, sexuality, disability, as well as religion/spirituality, which in this film is very specifically a bodily performance. So, for example, the film reinscribes a necessary heteronormativity by including the romance between Sully and Naytiri. The story of anti-colonialism does not need any romance to make it compelling, but the heteronormativity of the story adds an element of reinforced norms. However, the performance of masculinity and femininity are complicated by both Naytiri being a strong warrior and Sully being perceived as weakened in his paraplegic human state. His transference in the end to the stronger Na'vi body is not only a statement about the social unacceptability of disability in our current society, but particularly a statement about the need for a strong body for the performance of masculinity. This performed masculinity is reinforced by the way Sully is both able to control the largest flying beast, the Toruk, to become the Toruk Makto (the greatest warrior), as well as to bring the people together through his heroic deeds and leadership skills. The continual movement in the story from Sully's disabled body into the stronger, more masculine Na'vi body could be seen to highlight the necessity of continual performance of gender.

Ritual scholars such as Grimes may also have something to contribute to an understanding of the performativity of this film. The gender and sexuality performed are reinforced by ritual since the spirituality of the Na'vi people is inherently bodily and active. Sully and Naytiri's sexual encounter happens in a holy place and involves the integration of their energies in a spiritual way. Similarly, the transformation of Sully into the ultimate warrior involves the energy connection between him and the Toruk. When the Na'vi are ready to accept Sully into their tribe, he must first undergo the rite of bonding with an Ikran, what Sully ends up calling a Banshee. This rite of bonding involves Sully approaching a group of Ikran, a particular Ikran choosing him, and a fight to make the connection between Sully's energy cord in his hair and a similar energy cord in the animal. If the bond is not made, the Ikran will kill Sully, thus ending his initiation rite into the Na'vi. Sully adapts this rite by bonding instead with a Toruk, a larger version of an Ikran. Only a few times in Na'vi history has anyone been able to successfully fight with a Toruk to bond with it. The ultimate becoming Na'vi for Sully is also in the context of a rite, in which the entire community of Na'vi join their energy with their most sacred tree so that Eywa can flow freely into Sully to transfer his mind permanently into his Na'vi body. These ritual contexts do something, not just represent or symbolize something. The sexual rite binds Sully and Naytiri together in a way that cannot easily be broken. The connection between Sully and his beast allows him to control the animal and ride it. The rite at the end of the film transforms Sully permanently. Performance theorists would see this film as an example of the continued performance of heteronormativity and elements of hegemonic masculinity and femininity, thus contributing to the sense of these identities as normative and natural. Similarly the ritual contexts are performative rather than simply symbolic, showing rites as *doing* something—that is, making some sort of change.

Feminist Theories

Though some feminist theorists would follow the performativity model of Judith Butler others would look at different elements of this film. In one sense, the film models a kind of ecofeminism, or feminist approach to ecological concerns, by addressing the care of nature on the part of the Na'vi in contradiction to the exploitation on the part of the Company. Some ecofeminism is very much influenced by cultural feminism in that some ecofeminists view nature as feminine and/or view women as somehow essentially more connected to nature. That the Na'vi call their unity of all living energy, Eywa, a female being, seems to fall under this cultural feminist perspective and provide a model for cultural feminists to admire. However, as we saw with Dan Brown's *The Da Vinci Code*, not all feminists are happy with this more essentialized cultural feminist view on a sacred feminine. This example of the sacred feminine, while not particularly sexualized, as is Mary Magdalene in *The Da Vinci Code*, is associated with community, nurturance, and motherhood. This sacred feminine, it could be argued, then allows the masculine to be more aggressive. Thus, it is mostly through the military skills of the ex-marine, Sully, that the Na'vi, and the endangered sacred feminine, Eywa, are saved. This formula could be a particular problem for cultural, and many other, feminist theorists who see the military as part of the patriarchal order, while the girl power emphasized in the hunting and fighting prowess of Naytiri could be applauded by post-feminist theorists. However, again, her romantic relationship with Sully and her ultimate reliance on him as the great warrior to save her people diminishes this power.[1]

---

1. See Klassen 2013 for more on the themes of gender and feminism in *Avatar*.

Race and Racism

Anti-racism theorists such as Gilroy and hooks are concerned both with the racist history of the Black Atlantic and the collusion of Black people in white supremacy, particularly for hooks, in internalizing a hatred of their own Blackness. hooks calls for a loving of Blackness as a way to fight white supremacy. Gilroy calls for a transnational anti-racism that recognizes migrations and shaping multiple identities. He is highly critical of Black nationalist movements that want to reclaim some sort of pristine Africanness, just as hooks is critical of Black nationalist movements that privilege men over women. For hooks, racism is integrally connected to gender and class.

With these theorists in mind we can see two possible responses to *Avatar*. In one interpretation we can see that the Na'vi as a people are originally represented as primitive and dangerous, much like other indigenous peoples were deemed by European colonialists. However, unlike in the situation in our human histories, they are able to come together to conquer the colonists. As we sit through the film, we, as viewers, are encouraged to increasingly identify with the Na'vi, rather than the humans, and come to love their differences from the humans. They are not primitive, but in tune with their surroundings. They are beautiful and strong and determined to save their environment, which is also their religion. Thus the film could be seen as providing an anti-racist message. However, Gilroy's concern about Black nationalist movements could complicate this positive image. There is little collaboration between the humans and the Na'vi, with the exception of Sully, the scientist Dr Grace Augustine (who dies), the fighter pilot Trudy Chacon (who dies), and a couple of other techy guys. There is no reconciliation between fighting groups, and the Na'vi cast the humans off their moon. Even Sully's eventual permanent identity as Na'vi suggests a type of Na'vi nationalism that permeates the ending of this film. So, perhaps one could also argue that this is an anti-racist film that reinforces the very nationalism Gilroy sees as problematic to a truly successful anti-racist. It certainly leaves open the opportunities for a future film where the humans return to pay back the Na'vi for their revolution.

Orientalism

Though *Avatar* shows a very positive image of the Na'vi, such that one could argue that the film has an anti-racist message, some could argue[2] that there is also an orientalist lens in place in this film, particularly of the variety focused on indigenous peoples. There is a long history of accounts of white people wanting to become like

---

2.   as I have in Klassen 2013.

the "Indians," or become the "noble savage,"—the wise, earthy warrior who knows his or her environment fully and can teach the colonizing, technological world how to live more peacefully with the earth. This same narrative could be seen in the depiction of Sully as he literally becomes Na'vi once he has learned their ways and sees them as superior to the militaristic, technological ways of the humans. Though this orientalism is not a negative image like the Islamic terrorist, it is still an image that reduces a whole people into a stereotype. The Na'vi are not a representation of a specific indigenous people on Earth, however they hold the same image as the trope of the noble savage: they are in tune with nature, see nature as a spiritual mother, and have much wisdom about their world. They also, like in the Oriental Monk version of orientalism, cannot save themselves. Their wisdom must be taught to the outsider who will save them. Sully becomes the ultimate Na'vi because he is not really Na'vi. The Na'vi are essentially saved by a member of the colonizing force.

Subcultures and Post-Subcultures

Those theorists interested in subcultures and post-subcultures would look at the fan community of this film. Some of this concern with fandom was already alluded to when looking at the culturalist position of viewer interpretation. However, subculturalists might look to see if there have been any cases of fans embracing the Na'vi way to the extent of creating Na'vi religious rites and communities. Holtmeier (2010) points to some of this with his discussion of Na'vi sympathizers, though these tend not to fully recreate Na'vi contexts outside the film. You can, however, create a picture of yourself as a Na'vi at www.avatarizeyourself.com. You can also learn the Na'vi language on a number of different websites. Could these develop into full grown subcultures? Maybe. But post-subcultural theorists would argue that as we are living in a postmodern age, people are less likely to adopt one subculture and would rather identify with diverse kinds of movements, activities, and ideologies. They are more flexible. Thus post-subcultural theorists may ask how Na'vi spirituality, practices, ideas have infiltrated other contexts. Is there a Na'vi camp at Burning Man? Do Pagans engage with Eywa as one of their multiple interpretations of a nature deity? More empirical study would be needed to fully answer these kinds of questions.

Digital Media

Avatar was filmed in 3D with fully Computer Generated Images (CGI). This film, without a doubt, is a prime example of a digital medium. This has some implications for the kind of message it can present, as well as the kind of experience one can have watching it. CGI is technological and we, as viewers, know it is technological. As such, we know the "nature" we see is not really out there somewhere but was constructed digitally. So is it really nature? For all the people who were profoundly moved by the environmental message of this film, its awesome natural beauty, and its spirituality embedded in the natural world, there are equal numbers who are profoundly moved by its awesome technological construction and the triumph of the human ability to create a nature that is even better than the "real" nature: the animals are bigger and fiercer; the plants are cooler—they are luminescent; the people are bigger; mountains can float. If there was ever an example of hyper-reality, it is in the representation of nature found in *Avatar*. There are definitely no real life referents to the Hallelujah Mountains.

While *Avatar* may provide a message of environmental care based on a nature spirituality, it also very clearly provides a message of human technological prowess, which is a common theme in James Cameron's films. My concern, as I wrote in 2012, is "When what is represented through this technology is a pristine, natural world embedding spiritual values of interconnection, I cannot help but ask what kind of spirituality is born of this construction" (85). It seems that it is a spirituality of optical illusion and thus not really a nature spirituality. However, other scholars interested in digital media, such as Adam Possamai or Stef Aupers, would argue with me and suggest that the spirituality embedded in this technological world can be as real for participants as any other spirituality. The implications of digital media on religion and spirituality are complex and open to continual negotiation.

This example of *Avatar*, like all the other examples included in this text, shows that there are multiple readings available for any given popular cultural text. There are also multiple relationships between religion and popular culture. In some contexts it is, in fact, difficult to separate the religious aspects from the popular cultural aspects. The performances of popular culture can speak to, about, and within religion, just as religious ritual can take the form of popular cultural performance. The hybridity of cultures and religions interacting in the world create and recreate religio-cultural images, sounds, and practice. We use popular culture to limit our visions of the "Other" through reinforced stereotypes and static imagery, and we use popular culture to expand our understandings of the world, interact with, and reshape our sense of both local and global community.

Popular culture resists and maintains religion; religion resists and maintains popular culture. In the digital age, popular culture can *be* religion just as religion can *be* popular culture. The way we approach religion and popular culture makes a difference to how we understand these multiple relationships. If we follow the Frankfurt School, we are limited to one possible reading: what do the producers intend. If we follow the culturalists we open that up to allow consumers some agency in articulating their own meanings. When we take seriously anti-racism theory, gender and queer theory, and critiques of Orientalism, we are able to add nuance to our readings and further specify the varying contexts of development, consumption, and replication of popular cultural products and processes. The various theories of cultural studies show how both religion and popular culture continue to shape our world, while at the same time demonstrating how religion and popular culture are shaped by us and our various communities.

Useful Resources

Print

Holtmeier, Matthew. 2010. "Post-Pandoran Depression or Na'vi Sympathy: *Avatar*, Affect, and Audience Reception." *Journal for the Study of Religion, Nature and Culture*. 4(4). 414–24.

Istoft, Britt. 2010. "*Avatar* Fandom as Nature-Religious Expression?" *Journal for the Study of Religion, Nature and Culture*. 4(4). 394–413.

Klassen, Chris. 2012. "*Avatar*, Dark Green Religion, and the Technological Construction of Nature." *Cultural Studies Review*. 18(2). 74–88.

Klassen, Chris. 2013. "Becoming the 'Noble Savage': Nature Religion and the 'Other' in *Avatar*." In *Avatar and Nature Spirituality*. Ed., Bron Taylor. Waterloo: Wilfrid Laurier University Press.

Video

James Cameron. 2009. *Avatar*. 20th Century Fox.

Glossary

agency The capacity of an individual to negotiate or act with self-determination in the world.

alienation A separation or disconnect from the social world or elements within it. According to Marxist theory, under capitalism labourers are separated from what they produce because they do not own the products they produce leading to alienation, or separation, from the economic privileges of production.

animism The belief that all, or some, of the material world is animated with spiritual force(s) or souls.

anticipation The realization of something in advance of experiencing it. Judith Butler uses this term to refer to the way we perform gender to construct it. In other words, we anticipate what gender should be or look like, we then act in that way, and thus we construct it through our performance. Rather than gender existing prior to our performance, it is anticipated by our performance.

articulation The practice of appropriating a cultural product or process for one's own. This term is used within cultural studies to refer to consumer interpretation and use of popular culture. Consumers articulate a specific meaning, whether it is the intended meaning of the producer or not.

avatar A graphic image that represents a person in virtual reality coming from Hindu mythology in which an avatar is the human-like embodiment of a god.

base In Marxist theory the foundation of any society is the economic system or mode of production. Thus, the way we produce and exchange our necessary products is the base. Examples are hunting and gathering, feudal agriculture, and industrial capitalism.

binary A whole composed of two parts.

Black theology A type of Christian liberation theology that specifically addresses the injustices faced by African and African-diasporic peoples due to colonialism, slavery, and racism.

bokor A priest or priestess in Haitian vodou who practises both light and dark magic, and has the power to create zombies.

bourgeoisie The middle class who are concerned with property ownership and increasing capital.

capitalism An economic system in which production is owned by individuals or corporations, rather than by the state. Those who own the production hire others to labour in the creation of products, thus increasing the profit of the owners.

catholic (Universal). This term was originally used for the universal orthodox Christian church as a description of its unity. As groups split off, such as the Eastern Orthodox Church, and later the Protestants, *Catholic* (with a capital C) became the term used for one specific form of Christianity.

cognitive approach An approach to studying religion that begins with belief systems, including a concern with psychological or neurological wiring towards religious belief.

cold media Media that give minimal data, thus requiring higher participation from the consumer through interpretation or interaction. See **hot media**.

collusion Being complicit in the perpetuation of stereotypes and oppression; by living as if these stereotypes are correct or natural and through internalizing this oppression, racial minorities can collude in the maintenance of racism, women can collude in the maintenance of sexism, and gays and lesbians can collude in the maintenance of heterosexism.

commodification The making of something into a **commodity** that previously was not thought to be a commodity, such as religion, or a religious icon or symbol.

commodity An object or service produced for consumption by someone other than the producer. Commodities require an economic exchange.

communism A system of social organization in which all property is owned collectively. In Marx's articulation, communism would result from human goodness and unselfishness, by everyone thinking of the good of their neighbours. Thus, for him, communism would not require any governmental system at all.

compulsory heterosexuality The expectation or assumption that everyone is naturally heterosexual or that everyone must live a heterosexual life.

connotative meaning The subjective meaning of a word or phrase that is culturally determined. See **denotative meaning**.

convergence The coming together of distinct things. In media studies, Jenkins uses this term to refer to the coming together of various functions and technologies of media, as well as the coming together, or interaction between, producers and consumers.

critical theory A form of neo-Marxist theory that analyzes capitalism with a goal of challenging it, rather than simply thinking about it.

cultural feminism A form of feminism which suggests that women and men have different needs and thus must have separate cultural, including religious, spaces.

culturalism The cultural studies perspective that consumers are able to articulate meaning in cultural productions, rather than assuming the meaning of the producer is passively absorbed.

culture industry thesis The idea that there is a single culture industry managed by the elites designed to promote **hegemony** and keep people happy with the status quo. This thesis is promoted by the Frankfurt School.

decoding The reading, and articulation of meaning, of a cultural product by the consumer. See **encoding.**

decolonization The process of gaining self-determination by colonized people. This term can be used for nations and individuals.

denotative meaning The literal meaning of a word or phrase. See **connotative meaning**.

diaspora The movement of people from their homelands. Diasporic communities typically retain some connection with the homeland, while integrating into the new context, thus creating hybrid identities and cultures.

discourse Areas of social knowledge that shape social reality. Through discourse—speech, written accounts, interpretations, etc.—the boundaries of reality are drawn. It is virtually impossible to step out of the discourse and still be socially intelligible.

documentary culture All the cultural products of any given society regardless of quality or presumed social importance.

dominant reading The interpretation of a cultural product that is intended by the creator or producer of that product. See **negotiated reading, oppositional reading**.

drag The performance of a gender that does not match one's sexual assignment. Typically drag performances are ultra-feminine (by males) or ultra-masculine (by females). In Judith Butler's work, drag is an instance of showing the constructedness of all gender.

encoding The placing of meaning into a cultural product by the producer. See **decoding.**

enlightenment The end goal of Buddhism. Enlightenment involves the realization that life is suffering and the cause of suffering is desire. The enlightened person is able to let go of this desire and embrace their Buddha-nature.

essentialism The idea that certain properties or characteristics are natural and necessary to a type of person. For example, the idea that women are naturally nurturing is essentialist.

ethnography The practice of studying a group of people by long-term participant observation within their specific cultural context.

ethos A preferred way of acting in the world based upon one's cultural understanding of the world.

evangelize To spread one's religious beliefs to other people. Evangelical Christians, for example, are characterized by their desire to spread Christianity to all people because it is understood to be the only Truth.

existentialism A philosophical perspective that focuses on the individual experience rather than some shared human nature. In existentialism the individual is responsible for his or her own choices and should not simply follow the rules of an authority system such as religion.

fascism A governmental system that is ruled by a dictator and in which all opposition is suppressed. Fascist states tend to be associated with ultra-nationalism.

folk culture Cultural products and activities created by the people rather than by elites or governmental structures.

hegemony The normative ideal of the elite, dominant class. In order to maintain the hegemony, the elites need to convince the masses that the dominant ideology is in everyone's best interest. Hegemony is not maintained by force, but by the promise of benefit.

heretical Having beliefs or practices that go against the orthodox religious system.

hermeneutic The way one interprets or reads texts.

heteronormative Connected to compulsory heterosexuality where only heterosexuality is perceived as normal and natural. All other sexual orientation is presumed to be deviant—sometimes pathological or criminal.

high culture Cultural products created or enjoyed by the elites of a society, usually contrasted with **mass culture**.

historical materialism Marx's approach to history, economics, and society, whereby all social institutions and changes in human cultures are determined by modes of production.

history of religions The study of world religions with the purpose of finding universal patterns of symbolism and mythology.

hot media Media that give a large amount of data and thus do not require extensive interpretation by the consumer. According to McLuhan, hot media are more conducive to passive consumption than **cold media**.

humanism The idea that all human life has inherent worth, and that humans can create a better world for themselves without the need to rely on external supernatural forces.

hybridity The blending of two or more cultures to create a third, unique culture. This term is often associated with **diaspora**.

hypermodernity An intensification of modernity that is characterized by an optimistic belief in the power of human technology to create a better world.

hyper-real A simulation of something that is so intense it is perceived to be better than what it refers to. According to Baudrillard, the hyper-real has become more important than any reality to the point that the reality no longer exists, only the hyper-real simulation.

ideology A set of beliefs and values, assumed to be natural and necessary, that support hegemonic systems. For Marx, ideology was spread through the superstructures, such as religion, government, news media, etc., to uphold the base economic system.

implicit religion The functions of religion as they operate within secular contexts. When secular groups or activities function in a similar way as an explicit religious organization does, they can be seen as functioning as implicit religion.

inerrancy With no errors. The belief that the Christian Bible has no errors. This has led some evangelical Christians to argue against scientific discoveries that go against stories, doctrines, and teachings in the scriptures.

inner-worldly asceticism The practice of working hard at one's employment to gain wealth, yet living simply and not spending that wealth on frivolous things or luxuries.

infelicitous Inappropriate or ineffective.

Islamism The integration of religion and politics in Muslim contexts. Many Islamic states are governed by *shari'a* law and are determined to resist Western liberal secularism.

Islamophobia The fear or hatred of all Muslims.

liberal feminism A form of feminism that fights for women's equality to men under the law and social policy.

liberalism The philosophical and political movement that values above all other things rationality, equality, and utilitarianism.

liberation theology A Christian theological position which argues that God is on the side of the poor and the oppressed and thus the Christian church must act accordingly. Liberation theology is concerned with issues of social justice such as poverty, racism, sexism, globalization, and war.

liminal stage The middle point in some ritual processes in which one is outside of social roles. One is transformed as one leaves the liminal stage into a new or renewed social and cultural position in one's group.

masquerade The taking on of a persona that is false or constructed. In performative theory, a masquerade is a performance that highlights the constructed nature of all identity performance.

mass culture Cultural products created by the elite producers to maintain their **hegemony** on the masses.

media studies The study of the development and uses of all types of media (radio, television, computer, Internet, etc.).

metanarratives Stories about human life that are presented as universal truths. Metanarratives, such as history and science, are components of modernism developed to try to make sense of human existence. Postmodernism dismisses metanarratives as constructions based on false universality.

misogyny The hatred or fear of women.

MMORPGs Massive Multiplayer Online Role-Playing Games. In these games one constructs an **avatar** and guides that avatar through a series of quests with the participation of other players. The games are run on large servers, which give access to players across the globe.

monotheism The belief in the existence of only one god. Christianity, Judaism, and Islam are monotheistic religions. See **polytheism**.

moral panic A community-wide fear of an "Other" leading to an attack on anyone who might be associated with that "Other." For example, a fear of Satanism could lead to an attack on anyone thought to be associated with Satanism, such as Goths, regardless of an actual threat.

mysticism The spiritual experience of union with the divine.

nationalism A strong identification with a group of people making up a nation. Nationalist identities promote the commonalities of citizens and minimize the differences. In ultra-nationalism, nationalist identity is often associated with singular ethnic or racial identities.

naturalized Made to seem natural. Much of hegemonic ideology and values are naturalized so that people do not think it possible to challenge these ideas; they are thought to be inevitable and necessary.

negotiated reading An interpretation of cultural products that recognizes the producer's intended meaning, yet alters that meaning to meet the needs of the consumer. See **dominant reading, oppositional reading**.

neo-liberalism The political movement to remove government influence in economics through privatization of all services, deregulation of trade, and the removal of a social safety net. Neo-liberalism is associated with a free market economy and globalization.

neo-Marxism Various twentieth-century uses of Marxist economic theory to think through cultural constructions. Both the Frankfurt School and the culturalists use neo-Marxist theory to approach popular culture, though they come up with very different evaluations. However, both are concerned with structures of power, class, and hegemonic ideology and the way popular culture can either maintain **hegemony** or be a source of resistance.

neo-tribalism The idea that society has shifted from a mass society to a tribal society. This idea was first promoted by Maffesoli, who argued that we are increasingly associating ourselves with small groups of like-minded people through various social networking activities. The idea of neo-tribalism has been used by post-subcultural theorists to counter the notion of one singular dominant culture.

New Age A set of spiritual beliefs and practices based on the integration of an eclectic variety of world traditions that meet an individual's personal needs. New Age practitioners draw on ancient traditions, Eastern spirituality, indigenous spirituality, and marginalized Western magical traditions.

nonattachment The Buddhist practice of being aware of the nature of suffering and desire. To live with nonattachment one must be able to detach from both pain and pleasure and recognize the impermanence of all things.

occult That which is hidden. This term is typically used today to refer to magical or secret traditions concerned with accessing hidden knowledge through the practices of divination, spiritual intercession, or mysticism. Partridge argues that in the West we are seeing an increase in interest in the occult leading to a wider "occulture," which may or may not be tied to specific religious traditions, such as **Paganism** or **New Age**.

oppositional reading An interpretation of a cultural product that goes against and resists the producer's intended meaning. See **dominant reading, negotiated reading**.

Orientalism The lens through which Western state and scholarly leaders have seen and represented the East. Said argues that Orientalism shapes the East as primitive, static, and in need of Western progress. This ideology was used to justify colonialism and other military actions in the Middle and Far East.

Paganism A contemporary religious movement that draws on the mythologies of ancient Europe, the concept of the sacredness of nature, and a ritual system utilizing occult magic. Contemporary Pagans take their name from the term for pre-Christian people of Europe, such as the ancient Greeks and Romans.

parareligious The use of practices and symbols that are religious-like, yet outside of institutional religion. Powell uses this concept to explain the Goth use of religious imagery in their style even though most are self-declared secularists.

patriarchy The rule of the fathers. In patriarchal societies a certain group of elite men hold social, economic, and political power over all women and non-elite men.

performance theory A complex theory about the way we continuously perform our identities, particularly our sexual and gender roles.

performative utterance The use of words to make something happen. For example, when a priest says, "I pronounce you husband and wife," the words make the marriage happen.

phenomenological Concerned with the experience of people. In the study of religion, phenomenology takes seriously people's accounts of interacting with the sacred without explaining that interaction in terms of social or psychological function.

phenotypes Observable traits in an organism. In humans, phenotypes refer to skin, hair, and eye colour, hair texture, the shape of one's face, eyes, nose, etc.

philology The study of language through literary studies, linguistics, and history.

plantation colonies Colonies designed to cultivate, extract, and export resources. In the Americas, the plantation colonies had a much higher percentage of slaves and workers than European owners and other settlers. The goal of these colonies was profit rather than resettlement. See **settlement colonies**.

polyamorous In a sexual relationship with multiple people. Polyamory is different from polygamy in that all the members of a polyamorous group may be involved with all other members, rather than one man having multiple wives, or one woman having multiple husbands.

polyrhythmic Characterized by multiple musical rhythms, such as a four-beat rhythm overlaid by a three-beat rhythm. West African religious ritual used polyrhythmic music to instigate a trance state conducive to communication with the spirits. This rhythmic style was carried into the Americas to become the base of African-American music such as blues and, later, rap music.

polytheism The belief in the existence of many gods, who are typically in relationship with one another. Hinduism and many indigenous religious traditions are polytheistic. See **monotheism**.

postmodernity The time period after modernity characterized by a fragmentation of metanarratives and a concern for contextual knowledge.

post-subcultures Small groups within society that are characterized by diversity and fluidity. Post-subcultural scholars argue that in a postmodern society there is no longer a hegemonic mainstream to resist, but multiple post-subcultures that people flow in and out of. Some of these post-subcultures do take political stances that vary from dominant ideologies.

proletariat A member of the working class. In Marxist theory, the proletariat needs to rise up against the bourgeoisie to reclaim the production of their labour.

Protestant Reformation The movement in sixteenth-century Europe which split the Western Christian Church into the Roman Catholic Church and various Protestant denominations.

pseudo-individuality An element of the culture industry thesis. Adorno and Horkheimer argued that in the culture industry cultural products are superficially varied in order to make it look like consumers have multiple choices to meet individual tastes, when in reality these products are standardized and there is no real freedom of choice.

queer theory A deconstruction of heteronormativity that also challenges identity politics and the essentialisation of all gendered and sexual identities.

radical feminism A form of feminism that focuses on liberation from current patriarchal structures (such as marriage) to free women from bondage.

rite A specific patterned event within a religious ceremony, such as a baptism or a prayer service.

ritual The practices of religious groups or individuals. Ritual includes specific **rites**, **ritualization**, and **ritualizing**.

ritualization Doing activities in a patterned way similar to rites. For example, some people attend sporting events regularly and with devotion, almost "religiously." This participation could be seen as ritualization.

ritualizing The creation of new ritual processes to meet needs not previously acknowledged by religious institutions. For example, a transformation ceremony for someone completing sexual reassignment surgery could involve ritualizing.

Satanism The practice of appealing to the myths of Satan to create an individualistic, hedonistic, and often anarchistic worldview and ethos. Many people have feared Satanists as people who conduct ritual murder and call on Satan to curse others. However, the majority of Satanists today do not actually believe in a being called Satan but rather see Satan as a metaphor for resistance to Christian values and for self-determination.

secular Being separate from religion. Secularism is not anti-religion, but promotes a structuring of society in which religion does not hold authority over other institutions.

secularization thesis The idea that, as our societies become more secular, religion itself will become less important to people.

semiotics The study of signs and symbols as elements of communication and language.

settlement colonies Colonies designed to create new communities, often due to over-population in the homeland. In the Americas, settlement colonies were populated by high numbers of Europeans and low numbers of slaves or other workers from Africa. See **plantation colonies**.

shari'a The sacred law within Islam which Islamist groups elevate above secular and international law.

sign A word or symbol used to communicate meaning. A sign is the symbolic representation of a physical thing, composed of a signified (cultural meaning) and a signifier (physical representation). For example, to communicate the concept of a "table" one must have both the physical thing and the meaning given to that physical thing (something you put things on rather than something you sit on). See **signified, signifier**.

signified In semiotics, the cultural meaning (or mental concept) associated with the signifier (the physical representation) of any given sign (the symbolic representation). For example, the signified of a "table" is the meaning associated with the word: something you put things on. See **sign, signifier**.

signifier In semiotics, the physical representation of any given sign (the symbolic representation). For example, the signifier of a "table" is the physical thing. This physical thing has no real connection to the sign "table" unless is has a signified association; the word/sign is arbitrary. See **sign, signified**.

simulacra Reproductions of something else. Baudrillard argues that the simulacra have become reproductions of something that no longer exists. There is no real thing the simulacra is simulating; there is now only the simulacra.

simulation The reproduction of something else, or as Baudrillard argues, the faking of something that does not exist.

social construction The construction of specific identities, ideologies, or activities through social processes. Social construction is typically opposed to the notion of natural identities, ideologies, or practices, allowing for a study of how cultures and societies develop their sense of gender, sexuality, race, politic systems, religions, etc.

socialist feminism A form of feminism that emphasizes the connections between class and gender divisions.

spirituality The experience of something that is greater than oneself. Some see spirituality as a personal or individual belief and practice while seeing religion as institutional.

structure of feeling The aura of any given culture determined by the themes and values of the entirety of its cultural products.

subcultural capital The cultural knowledge and the commodities acquired by members of any given subculture. Those with high subcultural capital are insiders; those with low subcultural capital are wannabes.

subcultures Smaller groups within society that challenge the hegemonic dominance of the mainstream and its presentation as natural.

suffrage Having access to the vote in a democratic context.

superstructure The institutions that create and disseminate ideology designed to maintain the **base** mode of production within Marxist theory. These could be religion, education, popular culture, etc.

syntactical Pertaining to the structure of language.

taste A person's individual and cultural patterns of preference. Taste is particularly relevant to choices of clothing style, popular cultural consumption, and manners. Taste can be associated with class as well as subcultural capital.

televangelism The practice of evangelical preaching, teaching, and ministering using television as a medium.

theology The study of the religious and ethical norms of any given religious tradition. Theology is typically conducted by insiders and is concerned with how one should believe, act, and interact in a given religious context.

totemism A religious system in which a group of people is spiritually connected to a particular animal or plant that then represents the group.

transnational feminism A form of feminism that acknowledges the differing experiences and needs of women in the various cultural and geographical contexts of the world. Transnational feminists focus on global support and interaction while emphasizing local needs and voices.

white supremacist capitalist patriarchy The concept articulated by bell hooks to represent the connected ideologies of racism, classism, and sexism. For hooks, one cannot address only one of these oppressions; one must address them all together.

Wicca A contemporary Pagan tradition. Wiccans believe in both a goddess and a god and practice **occult** ritual, that is, ritual which is secret and concerned with accessing hidden knowledge through various magical and divination methods. Members of Wiccan covens must be initiated in order to access the secret knowledge.

worldview A belief system that purports to explain the world, human existence, and any supernatural forces.

References

Achterbosch, Leigh, Robyn Pierce, and Gregory Simmons. 2008. "Massively Multiplayer Online Role-Playing Games: The Past, Present, and Future." *ACM Computers in Entertainment*. 5(4). 9:1–9:33.

Adams, Guy. 2010. "The Real 'Avatar': Cameron Shoots Amazon Tribe in 3D." *The Independent*, 8 September. http://www.independent.co.uk/arts-entertainment/films/news/the-real-avatar-cameron-shoots-amazon-tribe-in-3d-2073139.html

Adorno, Theodor and Max Horkheimer. 2002. *Dialectic of Enlightenment: Philosophical Fragments*. Trans., Edmund Jephcott. Stanford, CA: Stanford University Press.

Albanese, Catherine L. 1999. *America: Religions and Religion*. Third Edition. Belmont, CA: Wadsworth Publishing Company.

Allen, Chris. 2010. *Islamophobia*. Ashgate.

Ames, Melissa. 2010. "Twilight Follows Tradition: Analyzing 'Biting' Critiques of Vampire Narratives for Their Portrayals of Gender and Sexuality," In *Bitten by Twilight: Youth Culture, Media and the Vampire Franchise*. Eds. Melissa A. Click, Jennifer Stevens Aubrey and Elizabeth Behm-Morawitz. New York: Peter Lang. 37–53.

Andrews, Vernon L. 2011. "Rituals of the African American Domus: Church, Community, Sport, and LeBron James." In *God in the Details: American Religion in Popular Culture*. Second Edition. Eds., Eric Michal Mazur and Kate McCarthy. Londong: Routledge. 120–139.

Arnold, Matthew. 1960 [1869]. *Culture and Anarchy*. London: Cambridge University Press.

Aupers, Stef. 2012. "'An Infinity of Experiences.' Hyper-Real Paganism and Real Enchantment in *World of Warcraft*." In *Handbook of Hyper-real Religions*. Ed., Adam Possamai. Leiden: Brill. 225–45.

Austin, J.L. 1975. *How to Do Things With Words*. Second edition. Oxford: Clarendon Press.

Azzan, Maha. 2006. "Islamism Revisited." *International Affairs*. 82(6). 1119–32.

Bailey, Edward. 2012. "'Implicit Religion?': What Might That Be?" *Implicit Religion*. 15(2). 195–207.

Baudrillard, Jean. 1994 [1981] *Simulacra and Simulation*. Trans. Sheila Faria Glaser. Ann Arbor: University of Michigan Press.

Baumgardner, Jennifer, and Amy Richards. 2000. *Manifesta: Young Women, Feminism, and the Future*. New York: Farrar, Straus and Giroux.

Behm-Morawitz, Elizabeth, Melissa A. Click, and Jennifer Stevens Aubrey. 2010. "Relating to Twilight: Fans' Responses to Love and Romance in the Vampire Franchise." In *Bitten by Twilight: Youth Culture, Media and the Vampire Franchise*. Eds. Melissa A. Click, Jennifer Stevens Aubrey and Elizabeth Behm-Morawitz. New York: Peter Lang. 137–54.

Bell, Catherine. 1992. *Ritual Theory, Ritual Practice*. Oxford: Oxford University Press.

———. 1997. *Ritual: Perspectives and Dimensions*. Oxford: Oxford University Press.

Benjamin, Walter. 2008. *The Work of Art in the Age of Its Technological Reproducibility and Other Writings on Media*. Trans. Edmund Jephcott, Rodney Livingston, Howard Eiland, and Others. Eds., Michael W. Jennings, Brigid Doherty, and Thomas Y. Levin. Cambridge, MA: The Belknap Press of Harvard University Press.

Berger, Helen A., and Douglas Ezzy. 2007. *Teenage Witches: Magical Youth and the Search for the Self*. New Jersey: Rutgers University Press.

Berger, Peter. 2008. "Secularization Falsified." In *First Things*. No. 180. 23–7

Bernauer, Lauren. 2012. "Playing for Christ: Christians and Computer Games." In *Handbook of Hyper-real Religions*. Ed., Adam Possamai. Leiden: Brill. 227–357.

Blizzard Entertainment. 2010. "World of Warcraft Subscriber Base Reaches 12 Million Worldwide." http://us.blizzard.com/en-us/company/press/pressreleases.html?id=2847881 Date Accessed: August 21, 2012.

Boas, Franz. 1925. "What is Race?" *The Nation*. 120. 89–91.

Bourdieu, Pierre. 1984. *Distinction: A Social Critique of the Judgement of Taste.* Trans. R. Nice. Cambridge, MA: Harvard University Press.

Boyer, Horace Clarence. 1992. "Take My Hand, Precious Lord, Lead Me On." In *We'll Understand it Better By and By: Pioneering African American Gospel Composers.* Ed., Bernice Johnson Reagon, 141–63. Washington and London: Smithsonian Institution Press.

Boyer, Pascal. 1994. *The Naturalness of Religious Ideas: A Cognitive Theory of Religion.* Berkeley: University of California Press.

Breimeier, Russ. 2005. "Redeeming Harry Potter." *Christianity Today.* http://www.christianity today.com/ct/2005/novemberweb-only/redeemingharrypotter.html?paging=off Date Accessed: January 3, 2013.

Butler, Judith. 1990. *Gender Trouble: Tenth Anniversary Edition.* London: Routledge.

———. 1993. *Bodies That Matter: On the Discursive Limits of 'Sex'.* London: Routledge.

Byrne, Rhonda. 2006. *The Secret.* New York: Atria Books.

Calvert-Koyzis, Nancy. 2006. "Re-sexualizing the Magdalene: Dan Brown's Misuses of Early Christine Documents in *The Da Vinci Code.*" *Journal of Religion and Popular Culture.* Vol. 12. http://utpjournals.metapress.com/content/c76j022214t55k88/fulltext.pdf. Date Accessed June 3, 2013.

Cañas, Sandra. 2008. "*The Little Mosque on the Prairie*: Examining (Multi) Cultural Spaces of Nation and Religion." *Cultural Dynamics.* 20(3). 195–211.

Carrette, Jeremy and Richard King. 2005. *$elling Spirituality: The Silent Takeover of Religion.* London: Routledge.

Caterine, Darryl V. 2004. "Curses and Catharsis in Red Sox Nation: Baseball and Ritual Violence in American Culture." *Journal of Religion and Popular Culture.* 8. http://utpjournals.meta press.com/content/813512845704389j/full text.pdf. Date Accessed June 3, 2013.

Chidester, David. 2000. "The Church of Baseball, the Fetish of Coca-Cola, and the Potlatch of Rock 'n' Roll." In *Religion and Popular Culture in America.* Eds., Bruce David Forbes and Jeffrey H. Mahan. Berkeley: University of California Press. 219–38.

———. 2005. *Authentic Fakes: Religion and American Popular Culture.* Berkeley: University of California Press.

Clark, Lynn Schofield. 2002. "U.S. Adolescent Religious Identity, the Media, and the 'Funky' Side of Religion." *Journal of Communication.* 52(4). 794–811

———. 2003. *From Angels to Aliens: Teenagers, the Media, and the Supernatural.* Oxford University Press.

Cravens, Hamilton. 2010. "What's New in Science and Race Since the 1930s? Anthropologists and Racial Essentialism." *The Historian.* 72(2). 299–320.

Coakley, Sarah. 2002. *Powers and Submissions: Spirituality, Philosophy, and Gender.* Oxford: Blackwell Publishers.

Cockrell, Amanda. 2006. "Harry Potter and the Witch Hunters: A Social Context for the Attacks on Harry Potter." *The Journal of American Culture.* 29(1). 24–30.

Cohen, Stan. 1972. *Folk Devils and Moral Panics: The Creation of the Mods and Rockers.* London: MacGibbon and Kee.

Connell, Raewyn. 2008. "Masculinity Construction and Sports in Boys' Education: a Framework for Thinking About the Issue." *Sport, Education, and Society.* 13(2). 131–45.

Corona, Victor P. 2011. "Memory, Monsters, and Lady Gaga." *The Journal of Popular Culture.* doi: 10.1111/j.1540–5931.2011.00809.x. Accessed May 11, 2012.

Cressey, Paul G. 1932. *The Taxi-Dance Hall.* New York: Greenwood Press.

Dakroury, Aliaa. 2012. "Toward Media Reconstruction of the Muslim Imaginary in Canada: The Case of the Canadian Broadcasting Corporation's Sitcom *Little Mosque on the Prairie.*" In *Islam in the Hinterlands: Exploring Muslim Cultural Politics in Canada.* Ed., Jasmin Zine. Vancouver: UBC Press. 161–181.

Daniels, Les. 2000. *Wonder Woman: The Complete History.* San Franscisco: Chronicle Books.

Danna, Elizabeth, 2008. "Wonder Woman Mythology: Heroes from the Ancient World and Their Progeny." In *The Gospel According to Superheroes: Religion and Popular Culture.* Ed, B. J. Oropeza. New York: Peter Lang.

Davis, Wade. 1985. *The Serpent and the Rainbow*. Toronto: Stoddart.

Dawson, Lorne L. 1998. *Comprehending Cults: The Sociology of New Religious Movements*. Oxford University Press.

de Beauvoir, Simone. 1973. *The Second Sex*. New York: Vintage Books.

Diamond, Neil. 2009. *Reel Injun*. National Filmboard of Canada.

DiPaolo, Marc. 2011. *War, Politics and Superheroes: Ethics and Propaganda in Comics and Films*. Jefferson, NC: McFarland & Company, Inc.

Dozhansky, Theodosius and M. F. Ashley-Montague. 1947. "Natural Selection and the Mental Capacities of Mankind." *Science*. 105. 588–91.

Du Bois, W.E.B. 1989. *The Souls of Black Folk*. New York: Bantam.

Durkheim, Émile. 1995 [1912]. *The Elementary Forms of Religious Life*. Trans. Karen E. Fields. New York: The Free Press.

Dyson, Michael Eric. 2001. *Holler if You Hear Me: Searching for Tupac Shakur*. New York: Basic Civitas Books.

Eco, Umberto. 1983. *Travels in Hyperreality*. Trans. William Weaver. New York: Harcourt Brace Jovanovich.

Eliade, Mircea. 1959. *The Sacred and the Profane: The Nature of Religion*. Trans. Willard Trask. New York: Harcourt Brace Jovanovich.

Evans, Christopher H. and William R. Herzog II, eds. 2002. *The Faith of The Fifty Million: Baseball, Religion, and American Culture*. Louisville: Westminster John Knox Press.

Fausto-Sterling, Anne. 1993. "The Five Sexes: Why Male and Female are not Enough." *The Sciences*. 33(2). 20–6.

Fenn, Mavis L. 2013. "Buddhism." In *World Religions: Canadian Perspectives: Eastern Traditions*. Ed., Doris R. Jakobsh. Toronto: Nelson Education.157–203.

Fey, Julia Winden. 2000. "Spirituality Bites: Xers and the Gothic Cult/ure." In *GenX Religion*. Eds., Richard W. Flory and Donald E. Miller. New York: Routledge. 31–53.

Floyd-Thomas, Juan M. 2003. "A Jihad of Words: The Evolution of African American Islam and Contemporary Hip-Hop." In *Noise and Spirit:*

The Religious and Spiritual Sensibilities of Rap Music. Ed. Anthony B. Pinn. New York: New York University Press. 49–70.

Forbes, Bruce David and Jeffrey H. Mahan. 2005 [2000]. *Religion and Popular Culture in America*. Revised Edition. Berkeley: University of California Press.

Foucault, Michel. 1977 [1975]. *Discipline and Punish*. New York: Pantheon

Fouz-Hernández, Santiago and Freya Jarman-Ivens, eds. 2004. *Madonna's Drowned Worlds: New Approaches to her Cultural Transformations, 1983–2003*. Ashgate.

Frazer, James.1950 [1922]. *The Golden Bough: A Study in Magic and Religion*. Abridged Edition. New York: The Macmillan Company.

Gamman, Lorraine, and Margaret Marshment, eds., 1988. *The Female Gaze: Women as Viewers of Popular Culture*. London: The Women's Press.

Geertz, Clifford. 1993 [1973]. *The Interpretation of Cultures: Selected Essays*. Fontana Press.

Gilmore, Lee. 2010. *Theater in a Crowded Fire: Ritual and Spirituality at Burning Man*. University of California Press. Includes DVD.

Gilroy, Paul. 1991 [1987]. *"There Ain't No Black in the Union Jack": The Cultural Politics of Race and Nation*. Chicago: University of Chicago Press.

———. 1993. *The Black Atlantic: Modernity and Double Consciousness*. Cambridge: Harvard University Press

———. 2000. *Between Camps: Nations, Cultures and the Allure of Race*. London: Routledge.

Gramsci, Antonio. 1971. *Selections from the Prison Notebooks*. Eds. and Trans. Quintin Hoare and Geoffrey Nowell Smith. New York: International Publishers.

Gray, Richard J., ed. 2012. *The Performance Identities of Lady Gaga: Critical Essays*. Jefferson, NC: McFarland & Company, Inc.

Grimes, Ronald L. 1990. *Ritual Criticism: Case Studies in Its Practice, Essays on Its Theory*. Columbia: University of South Carolina Press.

Guilbert, Georges-Claude. 2002. *Madonna as Postmodern Myth*. Jefferson, NC: McFarland & Company, Inc.

Hall, Stuart. 1980. "Encoding/decoding." In *Culture, Media, Language: Working Papers in Cultural Studies, 1972-1979*. Eds. Stuart Hall, Dorothy Hobson, Andrew Lowe, and Paul Willis. Florence, KY: Routledge. 117-27.

Halperin, David. 2003. "The Normalization of Queer Theory." *Journal of Homosexuality*. 45(2-4): 339-343.

Hawkins, Stan. 2004. "Dragging out Camp: Narrative Agendas in Madonna's Musical Production." In *Madonna's Drowned Worlds: New Approaches to her Cultural Transformations, 1983-2003*. Eds., S. Fouz-Hernández and F. Jarman-Ivens. 3-21. Ashgate.

Hebdige, Dick. 1979. *Subculture: The Meaning of Style*. New York: Methuan & Co. Ltd.

Heelas, Paul. 2008. *Spiritualities of Life: New Age Romanticism and Consumptive Capitalism*. Oxford: Blackwell Publishing.

Herr, Corinna. 2004. "Where is the Female Body? Androgyny and Other Strategies of Disappearance in Madonna's Music Videos." In *Madonna's Drowned Worlds: New Approaches to her Cultural Transformations, 1983-2003*. Eds., S. Fouz-Hernández and F. Jarman-Ivens. 36-52. Ashgate.

Holtmeier, Matthew. 2010. "Post-Pandoran Depression or Na'vi Sympathy: *Avatar*, Affect, and Audience Reception." *Journal for the Study of Religion, Nature and Culture*. 4(4). 414-24.

hooks, bell. 1992. *Black Looks: Race and Representation*. Toronto: Between the Lines.

———. 1994. *Outlaw Culture: Resisting Representations*. Routledge.

Hulsether, Mark D. 2000. "Like a Sermon: Popular Religion in Madonna Videos." In *Religion and Popular Culture in America*. Eds., Bruce David Forbes and Jeffrey H. Mahan. Berkeley: University of California Press.

Hume, Lynne. 2006. "Liminal Beings and the Undead: Vampires in the 21st Century." In *Popular Spiritualities: The Politics of Contemporary Enchantment*. Eds. Lynne Hume and Kathleen McPhillips. Ashgate. 3-16.

Istoft, Britt. 2010. "*Avatar* Fandom as Nature-Religious Expression?" *Journal for the Study of Religion, Nature and Culture*. 4(4). 394-413.

Iwamura, Jane Naomi. 2000. "The Oriental Monk in American Popular Culture." In *Religion and*

Popular Culture in America. Eds., Bruce David Forbes and Jeffrey H. Mahan. Berkeley: University of California Press. 25-43.

———. 2011. *Virtual Orientalism: Asian Religions and American Popular Culture*. Oxford University Press.

James, William. 1929. *The Varieties of Religious Experience: A Study in Human Nature*. New York: The Modern Library.

Jenkins, Henry. 2006. *Convergence Culture: Where Old and New Media Collide*. New York: New York University Press.

Jhally, Sut. 1997. *bell hooks: Cultural Criticism and Transformation*. Media Education Foundation. VHS.

———. 1998. *Edward Said on Orientalism*. Media Education Foundation. VHS.

———. 2006. *Reel Bad Arabs: How Hollywood Vilifies a People*. Media Education Foundation. DVD.

Jindra, Michael. 2000. "It's about Faith in Our Future: *Star Trek* Fandom as Cultural Religion." In *Religion and Popular Culture in America*. Eds., Bruce David Forbes and Jeffrey H. Mahan. Berkeley: University of California Press. 165-79.

Johnson, Phylis, 2010. *Second Life, Media, and the Other Society*. New York: Peter Lang.

Jones, Steven T. 2011. *The Tribes of Burning Man: How an Experimental City in the Desert is Shaping the New American Counterculture*. Consortium of Collective Consciousness.

Klassen, Chris. 2008. *Storied Selves: Shaping Identity in Feminist Witchcraft*. Lanham: Lexington Books.

———. ed. 2009. *Feminist Spirituality: The Next Generation*. Lanham: Lexington Books.

———. 2012. "*Avatar*, Dark Green Religion, and the Technological Construction of Nature." *Cultural Studies Review*. 18(2). 74-88.

———. 2013. "Becoming the 'Noble Savage': Nature Religion and the 'Other' in *Avatar*." In *Avatar and Nature Spirituality*. Ed., Bron Taylor. Waterloo: Wilfrid Laurier University Press.

Knight, Jennie S. 2005. "Re-Mythologizing the Divine Feminine in *The Da Vinci Code* and *The Secret Life of Bees*." In *Religion and Popular Culture in America*. Revised Edition. Eds., Bruce

David Forbes and Jeffery H. Mahan. Berkeley: University of California Press. 56–74.

Kottler, Jeffrey A. 2011. *The Lust for Blood: Why We are Fascinated by Death, Murder, Horror, and Violence*. New York: Prometheus Books.

Lawson, E. Thomas, and Robert N. McCauley. 2006. "Interpretation and Explanation: Problems and Promise in the Study of Religion." In *Religion and Cognition: A Reader*. Ed., D. Jason Slone. London: Equinox. 12–35.

Leavis, F.R. 1933. *Mass Civilisation and Minority Culture*. Cambridge: Minority Press.

Lyden, John C. 2003. *Film as Religion: Myths, Morals, and Rituals*. New York University Press.

Lyotard, Jean-François. 1984 [1979]. *The Postmodern Condition*. Minneapolis: University of Minnesota Press.

Maddux, Kristy. 2008. "*The da Vinci Code* and the Regressive Gender Politics of Celebrating Women." *Critical Studies in Media Communication*. 25(3). 225–48.

Maffesoli, Michel. 1993. *The Shadow of Dionysus: A Contribution to the Sociology of the Orgy*. Albany: State University of New York Press.

———. 1995. *The Time of the Tribes: The Decline of Individualism in Mass Society*. London: Sage.

Magoulick, Mary. 2006. "Frustrating Female Heroism: Mixed Messages in *Xena*, *Nikita*, and *Buffy*." *The Journal of Popular Culture*. 39(5). 729–55.

Marx, Karl and Friedrich Engels. 1964. *The German Ideology*. Moscow: Progress Publishers.

———. 1975. *Collected Works*. Vol. 3. New York: International Publishers.

McCormick, Debbie. 2012. "The Sanctification of *Star Wars*: From Fans to Followers." In *Handbook of Hyper-real Religions*. Ed., Adam Possamai. Leiden: Brill. 165–84.

McGuire, Meredith B. 2008. *Lived Religion: Faith and Practice in Everyday Life*. Oxford University Press.

McLuhan, Marshall. 1964. *Understanding Media: The Extensions of Man*. New York: McGraw-Hill Book Company.

McMurray, Anaya. 2008. "Hotep and Hip Hop: Can Black Muslim Women be Down with Hip Hop?" *Meridians*. 8(1). 74–92

McRobbie, Angela. 2005. *The Uses of Cultural Studies*. London: Sage Publications.

———. 2009. *The Aftermath of Feminism: Gender, Culture and Social Change*. London: Sage Publications.

Miller, Monica R. 2009. "'The Promiscuous Gospel': The Religious *Complexity* and Theological *Multiplicity* of Rap Music." *Culture and Religion*. 10(1). 39–61.

Moreman, Christopher M. 2010. "Dharma of the Living Dead: A Meditation on the Meaning of the Hollywood Zombie." *Studies in Religion/sciences religieuses*. 39(2): 263–81.

Muggleton, David. 2006. *Inside Subculture: The Postmodern Meaning of Style*. Oxford: Berg.

Mulvey, Laura. 1975. "Visual Pleasure and Narrative Cinema." *Screen* 16(3). 6–18.

Oropeza, B.J., ed. 2005. *The Gospel According to Superheroes: Religion and Popular Culture*. New York: Peter Lang.

Orsi, Robert. 1999. *Gods of the City: Religion and the American Urban Landscape*. Bloomington: Indiana University Press.

———. 2003. "Is the Study of Lived Religion Irrelevant to the World We Live in? Special Presidential Plenary Address, Society for the Scientific Study of Religion, Salt Lake City, November 2, 2002." *Journal for the Scientific Study of Religion*. 42(2). 169–74.

Pagels, Elaine. 1979. *The Gnostic Gospels*. New York: Random House

Pals, Daniel L. 2006. *Eight Theories of Religion*. Second Edition. Oxford University Press.

Parrot, Douglas M. ed., 1990. "*The Gospel of Mary*." In *The Nag Hammadi Library in English*. Ed., James M. Robinson. San Francisco: Harper.

Partridge, Christopher. 2004. *The Re-Enchantment of the West*. Vol. 1. London: T&T Clark.

———. 2005. *The Re-Enchantment of the West*. Vol. 2. London: T&T Clark.

Peck, M. Scott. 1978. *The Road Less Travelled*. Touchstone.

Pendergrast, Mark. 1993. *For God, Country, and Coca-Cola: The Unauthorized History of the Great American Soft Drink and the Company that Makes It*. New York: Charles Scribner's Sons.

Pinn, Anthony B. 2000. "Rap Music and Its Message: On Interpreting the Contact between

Religion and Popular Culture." *Religion and Popular Culture in America*. Eds., Bruce David Forbes and Jeffrey H. Mahan. Berkeley: University of California Press. 258–75.

——. 2003a. "Introduction: Making a World with a Beat: Musical Expression's Relationship to Religious Identity and Experience." In *Noise and Spirit: The Religious and Spiritual Sensibilities of Rap Music*. Ed. Anthony B. Pinn. New York: New York University Press. 1–26.

——. 2003b. " 'Handlin' My Business': Exploring Rap's Humanist Sensibilities." In *Noise and Spirit: The Religious and Spiritual Sensibilities of Rap Music*. Ed. Anthony B. Pinn. New York: New York University Press. 85–104.

——. 2007. "Bling and Blessings: Thoughts on the Intersections of Rap Music and Religious Meaning." *Cross Currents*. 57(2). 289–95.

Pisters, Patricia. 2004. "Madonna's Girls in the Mix: Performance of Femininity Beyond the Beautiful." In *Madonna's Drowned Worlds: New Approaches to her Cultural Transformations, 1983–2003*. Eds., S. Fouz-Hernández and F. Jarman-Ivens. 22–35. Ashgate.

Porter, Jennifer. 2009. "Implicit Religion in Popular Culture: the Religious Dimensions of Fan Communities." *Implicit Religion*. 12(3). 271–80.

Possamai, Adam. 2012. "Yoda Goes to Glastonbury: An Introduction to Hyper-real Religions." In *Handbook of Hyper-real Religions*. Ed., Adam Possamai. Leiden: Brill.

Postman, Neil. 1985. *Amusing Ourselves to Death: Public Discourse in the Age of Show Business*. New York: Viking.

Powell, Anna. 2007. "God's Own Medicine: Religion and Parareligion in U.K. Goth Culture." In *Goth: Undead Subculture*. Eds., Lauren M. E. Goodlad and Michael Bibby. Durahm NC: Duke University Press.

Press, Andrea L. and Bruce A. Williams. 2010. *The New Media Environment: An Introduction*. Oxford: Wiley-Blackwell.

Price, Joseph L. 2000. "An American Apotheosis: Sports as Popular Religion." In *Religion and Popular Culture in America*. Eds., Bruce David Forbes and Jeffrey H. Mahan. Berkeley: University of California Press. 201–18.

Prieto-Arranz, José I. 2012. "The Semiotics of Performance and Success in Madonna." *Journal of Popular Culture*. 45(1). 173–96.

Raheja, Michelle H. 2007. "Reading Nanook's Smile: Visual Sovereignty, Indigenous Revisions of Ethnography and *Atanarjuat (The Fast Runner)*." *American Quarterly*. 59(4). 1159–85.

Rattansi, Ali. 2007. *Racism: A Very Short Introduction*. Oxford University Press.

Reagon, Bernice Johnson. 1992. "Pioneering African American Gospel Music Composers: A Smithsonian Institution Research Project." In *We'll Understand it Better By and By: Pioneering African American Gospel Composers*. Ed., Bernice Johnson Reagon, 3–18. Washington and London: Smithsonian Institution Press.

Reuters. 2006. "Madonna Defends Crucifixion." *The Sydney Morning Herald*. Sept. 22. www. smh.com.au/news/music/madonna-defends-crucifixion/2006/09/22/1158431871232.html Accessed May 9, 2012.

Romanowski, William D. 2000. "Evangelicals and Popular Music: The Contemporary Christian Music Industry." In *Religion and Popular Culture in America*. Eds., Bruce David Forbes and Jeffrey H. Mahan. Berkeley: University of California Press. 105–24.

Runnymede Trust: Commission on British Muslims and Islamophobia. 1997. *Islamophobia: A Challenge For Us All*. The Runnymede Trust.

Russell, Stephen. 2002. *Liberation: The Perfect Holistic Antidote to Stress, Depression and other Unhealthy States of Mind*. HarperCollins.

Said, Edward W. 2003 [1978]. *Orientalism*. Penguin Books.

Saunders, Ben. 2011. *Do the Gods Wear Capes? Spirituality, Fantasy, and Superheroes*. New York: Continuum.

Schenck, Ken. 2008. "Superman: A Popular Culture Messiah." In *The Gospel According to Superheroes: Religion and Popular Culture*. Ed., B. J. Oropeza. New York: Peter Lang. 33–48.

Scholes, Jeffrey. 2004. "Professional Baseball and Fan Disillusionment: A Religious Ritual Analysis." *Journal of Religion and Popular Culture*. 7. http://utpjournals.metapress.com/content/x1114238j6288812/fulltext.pdf. Date Accessed June 3, 2013.

———. 2012. "The Coca-Cola Brand and Religion." In *Understanding Religion and Popular Culture*. Eds., Terry Ray Clark and Dan W. Clanton, Jr. London: Routledge. 139–56.

Shaheen, Jack. 2001. *Reel Bad Arabs: How Hollywood Vilifies a People*. Interlink Publishing Group.

Sheldon, Suzanne. 1997. "Xena: Feminist Icon." *Whoosh! International Association of Xena Studies*. Issue 9. http://whoosh.org/issue9/index.html. Date Accessed January 10, 2013.

Smith, Jeffery A. 2001. "Hollywood Theology: The Commodification of Religion in Twentieth Century Films." *Religion and American Culture*. Vol 11, No. 2: 191–231.

Sorett, Josef. 2009. "'Believe me, this pimp game is very religious': Toward a religious history of hip hop." *Culture and Religion*. 10(1). 11–22.

Soulliere, Danielle M. 2010. "Much Ado about Harry: *Harry Potter* and the Creation of a Moral Panic." *Journal of Religion and Popular Culture*. 22(1)). http://utpjournals.metapress.com/content/010460l1145r1056/fulltext.pdf. Date Accessed June 3, 2013.

Spooner, Catherine. 2006. *Contemporary Gothic*. London: Reaktion Books.

St John, Graham. 2003. "Post-Rave Technotribalism and the Carnival of Protest." In *The Post-subcultures Reader*. Eds. David Muggleton and Rupert Weinzierl. Oxford: Berg. 65–82.

Storey, John. 2009. *Cultural Theory and Popular Culture: An Introduction*. Fifth Edition. Harlow, England: Pearson Education Limited.

Sylvan, Robin. 2002. *Traces of the Spirit: The Religious Dimensions of Popular Music*. New York: New York University Press.

Thornton, Cassandra. 2012. "Isn't Loving God Enough? Debating Holy Hip Hop." In *The Black Church and Hip Hop Culture: Toward Bridging the Generational Divide*. Ed., Emmett G. Price III. Lanham: The Scarecrow Press, Inc. 115–29.

Thornton, Sarah. 1996. *Club Cultures: Music, Media and Subcultural Capital*. Middletown, CT: Wesleyan University Press.

Thrasher, Frederic. 1927. *The Gang: A Study of 1,313 Gangs in Chicago*. University of Chicago Press.

Trothen, Tracy. 2009. "Holy Acceptable Violence? Violence in Hockey and Christian Atonement Theories." *Journal of Religion and Popular Culture*. Special Edition: Religion and Popular Culture in Canada. 21. http://utpjournals.metapress.com/content/u926307k42351742/fulltext.pdf. Date Accessed June 3, 2013.

Tubbs, Sharon. 2004. "The Gospel According to Dan Brown." *St. Petersburg Times*. http://www.sptimes.com/2004/01/25/Floridian/The_gospel_according_.shtml. Date Accessed January 8, 2013.

Turner, Richard Brent. 1997. *Islam in the African-American Experience*. Bloomington: Indiana University Press.

Turner, Victor. 1967. *The Forest of Symbols: Aspects of Ndembu Ritual*. Ithaca, NY: Cornell University Press.

———. 1974. *Dramas, Fields, and Metaphors: Symbolic Action in Human Society*. Ithaca, NY: Cornell University Press.

Tweed, Thomas A. 2006. *Crossing and Dwelling: A Theory of Religion*. Cambridge: Harvard University Press.

Twitchell, James. 2004. *Branded Nation: The Marketing of Megachurch, College Inc., and Museumworld*. New York: Simon and Schuster.

van Gennep, Arnold. 1960. *The Rites of Passage*. Trans., Monika B Vizedom and Gabrielle L. Caffee. London: Routledge and Kegan Paul.

Wagner, Rachel. 2012. *Godwired: Religion, Ritual and Virtual Reality*. Routledge.

Walliss, John. 2012. "The Road to Hell is Paved with D20s: Evangelical Christianity and Role-Playing Gaming." In *Handbook of Hyper-real Religions*. Ed., Adam Possamai. Leiden: Brill. 207–223.

Walters, Suzanna Danuta. 1995. *Material Girls: Making Sense of Feminist Cultural Theory*. Berkeley: University of California Press.

Warne, Randi R. 1998. "(En)gendering Religious Studies." *Studies in Religion/Sciences Religieuses*. 27: 427–36.

Watkins, Ralph Basui. 2011. *Hip-Hop Redemption: Finding God in the Rhythm and the Rhyme*. Grand Rapids: Baker Academic.

Weber, Max. 2003 [1930]. *The Protestant Ethic and the Spirit of Capitalism*. Trans. Talcott Parsons. Mineola, NY: Dover Publications.

Weinzierl, Rupert and David Muggleton. 2003. "What is 'Post-subcultural Studies' Anyway?" In *The Post-Subcultures Reader*. Eds., David Muggleton and Rupert Weinzierl. Oxford: Berg. 3–23.

Weissler, Chava. 2006. "Meanings of Shekhinah in the 'Jewish Renewal' Movement." *Nashim: A Journal of Jewish Women's Studies and Gender Issues*. 10. 53–83.

Whitehouse, Harvey. 2007. "Towards an Integration of Ethnography, History, and the Cognitive Science of Religion." In *Religion, Anthropology, and Cognitive Science*. Ed., Harvey Whitehouse and James Laidlaw. Durham, NC: Caroline Academic Press. 247–80.

Wilkins, Amy C. 2008. *Wannabes, Goths, and Christians: The Boundaries of Sex, Style, and Status*. University of Chicago Press.

Wilkins, Karin and John Downing. 2002. "Mediating Terrorism: Text and Protest in Interpretations of *The Siege*." *Critical Studies in Media Communication*. 19(4). 419–37.

Williams, Raymond. 1961. *The Long Revolution*. New York: Columbia University Press.

Williamson, Milly. 2005. *The Lure of the Vampire: Gender, Fiction and Fandom from Bram Stoker to Buffy*. London: Wallflower Press.

Wollstonecraft, Mary. 1993. *Political Writings*. Ed., Janet Todd. Toronto: University of Toronto Press.

Young, Msgr. T.W. 2003. "'The Da Vinci Code' is All Fiction, Keep in Mind." *The Georgia Bulletin*. www.georgiabulletin.org/local/2003/12/11/Da_Vinci_Code_Is_All_Fiction/. Date Accessed January 8, 2013.

Zanfagna, Christina. "Building 'Zyon' in Babylon: Holy Hip Hop and Geographies of Conversion." *Black Music Research Journal*. 31(1). 145–62.

Zuckerbrot, Donna. 2008. *Zombies: When the Dead Walk*. Reel Time Images and Vision TV.

Index